Learning in
Early Childh**ood**

Education at SAGE

SAGE is a leading international publisher of journals, books, and electronic media for academic, educational, and professional markets.

Our education publishing includes:

- accessible and comprehensive texts for aspiring education professionals and practitioners looking to further their careers through continuing professional development
- inspirational advice and guidance for the classroom
- authoritative state of the art reference from the leading authors in the field

Find out more at: **www.sagepub.co.uk/education**

Learning in Early Childhood

Edited by
Pat Beckley

A Whole Child Approach from Birth to 8

Los Angeles | London | New Delhi
Singapore | Washington DC

SAGE Publications Ltd
1 Oliver's Yard
55 City Road
London EC1Y 1SP

SAGE Publications Inc.
2455 Teller Road
Thousand Oaks, California 91320

SAGE Publications India Pvt Ltd
B 1/I 1 Mohan Cooperative Industrial Area
Mathura Road
New Delhi 110 044

SAGE Publications Asia-Pacific Pte Ltd
33 Pekin Street #02-01
Far East Square
Singapore 048763

Library of Congress Control Number: 2011926551

British Library Cataloguing in Publication data

A catalogue record for this book is available from the British Library

ISBN 978-1-84920-404-0
ISBN 978-1-84920-405-7 (pbk)

Typeset by C&M Digitals (P) Ltd, Chennai, India
Printed by MPG Books Group, Bodmin, Cornwall
Printed on paper from sustainable resources

MIX
Paper from
responsible sources
FSC
www.fsc.org   FSC® C018575

CONTENTS

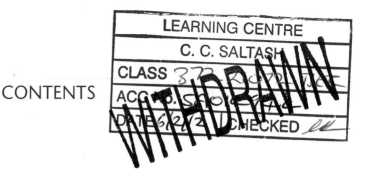

ACKNOWLEDGEMENTS

We would like to thank Michael Loncaster and early years staff at Molescroft Primary School, East Yorkshire, Janet Steward and staff at Barton St. Peter's Church of England Primary School, North Lincolnshire, and colleagues at Flekkenga Barneharge, Norway and Vestenga Kindergarten, Norway, for their kind support of this project. It has been greatly appreciated.

ABOUT THE EDITOR AND CONTRIBUTORS

THE EDITOR

Pat Beckley is the Academic Co-ordinator for 3–7 PGCE Primary course at Bishop Grosseteste University College Lincoln. She has taught children in the 3–11 age range, becoming the leader in each age phase and gaining NPQH. As an Advanced Skills Teacher for Early Years, Pat supported colleagues and settings, leading INSET and formulating Action Plans. Her work used research to inform her practice in schools. This included an Advanced Diploma in Special Educational Needs with a focus on early years, an M.Ed based on approaches to early years literacy and participation in the Effective Early Years Project. She has recently completed an Ed.D thesis which concerns a comparison of approaches to early years literacy between Lincolnshire, England and Hedmark, Norway. Her work has included liaison with educationalists in Norway, attendance at international conferences and participation as an executive member of the national organisation TACTYC (Association for the Professional Development of Early Years Educators).

THE CONTRIBUTORS

Nigel Appleton is Dean of the School of Teacher Development at Bishop Grosseteste University College Lincoln, where he is responsible for initial and continuing teacher education. He began his career as a mathematics teacher before moving into Higher Education at what is now the University of Cumbria, where he worked in initial teacher training.

Liz Creed is currently working as a Psychological Well-being Practitioner within a Primary Care setting for the National Health Service, providing brief guided self-help interventions using Cognitive Behaviour Therapy techniques to adults with mild to moderate mental health problems. Training for this involved successful completion of a Postgraduate Certificate in Low-Intensity Psychological Therapies awarded by The University of York. Prior to this, Liz gained three years' clinical experience working as a Support Worker for Child and Adolescent Mental Health Services in Leeds in an inpatient setting. Liz has been awarded an MSc Foundations of Clinical Psychology by the University of Wales, Bangor, after completing her undergraduate degree, a BSc (Hons) Psychology awarded by Nottingham Trent University.

Becky Glenton was a Foundation Year teacher for five years at Molescroft Primary School in Beverley, East Yorkshire. During this time, she implemented EYFS and developed provision in and around the county. She worked as an Early Years Lead Teacher and enjoyed supporting others in their teaching role. Her work has also included being the Gifted and Talented Co-ordinator and lead teacher for a cluster of 14 schools. She is a true believer in early years education and aims to work in this field for many years to come. She is currently working as a teacher in Melbourne, Australia, to gain a broader understanding of the international education system.

Helen Hendry is a Senior Lecturer at Bishop Grosseteste University College Lincoln. She is an early years specialist with particular interests in Communication, Language and Literacy, Inclusion, EAL and Social and Emotional aspects of learning. She has taught in all age groups in the primary phase and has managed the Foundation Stage departments of three Primary Schools in both rural and urban locations. She has worked as a lead Foundation Stage practitioner and profile moderator in Cornwall and has most recently supported and advised early years practitioners in a range of settings including the Private Voluntary and Independent sector, Childminders, Maintained Primary and Nursery schools and Children's Centres. Now lecturing in ITT she has completed a Masters degree, including research into peer collaboration in 3-year-olds' play and the preparation of ITT students for responding to the needs of pupils with EAL.

Alison Jakins is a Senior Lecturer in Primary Education at Bishop Grosseteste University College Lincoln. She is a science specialist who has taught across the primary age phases. Her research interests centre on how children learn and the development of modern foreign languages in the primary phase.

Jane Johnston is a Reader in Education at Bishop Grosseteste University College. She works extensively, both nationally and internationally, in three distinct areas: early childhood studies, primary science education and practitioner research. Her many publications reflect these interests and she is the author of many books, articles and chapters on early years and science education.

Sue Lambert is currently the Head of Department for Postgraduate Primary ITT at Bishop Grosseteste University College. Prior to commencing her post in HE she taught in mainstream primary schools for 19 years, teaching all ages in the primary phase. She was a SENCO for many years, which included responsibility for gifted and talented children. She was seconded for 18 months as an advisory teacher for history and was a subject leader for a number of subjects. She completed an MA in Education, the NPQH qualification and recently completed a CPSE and gained fellowship to the HEA.

Sharon Marsden is headteacher at Waddingham Primary School. She has worked in all age groups in the primary school. She recently completed her Masters degree based on thinking skills. This was based on action research at the school where she is the headteacher. The recommendations from the research were successfully implemented in the school.

Lindy Nahmad-Williams began her career as a teacher and became an early years LEA advisor. She currently works on the 3-year Primary Education course with QTS at Bishop Grosseteste University College. She recently co-edited the book *Early Childhood Studies* with Jane Johnston.

Anita Soni is a Senior Psychologist. She began her career as an early years teacher. She currently works part time as an Educational Psychologist for Worcestershire County Council. She also works for the Open University as an Associate Lecturer on Foundation Degree courses, and delivers training on 'Birth to Three Matters' and aspects of the Early Years Foundation Stage.

LIST OF TABLES AND FIGURES

TABLES

FIGURES

PREFACE

Providing appropriate learning contexts where young children thrive is vital for their progress and well-being. Professional practitioners, working in partnership with parents and carers and with support from local communities, seek to provide such contexts, often with the backing of government initiatives. Hence this book represents a timely reference for those interested in learning and development for children in their early years. Pat Beckley, Helen Hendry, Alison Jakins, Jane Johnston, Sue Lambert and Lindy Nahmad-Williams are colleagues at Bishop Grosseteste University College Lincoln, which received an 'outstanding' rating by Ofsted for its primary initial teacher education provision in 2010. Headteacher Sharon Marsden and early years practitioner Becky Glenton, bring views from their current experience of working with young children, while reflections underpinned by psychological perspectives are given by Anita Soni and Liz Creed. The contributors are experts in their field and together their input provides a range of viewpoints from their various professional backgrounds. Their collaboration with colleagues in Europe and the wider world, plus liaison with those using cutting-edge research, ensures the book is relevant to students, academics and those working with young children. This book furthers our understanding by exploring the crucial issues involved in taking an holistic view of the child.

Nigel Appleton
Dean of the School of Teacher Development,
Bishop Grosseteste University College, Lincoln

INTRODUCTION

This book provides discussions from a wealth of early years experts from a range of backgrounds; academics from Higher Education, psychologists, a headteacher and early years leader. It concerns an holistic approach which is becoming increasingly recognised as crucial for the well-being of young children in early years provision and for their welfare in the changing times ahead. The book is divided into four sections.

PART 1

Part 1 concerns how children learn. It was written by Pat Beckley who has recently completed her doctoral studies with colleagues in Norway and practitioners in settings in England researching early years literacy approaches. She is currently working with colleagues in Sweden, Italy and Israel researching approaches to early years teacher training, and colleagues throughout Europe and neighbouring countries, including Israel, Switzerland, Germany, Slovakia and Estonia to compile a programme to support multi-cultural teacher training.

Chapter 1 considers historical and contemporary perspectives relevant to the challenges faced by practitioners. It gives an exploration of relevant contemporary issues, such as international recommendations and how they impact on policy, parental needs for childcare, care and education for young children, accountability, government initiatives and the role of the professional in a changing world where children are perceived as global citizens.

Chapter 2 incorporates discussions of changing views as to what education for young children entails, for example the challenges for early years teachers when becoming facilitators of learning rather than instructors, the learning environment, indoors and outdoors, as a space for children's explorations, and working with other disciplines to promote holistic learning. It covers the range of theories regarding learning and development, including the research which is changing our views of the way we meet the needs of young children. The significance of parents/carers as a child's first social bond and the transmitters of cultural values and mores is discussed in Chapter 3, where practitioners can provide strategies to promote the partnerships, sharing and collaborating with those closest to the child. As a child's first and possibly most significant influence, discussion includes recent findings which highlight the importance of effective partnerships with parents and carers.

Chapter 4 considers some of the key figures in promoting pedagogical thinking and the influence which remains to this day. Challenges arising from the movement towards a new era are discussed in terms of the impact this has on the philosophy of learning and teaching for young children. The chapter goes on to explore some of the approaches to learning in early childhood in settings in England and Norway and how the strategies are used within the settings, with comments regarding practitioners' perceptions of the challenges when implementing the strategies.

PART 2

Part 2 introduces aspects of ways to support children's learning in challenging, changing times. This includes motivation and self-esteem, inclusion, diversity and thinking skills. Chapter 5 aims to promote an awareness of a range of communication strategies to aid interactions and dialogue between children and adults, suggestions to enhance perseverance and gives ideas to support planning for personalised learning and celebrating children's achievements. Part 2 introduces Sue Lambert and Helen Hendry who are members of the postgraduate team at Bishop Grosseteste University College Lincoln. Sue leads the Professional Issues courses on the PGCE team, where the subject of inclusion and relevant documentation such as the Every Child Matters agenda plays a large part and this is considered in Chapter 6. She highlights the key principles which aim to ensure all children have the opportunities to reach their full potential, that their well-being should be central to the process, that services should be responsive to children, young people and families, not designed around professional boundaries and that it is better to prevent failure than tackle crisis later. Helen recently completed a research project based on diversity matters which was presented at the British Educational Research Association conference in 2009. Her work is presented here, in Chapter 7. Helen feels that providers must act upon individual circumstances with specific support and intervention but can also support all the children in their care through careful choices of inclusive policy, practice and procedure and perhaps even more importantly through their own personal level of understanding.

Sharon Marsden is a successful headteacher at a school in Lincolnshire and completed her study of thinking skills in her school which is being disseminated in the locality as exemplary good practice. Sharon suggests that using thinking skills with children allows for a more balanced approach of knowing how rather than knowing what. It creates opportunities for enthusiasm and motivation which enable creativity and individuality to emerge in the children and leads to them wanting to learn more and take an active part in their development rather than being a passive, bored observer. Her contribution is welcome as the focus on thinking skills in Chapter 8.

PART 3

Part 3 concerns organising the learning environment to promote an holistic approach. The well-respected authors Lindy Nahmad-Williams and Jane Johnston discuss approaches to play and enabling environments respectively. In Chapter 9, Lindy considers that the significance of play on children's learning and development has been recognised for many years and was brought into prominence by philosophers such as Rousseau (1911) and Froebel (1826) who believed that play is the purest, highest and most natural form of learning. Chapter 10, written by Jane, aims to provide an understanding of what an enabling environment entails, how this can be achieved through appropriate planning and ways to support cooperation and collaboration to enhance the progress and development of children.

Alison Jakins draws on her many years of teaching about effective teaching and learning styles to write Chapter 11. It aims to provide an awareness of the breadth of teaching and learning styles to accommodate the development of different skills and give an overview of teaching and learning strategies that will help to strengthen the provision for all learners and promote independent thinking. Chapter 12 completes this section with a discussion of early years leadership and management styles, which seek to enable an holistic approach to be effectively implemented as a shared vision benefiting every child in the setting.

PART 4

Part 4, the final section, explores issues in practice. In Chapter 13, birth to eight matters are scrutinised by an experienced early years leader Becky Glenton, who supports others in their practice. In Chapter 14, Pat Beckley uses an holistic approach as the lens to explore the social context for inclusive practice in the locality, the wider community and consideration of the child as a member of a global community and a future world citizen. Pat feels that the use of the whole environment, both indoors and outdoors, has significance as a place where interactions between adults and children take place. The importance of providing children with 'real' experiences is discussed, where children are able to use their senses to explore the surroundings around them, take risks and enjoy and learn about their world. To promote an holistic approach there needs to be an awareness of children's needs, both their immediate ones and those reflecting academic progress. Multi-agency working is deemed a vital component of an holistic approach and this is described by Anita Soni who works as part of a multi-agency team. Anita notes that the skills and knowledge listed in this chapter form a useful foundation for practitioners in the early years to reflect upon when considering their strengths and areas for development within the area of effective multi-agency working.

Liz Creed closes the book with a discussion of her work with young children and adolescents. She sets out how they can be supported by strategies in the early years. This leads to consideration of ways to help children become strong, independent and resilient in the face of changes. It describes how our work in the early years is crucial for the well-being of the children in our care, for their precious childhood and to help them meet the challenges of the future.

PART 1

HOW YOUNG CHILDREN LEARN

Part 1 opens with the rationale for an holistic approach concerning the whole child. There are differing views of what constitutes an holistic approach, for example whether it is cross-curricular subject knowledge or a broader view of a whole child's development and welfare. This book seeks to consider the latter viewpoint and gains the perspectives of colleagues concerned with provision for young children.

Chapter 1 begins with a discussion of historical perspectives of education for young children and how they evolved. This is developed into consideration of pressures on provision through contemporary issues. 'In the twenty-first century it is probably evident to every parent, professional childcare worker, kindergarten and primary teacher that early childhood is high on the political agenda' (Gammage 2006: 235). But what constitutes appropriate provision? David Blunkett, the then Secretary of State for Education, in the Foreword to a key government green paper, The Learning Age (DfEE 1998) described the purpose of learning as:

> the key to prosperity – for each of us as individuals, as well as for the nation as a whole. Investment in human capital will be the foundation of success in the knowledge-based economy of the twenty-first century. This is why the Government has put learning at the heart of its ambition (Bottery 2001: 206).

The need for children's learning to be deemed as 'investment in human capital' focuses attention on the perceived economic value of education. This was emphasised by Tony Blair in 2005, who stated 'We have to secure Britain's future in a world ... driven by globalisation. We have to change and to modernise ... to equip everyone for this changing world' (cited in Cole, 2008: 86). Such notions for the rationale concerning provision for children are discussed in the first chapter which gives an exploration of relevant contemporary issues, such as international recommendations and how they impact on policy, parental needs for childcare, care and education for young children, accountability, government initiatives and the role of the professional in a changing world where children are perceived as global citizens.

Chapter 2 provides an overview of prominent theories of learning and considers their impact on educational philosophy. It describes key terms relevant to the theories and notes theorists who influenced educational thinking, such as Piaget, Vygotsky and Bruner. The work of notable pioneers of educational theories in practice are described, for example those of Froebel and Montessori. Changing views as to what education for young children entails, for example the challenges for early years teachers when becoming facilitators of learning rather than instructors, the learning environment, indoors and outdoors, as a space for children's explorations and working with other disciplines to promote holistic learning, are all discussed. Different ways of implementing theories are described, such as constructivist, socially constructive and instructive means through adult-led, adult-initiated and child-initiated methods. Changes in the delivery towards an open constructivist approach are considered, with possible reasons why this has occurred.

Chapter 3 focuses on partnerships with parents and carers and the strategies practitioners can use to support effective liaison between them and the children's first educators. As a child's first and possibly most significant influence, discussion includes recent findings which highlight the importance of effective partnerships with parents/carers, such as the Parents as Partners in Early Learning (PEEP, 2005, Sylva et al. 2005) project. This project, based in Oxford, sought to provide an early intervention programme, working with parents and carers to support their children in their role as the child's first educators. The chapter suggests ways in which successful relationships can be promoted in early years practice, based on research findings and observations from practice. Reflections are made on strategies to foster shared practice, such as assessment strategies, booklets, family learning groups, home/school projects, Open Days and celebration events. Attention is given to ways of developing harder to reach groups such as fathers, working parents or those who do not speak English. Strategies are discussed of ways to work with the wider community. The General Teaching Council in a statement of Professional Values and Practice for Teachers (GTC 2006) claims that 'Teachers should respond sensitively to the differences in the home background and circumstances of young people recognising the key role that parents and carers play in children's education'. Practitioners can share their knowledge and understanding of those concerned with a child's learning and development.

Chapter 4 explores how pedagogy informs practice. 'Practitioners interpret policy with their own histories, values, and purposes' (Bray et al. 2007: 250).

Aspects of practice are scrutinised including the perceptions of those implementing theories of learning and transition issues. Reflection is made of practice in other countries, with particular reference to observations and case studies in Norwegian settings. This is considered through reflections on approaches to learning in settings in different countries and how those working there have responded to changes taking place.

The *Guardian* (2001) stressed, following the aftermath of the 2001 disaster in New York, 'one illusion has been shattered on September 11th; that we can have the good life in the west, irrespective of the state of the world' (cited in Cole 2008: 87). Issues happening on a global scale impact on the lives of individuals throughout the world. Environmental destruction and global warming heighten concerns for the future. The effects of globalisation on early years provision and practice are explored. 'We live in a period of great change, some would even say of paradigmatic transition or movement from one epoch to another' (Dahlberg and Moss 2007: 176). Challenges arising from this movement towards a new era are discussed in terms of the impact this has on the philosophy of learning and teaching for young children. Through these reflections possible reasons are explored as to why these changes are taking place in learning and development for young children, the impact this has on provision, and the challenges posed for those who attempt to respond flexibly to meet these new trends, initiatives and policies. The section begins to provide an insight into the background for these dilemmas and leads towards further chapters in the book which consider specific aspects where challenges are posed for practitioners when attempting to positively resolve contemporary issues in practice.

References

Bottery, M. (2001) *Globalisation and the UK Competition State: No Room for Transformational Leadership in Education?* University of Hull, School Leadership and Management, Vol. 21.

Bray, M., Adamson, B. and Mason, M. (eds) (2007) *Comparative Education Research: Approaches and Methods.* Hong Kong: Comparative Education Research Centre and Springer.

Cole, M. (2008) *Marxism and Educational Theory.* London: Routledge.

Dahlberg, G. and Moss, P. (2007) *Ethics and Politics in Early Childhood Education.* London: RoutledgeFalmer.

DfEE (1998) *Green Paper: The Learning Age.* London: The Stationery Office.

Gammage, P. (2006) *Early Childhood Education and Care: Politics, Policies and Possibilities* TACTYC, Colchester: Routledge.

GTC (2006) *Professional Values for Teachers.* London: GTC Whittington House.

Sylva, K., Evangelou, M. and Brooks, G. (2005) *Enabling Parents: An Evaluation of Parent Early Education Programme* (PEEP). Learning Skills Council, 2002–2004.

HISTORICAL PERSPECTIVES

Pat Beckley

Learning objectives

- To gain an understanding of key features of the historical development of early years provision in England
- To have an awareness of global recommendations to support an holistic approach
- To gain an understanding of the effects of globalisation on young children's learning

An holistic approach is a crucial aspect to incorporate as a central foundation for young children's learning. This chapter explores the rationale for this and the reasons why this is as highly relevant in modern times as in previous eras. Ongoing changes are taking place regarding early years provision for children aged from birth to eight, responding to numerous factors. These will be discussed and the historical background to the changes in England will be considered.

HISTORICAL FEATURES

England was the first country to experience the industrial revolution. Workers, including numbers of young children, were employed in harsh conditions until reforms were introduced. The notion of gaining skills and knowledge in preparation for future employment to gain a satisfactory job and to provide a compliant workforce, was a powerful pressure for systems concerning provision for young children. This affected young children who were, or were preparing to become, part of the workforce. When debating the school starting age the importance of earning a living was considered, with beginning and ending statutory schooling early seen as a solution for children to begin work at an early age. In 1876, children from three years old could be taken into school 'babies'' rooms which offered training in alphabet recitation, picture recognition and marching to music (Anning 1991: 3). Early years provision developed from a need for childcare

to support working parents and to give disadvantaged children the opportunity to 'catch up' with their progress in readiness for school and employment.

PREPARATION FOR EMPLOYMENT

The emphasis on a preparation for an industrial workforce fostered the encouragement of strategies to promote a compliant workforce. Any successes were developed on an individual basis with strategies such as the 11+ testing for the school system implemented in the Butler Education Act, which determined the next steps and exerted a 'top-down' pressure on those working with younger children.

Yet changing family structures and employment goals encouraged new perspectives on appropriate arrangements for children. In 1967 the Central Advisory Council for education claimed, 'mothers with young children who also worked were to be deplored' (Brannen and Moss 2003: 33).

POLICIES AND PRACTICE

Callaghan's Ruskin speech in 1976 emphasised the financial implications of government policy, demanding 'value for money' and stressing the need for a monitoring system in order to 'maintain a proper national standard of performance'. He argued there was a strong case for the so-called 'core curriculum of basic knowledge' (Anning 1991: 7). The National Commission for Education in 1995 promoted the belief that investment of taxpayers' money in increased support for children aged 3–8 years would ensure that all children achieved a good grasp of basic skills early, to provide a foundation for future learning. Government control covered guidelines and frameworks for what was to be delivered, with regulations and accountability to ensure funding could be accessed. While maintaining this oversight of the provision, parents could access the setting of their choice. The Department for Education and Employment (DfEE) in 1998 stated 'It is up to parents to decide what kind of childcare they want for their children. This is not a matter for the government' (Brannen and Moss 2003: 29). Private providers played a central role in delivering services in the childcare market. The growth in numbers of working mothers created a need for childcare arrangements and provision which were to follow government guidelines. The findings of the external regulators had a profound impact on the viability of the provision, with adults readily able to transfer their children to other childcare arrangements. By the end of the twentieth century childcare was not just for children in need but a desirable commodity for working families. National standards and regulations existed for all providers.

The background to New Labour's approach drew heavily on the USA Headstart programme. The purpose of Headstart was to give children from low-income families a 'head start', to support the transition from early years provision to formal schooling with an emphasis on school 'readiness' and an outcomes-based approach. Consideration was also given to European guidelines and targets. When England referred to the European Union agenda regarding early years provision, account was taken of proposals such as the European Commission's 10-year strategy in 1996–2006.

However, while in 1951, 12% of the workforce in England were women, by 1998 this had risen to 30%. Although childcare was the subject of public policy, the responsibility for accessing the provision was up to the individuals concerned with the responsibility of the children. This encouraged a view of the provision as a commodity and parents as the consumers. It led to a diversity of provision, with local authorities organising nursery classes and extending reception classes to enable younger children to attend. The private sector also supplied places to meet the demand in a variety of forms such as playgroups or private day nurseries. Ofsted publicly identified those settings deemed to be failing.

YOUNG CHILDREN IN SCHOOL

With the rise of four-year-olds in school and the number of working women, views regarding children in early years started to change. It became financially attractive for younger children to attend school and fill spare places. The view grew that it was a beneficial requirement for young children, rather than a necessity.

Therefore, early years provision was perceived as a significant factor in preparing children to be successful in school, providing a workforce for the future which could in turn strengthen the economic position of the country.

CHANGES AND CHALLENGES IN THE CONTEMPORARY WORLD

According to Lauder et al. we live in a 'world of collective consciousness, where we see our problems as interconnected' (2008: 4). Ideas of best provision for early childhood care can be shared globally and can respond to global influences, with an interaction of thoughts and reflections. We have become used to living with uncertainty and change and this is reflected in the constantly changing nature of early years education and care. Besides global effects requiring assimilation by the providers of early years provision, practitioners are faced with national political agendas featuring new initiatives. 'In the twenty-first century it is probably evident to every parent, professional childcare worker, kindergarten and primary teacher that early childhood is high on the political agenda' (Gammage 2006: 235).

Changing patterns of work, where both parents seek employment, has led to an increased need for childcare arrangements to support this. A growing desire to support families in need strengthened the growth of childcare facilities and requirements. As early as 1997 Oberhuemer and Ulich (1997: 6) noted there was a 'common underlying thread' in Europe, where 'provision sprang to meet perceived needs'. Anderson and Eliassen, cited by Parsons (1995) consider a 'Europeification of national policy-making' where policies are discussed in a collaborative European context. Therefore the diverse early years settings which were developing in Europe not only sought to exist in the locality but questioned the quality of provision by sharing pedagogical ideas with colleagues further afield.

This questioning and sharing were responses to various factors. Tony Blair (2005) stated 'We have to secure Britain's future in a world ... driven by globalisation. We have to change and to modernise ... to equip everyone for this changing world' (cited in Cole 2008: 86). The notion that globalisation affects early years provision is implicated in the argument, through a response to changing forces in the contemporary world. This influences the approach to learning to prepare young children for a future workforce.

However, learning in the early years is also concerned with valuing the moment of childhood, rather than as the preparation of goals to strive for when children get older. 'At the heart of educational quality means meeting learners' diverse needs and opening rather than foreclosing opportunities to develop as individuals and as valuable members of local and global society' (Lauder et al. 2008: 16). This view requires a broad, holistic approach to address the needs of the developing child and provide challenges to learn through personal constructions of the world. Provision could become similar and standardised. Shared discussions between those interested in early years matters fosters collaboration of ideas and practice, while developing provision within local deliberations regarding appropriate practice. Therefore, early years practitioners use their professional skills to weave the requirements of national policies, influenced by global organisation recommendations, with their understandings of the individual children within their setting.

Environmental concerns, faster transport links, internet access and international organisations and companies have blurred national boundaries. These links can forge an international sharing of ideas regarding early years provision, through networking and collaboration. Prospective headteachers in England were encouraged to consider approaches used in other countries. 'Our children will become world citizens. The similarities between issues for education within a similar economic and developmental framework are appreciable whilst cultural differences can bring new thoughts to approaches to development in our countries' (NPQH Think Piece, National College for School Leadership, 2006).

Globalisation appears in literature regarding early years (Dahlberg and Moss 2007; Lauder et al. 2008) in terms of the need of the provision to prepare for future challenges. Parental need and the desire to obtain employment imposes further pressure on the demands of appropriate provision. In the current credit crisis, awareness of the desire to maintain and sustain economic viability is evident, as demonstrated in the G20 meeting in London in 2009, where leaders of countries met to decide strategies to deal with the situation. The uncertainty helps to drive discussions concerning the purpose of provision for young children, including a spectrum of views ranging from whether it should have a narrow curriculum focus as a means to gain specific skills or be viewed in broader terms as a period of childhood to enjoy in its own right. The United Nations International Children's Emergency Fund (UNICEF 2002) urged 'no nation today can afford to ignore opportunities for maximising investments in education'. Within this book, consideration of what knowledge and skills would be desired have been placed in an holistic manner.

Certain European countries share notions of good early years practice as a united response to international change. These dialogues between practitioners in different countries lead to changing practice. In Europe these can include networks for those concerned with the care and education of children, such as the European Early Childhood Education Research Association (EECERA). The character of communities changes as migrant workers and their children add new dimensions to the nature of the areas they move to. Inclusive practice in the early years settings flourishes, for example incorporation of modern foreign languages from an early age as part of learning about the world. Early years settings need to be viewed as diverse and multicultural environments, for example, in giving support for children who have English as an additional language.

RECOMMENDATIONS FROM INTERNATIONAL ORGANISATIONS

Recommendations from international organisations have had a profound impact on national agendas.

The United Nations

The United Nations Educational, Scientific and Cultural Organisation (UNESCO) was set up in November 1945, after the Second World War, with the aim to 'build peace in the minds of men'. It serves to 'function as a laboratory of ideas and a standard setter to forge universal agreements on emerging ethical issues' (www.portal.unesco). It provides a means of disseminating and sharing information and knowledge. UNESCO (2003) affirmed 'that children's holistic development can only be ensured if there is close co-ordination or preferably integration of the education, social and health sectors, and they strongly urge governments to tackle this integration as part of their social and economic planning' (Woods 2005: xi). It included Article 6 which stated development should be interpreted holistically, that is including emotional, cognitive, social, cultural and mental as well as physical aspects of development.

In 2007 UNESCO had 193 member states. Jarvis (2008: 39) suggests that UNESCO is a 'champion of lifelong learning' which is always presented 'within a humanistic perspective'. He mentions the Faure Report which was the outcome of a UNESCO Commission on the Development of Education (1972). 'Throughout the report the whole of the person is constantly emphasised: The physical, intellectual, emotional and ethical integration of the individual into the complete man is a fundamental aim of education.' (Jarvis 2008: 40)

The United Nations Convention on the Rights of the Child (UNCRC) is a 'universally agreed set of non–negotiable standards and obligations. These basic standards – also called human rights – set minimum entitlements and freedoms that should be respected by governments' (www.unicef.org).

Article 2 stated that the Convention applied to all children. An inclusive practice was promoted to ensure all children were to be included in provisions made for them. This would require inclusive practice to support those who might need it, to access the available provision. Article 4 stated the adherence to a multi-agency approach where social services, legal, health and educational systems were involved. It recognised a possible need to change existing laws or create new ones to accommodate this target. Article 29, the goals for education, stated children's education should develop each child's personality, talents and abilities to the fullest.

In the UNESCO World Education for All Monitoring Report 2009 two of three top policy recommendations for Early Childhood Education and Care stated:

- Prioritize early childhood education and care in planning for all children.
- Strengthen the links between education planning and health provision.

The Organisation for Economic Co-operation and Development

The OECD was established in 1960 'to achieve the highest possible economic growth and employment and increase the standard of living in member countries, to contribute to economic expansion in both member and non-member countries and to increase world trade' (Jarvis 2008: 42).

OECD 2006 guidelines for practice incorporate the targets identified in the European Commission report. Ten policy areas proposed for consideration by governments included:

2. To place well-being, early development and learning at the core of ECEC (Early Childhood Education and Care) work, while respecting the child's agency and natural learning strategies.

8. To improve the professional education of ECEC staff.

10. To aspire to ECEC systems that support broad learning.

The European Commission

The European Commission has been included in the discussions as a significant player in broader deliberations. It was believed amongst member states of the Council of Europe that there were 'as many patterns of pre-school organisation' as there were 'terms to describe them,' where the 'precise levels and patterns of use reflected national history and policies' (Woodhead 1979: 2). However, by 1991, Anderson and Eliassen (cited by Parsons 1995) described a 'Europeification of national policy-making' where a level of policy making developed following European guidelines and recommended targets (cited in Parsons 1995: 236).

The European Commission formulated recommendations to provide standards for quality, while giving examples of good practice throughout Europe. This led to the European Commission's *Quality Targets in Services for Young Children* (1996), incorporated into a 10-year plan, for states to achieve within the time scale. The 40 targets included those based on the issues concerning an holistic approach, multidisciplinary working and a framework for literacy, namely:

- Target 1 Governments should provide a published and coherent statement of intent for care and education services to young children aged birth to six years and explain how such initiatives will be co-ordinated between services.
- Target 14 All services should positively assert the value of diversity.
- Target 18 The educational philosophy should be broad and include linguistic and oral skills.

The report stated:

> Most countries in the industrialised world have accepted that children below the age of formal schooling benefit from some kind of collective provision, whether it is viewed as preparation for school, an opportunity to socialize with other children and adults beyond the family, or in order to enable parents to work (EC 1996: 18).

National states were strongly encouraged to address the recommendations, or at least attempt to implement many of the targets.

Moss et al. (2003) identified key features of early years policy in Europe:

- A legal right for parental leave
- Public support for the childcare needs of employed parents
- Public support for at least two years of education for all children before they start compulsory schooling. (Moss et al. 2003).

National governments were required to address the growing needs of provision for young children to support working parents, while provision attained certain standards. Esping-Andersen (Moss et al. 2003: 5) notes the 'open method of co-ordination' adopted by the European Union at its Lisbon Summit in 2000, which concerned a 'practice of cross-national policy' and where the objective was to 'institutionalise processes for sharing policy experience and the diffusion of best practices'. He continues that the 'key advantage of the open method of co-ordination for the advancement of a social Europe lies in its potential of reconciling national diversity and democratic accountability of the nation-state with common policy ambitions and measures of policy effectiveness through benchmarking and monitoring'. Jarvis (2008: 44) agrees, stating that 'throughout the European documents' one of the main aims is 'to create a united Europe'. The objective is also stated 'to provide employment for all its workers and to advance the knowledge and technological level of its workforce'. Thus, while highlighting specific examples of good practice throughout Europe, the standardisation of provision appears to be at the forefront of the European Commission's recommendations, in order to meet the needs of working parents and the children in early years settings.

The Enterprise Development website maintains 'for any country to transform itself into a viable, knowledge-based economy, internal, institutional change will be crucial' (www.govmonitor). Local and individual settings have responsibility for providing the framework for learning, within national guidelines, to ensure young children's development and progress.

EARLY YEARS EDUCATION AND CARE IN ENGLAND

In England children were perceived as 'not there yet' with educational aims to prepare children for later schooling. This went alongside universal goals of development to form the progression for learning, with a consideration of those who do not conform possibly at risk of failing to achieve prescribed goals.

Activities were devised based on enabling the child as an individual to progress through developmental stages. Rather than waiting for the child to accumulate enough experience to move on to the next stage, the adult or more experienced child supported the learner's progression. Progression was devised through such theories as those of Piaget (1950), Vygotsky (1962) and Bruner (1966). Settings were therefore highly 'organised and planned and there is less emphasis on children's self-initiative' (McQuail et al. 2003: 14).

The emphasis was on teacher initiated and directed tasks with basic academic skills within a structured framework comprising core knowledge for the children to learn. Links were sought with schools for 'in the UK ... there is a strong emphasis on school "readiness" with parents being encouraged to "educate" their children in the skills and knowledge which will allow them to succeed in school' (Smidt 2006: 85). According to Brannen and Moss (2003: 25) 'England has a National Childcare Strategy in 1998, although for those settings linked to schools the focus could have been on education for early years rather than an emphasis on care.'

A basic curriculum was sought for all children to succeed as part of the future workforce. David Blunkett, the then Secretary of State for Education, in the Foreword to a key government green paper, *The Learning Age* (1998), described the purpose of learning as

> the key to prosperity – for each of us as individuals, as well as for the nation as a whole. Investment in human capital will be the foundation of success in the knowledge-based economy of the twenty-first century. This is why the Government has put learning at the heart of its ambition (cited in Bottery 2001: 206).

The curriculum was linked to the perceived requirements for the future economic wealth of the country. The introduction of the National Literacy Strategy in 1998 gave rise to pressure for some practitioners who were encouraged to implement the strategy in Foundation Stage settings for three- and four-year-olds. In 1999 the Chief Inspector of Schools argued that the inclusion of reading, writing and numeracy in the early years curriculum would help to overcome educational disadvantage experienced by children from poorer backgrounds. The desire to ensure all children had the necessary skills needed for the workforce led to further guidelines for early years practice. The introduction in 2000 of the Curriculum Guidelines for the Foundation Stage aimed to give parity of provision to all three- and four-year-old children.

The OECD publication *Starting Strong* (2006: 141), noting key features of the English early years system, included the following curricula traditions:

- The child is a person to be formed.
- An early years centre is a place of development, learning and instruction. Children are expected to reach pre-determined goals.
- There is a prescribed ministerial curriculum, with goals and outcomes.
- There is a focus on learning and skills, especially in areas of school readiness.
- The national curriculum must be 'delivered' correctly.
- It incorporates a growing focus on individual competence in the national language. There is an emphasis on emergent literacy practices.
- Prescribed targets are set at a national level.
- Indoors is the primary learning space, with resources focused here.
- Learning outcomes and assessment are required.
- Quality control is evident with inspection undertaken by external regulators.

This approach to learning strives to enable children to progress in their learning, yet Gammage argues that the best care and education possible is 'not about "hot-housing" children, or about forcing them into early academic endeavour' (2006: 241). He cites evidence from neuroscience research which states 'early childhood is the period when the human organism responds to the environment with such malleability that the very architecture of the brain is affected' (Gammage, 2006: 236).

Urban (2008: 140) claims 'There is a powerful top down stream of knowledge presented as relevant for practice. Practitioners at the bottom are required to implement the policies'. This was emphasised in the *Children's Plan*, which stated: 'The single most important factor in delivering our aspirations for children is a world class workforce able to provide highly personalised support, so we will continue to drive up quality and capacity of those working in the children's workforce' (Balls 2007: 11). Practitioners could find the aspect of implementing the many policies and new initiatives to 'drive up quality' challenging. A creative approach is needed where children can respond to changing factors, such as employment and new, developing industries. Lauder et al (2008: 7) state 'improving early childhood education and childcare is linked to lifelong learning and a number of international policies where the rationales are those of economic development'. As early as 1978 Eyre stressed the need to be literate and have an holistic, creative, knowledge base to survive. Those who were not able to achieve this would have difficulties for 'a situation exists in which the population continues to increase but where human labour is increasingly dispensable' (Eyre 1978: 169). Emphasis is placed on transferable skills where children are 'learning to learn' rather than receiving formal prescriptive teaching.

The welfare state includes an ageing population who are not working but need to be provided for. In the global credit crisis the cost of early years provision is a concern. Clark and Waller (2007: 27) question 'Might there be a dichotomy ... between the ideology of improving childhood but without the financial investment to make it a reality?' Training needs could be incorporated into work-based learning, for example, as demonstrated in the growth of the Early Years Professional Status qualification. Nursery schools could be deemed expensive to maintain, with costs cut through closure and children moved to nursery classes linked to existing schools. The Rose Review of admission policies recommended young children should be admitted to early admission classes in schools. Birth to three provision could then be accessed through private facilities on site. This supports parental employment when the 'new discourse of policy now tells parents that childcare is not just acceptable but positively to be desired' (Brannen and Moss 2003: 33). The rationale is that children achieve more when given access to early years provision. However, to further achieve the aim of meeting the needs of working parents, flexible hours are required, which is facilitated through such means as extended schools and Children's Centres.

ACCOUNTABILITY

One of the means of judging achievements is through results from the EYFS (Early Years Foundation Stage) profiles. Pressure from colleagues teaching classes of older children could also be apparent, through the importance of results and a satisfactory report from Ofsted. The new Ofsted (Office for Standards for Education, Children's Services and Skills) came into being in 2007. It brings together four formerly separate inspectorates. It inspects provision for children and young people and inspects education and training for learners of all ages. This strengthens the remit of the inspectorate and in turn, accentuates the importance of the findings.

Evidence is needed to support the assessments which could lead to practice where documentation can be readily accumulated. When the profiles were initially introduced, John Bangs, head of education at the National Union of Teachers (NUT), was concerned the profiles attempted to 'ride two horses, to provide information for value-added scores and to be diagnostic' (Rodger 1999: 43).

The introduction of Letters and Sounds, following the Rose Review, provides a developmental approach in a pack of information and activities to use while children are in the early years leading through primary school. However, practitioners should be aware of what children need to understand before they can learn to read and write, what they have to do before they become literate and what type of adult support and environment best supports literacy learning. In order to implement the strategies effectively the approach the practitioner uses is personal to them in their daily interactions with children.

Case Study

In a moderation exercise with a group of practitioners from different providers it was found that practice to collate evidence for assessments varied. In some settings assessments formed part of a natural information gathering through on-going activities, while in others specific activities were devised to gain evidence to show children's progression in learning. It was felt at the meeting that the way information gathering for assessments was made had major concerns for the planning of activities and organisation of the learning environment.

AN HOLISTIC APPROACH

In 1994 SureStart used the term 'educare' to describe the way education and care could be combined in early years settings. This was reflected in the development of Children's Centres where early education was integrated with health and family support services. Flexible timings of the sessions, usually open from 8am to 6pm, supported parents' working patterns. It was proposed that by 2010 there would be 3,500 in England. These Centres could form a competition to ensure children access places available in Centres or local schools. Children's Centres have been given the proviso that they must be self sustaining within three years of opening. This tension heightens the stakes for the provision to gain sufficient funding for the places available. If places are unfilled the Centre could close through lack of funding. Decisions regarding appropriate provision for young children could be influenced by the ramifications of closing existing settings to provide access for children in a setting which incorporates flexible timing and multidisciplinary working. The cost of changing provision could be a factor where an existing add-on to school could be the cheaper option. Early years practitioners involved with the existing provision voiced their concerns about changes, although the closure of nursery schools to place young children in early years settings in schools appears to be continuing.

Questions for Discussion

How has globalisation affected an aspect of provision you are familiar with? What are the implications for your practice?

THE EARLY YEARS FOUNDATION STAGE FRAMEWORK

The Early Years Foundation Stage framework, which was introduced in 2008, is underpinned by the Every Child Matters agenda. This agenda, introduced in 2003, promotes an holistic approach to learning through specific outcomes identified for children aged birth to 19, that is; be healthy; stay safe; enjoy and achieve; make a positive contribution; and achieve economic well-being.

Legislation in 1989 from the UNCRC highlighted the need for professionals from a range of disciplines to work together to promote the well-being of children. The Children's Act in 2004 sought to increase multidisciplinary working to provide holistic care for children. Multidisciplinary working brings together professionals from differing disciplinary backgrounds to collaborate and co-operate to promote the well-being of the children they are responsible for.

The Early Years Foundation Stage framework, statutory in 2008, developed the holistic approach to learning for young children. It is underpinned by four principles: the unique child; positive relationships; an enabling environment; and learning and development. These broad aims can be implemented by practitioners to meet the needs of the individual children in the settings, providing a play-based learning environment for children. Within this framework, practitioners can create the environment that best enables children in the setting to construct their understanding of the world around them.

Further Reading

Beckley, P., Elvidge, K. and Hendry, H. (2009) *Implementing the Early Years Foundation Stage: A Handbook*. London: Open University Press.

Johnston, J. and Nahmad-Williams, L. (2008) *Early Childhood Studies*. Harlow: Pearson/Longman.

Moyles, J. R. (ed.) (1994) *The Excellence of Play*. Buckingham: Open University Press.

Neuman, M. J. (2005) *Governance of Early Childhood Education and Care: Recent Developments in OECD Countries*. TACTYC, Colchester: Taylor and Francis.

Petrie, P. (2005) 'Extending Pedagogy', *Journal of Education for Teaching* 31(4). London: Routledge.

Pugh, G. (ed.) (2008) *Contemporary Issues in the Early Years: Working Collaboratively for Children*. London: Paul Chapman.

Sylva, K., Melhuish, E., Sammons, P. and Taggart, B. (2004) *Effective Provision of Pre-School Education (EPPE) Project*. Nottingham: DfES Publications.

Taylor, J. and Woods, M. (eds) (2005) *Early Childhood Studies: A Holistic Approach*. London: Hodder Arnold.

Waller, T. (ed.) (2010) *An Introduction to Early Childhood* (2nd edn). London: Sage.

This book is edited by Tim Waller and contains contributions from many experts in their field. Contents in the book include discussions of children's rights to participation, with consideration of the United Nations Convention on the Rights of the Child (1989). It also features a chapter based on international perspectives.

Useful Websites

www.egovmonitor.com
www.portal.unesco
www.unicef.org
www.wsrcsocietytoday.ac.uk

References

Anning, A. (1998) *The Co-construction by Early Years Care and Practitioners of Literacy and Mathematics Curricula for Young Children*. University of Belfast. BERA.

Balls, E. (2007) *The Children's Plan – Building Brighter Futures*. Norwich: HMSO.

Bottery, M. (2001) *Globalisation and the UK Competition State: No Room for Transformational Leadership in Education?* University of Hull, School Leadership and Management, Vol. 21.

Brannen, J. and Moss, P. (2003) *Rethinking Children's Care*. Buckingham: Open University Press.

Clarke, M. M. and Waller, T. (2007) *Early Childhood Education and Care*. London: Sage.

Cole, M. (2008) *Marxism and Educational Theory*. London: Routledge.

Dahlberg, G. and Moss, P. (2007) *Ethics and Politics in Early Childhood Education*. London: RoutledgeFalmer.

Dahlberg, G., Moss, P. and Pence, A. (1999) *Beyond Quality in Early Childhood Education and Care*. London: Routledge Falmer.

Eyre, S.R. (1978) *The Real Wealth of Nations*. London: Edward Arnold (Publishers) Ltd.

European Commission (1996) *Quality Targets in Services for Young Children*. University of Toronto: Childcare Resource and Research Unit.

Gammage, P. (2006) *Early Childhood Education and Care: Politics, Policies and Possibilities*. TACTYC, Colchester: Routledge.

Jarvis, P. (2008) *Democracy, Lifelong Learning and the Learning Society*. London: RoutledgeFalmer.

Lauder, H., Lowe, J. and Chawla-Duggan, R. (2008) *Primary Review Interim Report: Aims for Primary Education: Changing Global Contexts*. University of Cambridge.

McQuail, S., Mooney, A., Cameron, C., Candappa, M., Moss, P. and Petrie, P. (2003) *Early Years and Childcare International Evidence Project*. London: Thomas Coram Research Unit, Institute of Education.

Moss, P., Cameron, C., Candappa, M., McQuail, S., Petrie, P. and Mooney, A. (2003) *Early Years and Childcare International Evidence Project*. University of London: Thomas Coram Research Unit.

NPQH (2006) *NPQH Think Piece*. Nottingham: National College of School Leadership.

Oberhuemer, P. and Ulich, M. (1997), *Working with Young Children in Europe*. London: Paul Chapman.

OECD (2006) *Starting Strong II: Early Childhood Education and Care*. Paris: OECD Publishing.

Parsons, W. (1995), *Public Policy*. Aldershot: Edward Elgar Ltd.

Rodger, R. (1999) *Planning an Appropriate Curriculum for the Under Fives*. London: David Fulton.

Smidt, S. (2006) *The Developing Child in the 21st Century*. Abingdon: Routledge.

Urban, M. (2008) 'Dealing with Uncertainty: Challenges and Possibilities for the Early Childhood Profession'. *European Early Childhood Research Journal* 16(2): 135–52.

Woodhead, M. (1979) *Pre-School Education in Western Europe; Issues, Policies and Trends*. London: Longman.

2 THEORIES OF LEARNING

Pat Beckley

Learning objectives

- To become aware of the range of theories of learning
- To know some of the key theorists who influenced thinking about learning
- To consider issues concerning the theories

This chapter incorporates discussions of theories of learning, for example those of Rousseau, Piaget, Vygotsky and Bruner, with findings from research, such as Bowlby's attachment theory, to support arguments for an holistic approach. It recognises a range of theoretical perspectives of child development and builds an appreciation and understanding of the relationship between theory and practice. It explains how aspects of child development are interrelated and the importance on individual development within a social context.

JEAN JACQUES ROUSSEAU (1712–1778)

Rousseau was born in Geneva. His mother died shortly after his birth and, after living for a while with his father, then his uncle, he supported himself wandering in Italy and France. He became a companion and secretary to Madame de Warens, later going to Paris where he worked as a music teacher and political secretary.

Rousseau believed that humans are born good but are influenced by society. His philosophy of education is not concerned with particular techniques of imparting information and concepts, but rather with developing the pupil's character and moral sense, so that he may learn to practice self-mastery and remain virtuous even in the unnatural and imperfect society in which he will have to live. Rousseau felt that children learn right and wrong through experiencing the consequences of their acts rather than through physical punishment.

Rousseau was one of the first to advocate developmentally appropriate education and his description of the stages of child development mirrors his conception of the evolution of culture. He divides childhood into stages: the first is to the age of about 12, when children are guided by their emotions and impulses. During the second stage, from 12 to about 16, reason starts to develop and finally the third stage, from the age of 16 onwards, when the child develops into an adult.

Rousseau has been called the 'Father of Education' and his emphasis on child-centredness has influenced thinking on education and learning to this day.

JOHN LOCKE (1632–1704)

Locke, an English philosopher and physician, considered nurture or external forces as routes for development. He believed interactions with people and the environment affected children's development and that parents were the first educators. Locke was the first to define the self through a continuity of consciousness. He claimed that the mind was an 'empty cabinet' and that it was only through experiences that knowledge was formed.

JOHANN HEINRICH PESTALOZZI (1746–1827)

Pestalozzi studied theology at the University of Zurich. In 1775 he opened a school for the children of the poor on his estate in Zurich. In 1798 in Switzerland Pestalozzi cared for a number of orphans who had been left without food or shelter during the French invasion. Although his schools ran into difficulties his ideas were discussed throughout Europe and in 1805 when he opened a school in Yverdon pupils from all over Europe attended. He emphasised that every aspect of the child's life contributed to the formation of personality, character, and reason. His educational methods were child-centred and based on the child as an individual.

SIGMUND FREUD (1856–1939)

Freud was born in Austria in 1856. He began his study of medicine at the University of Vienna. He proposed a psychoanalytical theory. Psychoanalysis has three main components comprising a method of investigation of the mind and the way one thinks, a systematised set of theories about human behaviour, and a method of treatment of psychological or emotional illness. He considered that a personality consists of three aspects; the id – this aspect dominates early life and refers to things which give us pleasure; the ego – this is the awareness of themselves children develop as they gain understanding of themselves and the world around them; and the superego – moral reasoning, following a recognition of the id and ego.

Freud favoured treatment where the patient talked through his or her problems. This came to be known as the 'talking cure' and the ultimate goal of this talking was to locate and release powerful emotional energy that had initially been rejected or imprisoned in the unconscious mind. Freud called this denial of emotions repression, and he believed that it was an impediment to the normal functioning of the psyche, and was even capable of causing physical retardation which he described as psychosomatic. Talking therapies are widely used and thought to be beneficial today.

JOHN DEWEY (1859–1952)

Dewey was born in America. He attended the University of Vermont and John Hopkins University. He argued in his writings that social interaction is needed for children to learn. He believed that pupils thrive in an environment where they actively interact with the curriculum and their surroundings. Dewey was elected president of the American Psychological Association in 1899.

CHILD DEVELOPMENT

Child development is concerned with a range of areas, including speculation on the way in which a child will grow up, consideration of factors which influence development, an understanding of the uniqueness of the developing child, an understanding of the beliefs of how to bring up children, an awareness of differences in child rearing practices, and examination of the theories, research and explanations in order to gain an understanding of the ways in which a child develops.

In order to consider what forms a child into an adult an understanding of the nature of the subject and its concepts and ideas is of importance. These include:

- **Development** The total process whereby individuals adapt to their environment.
- **Developmental Theory** A body of psychological theories concerned with the development of children from birth to maturity.
- **Growth** Ordinarily refers to such physical changes as increasing height or weight.
- **Childhood** An arbitrary division in the sequence of human development when the beginning and end of the period can be queried.
- **Heredity** The transmission of physical and personality characteristics and predispositions from parent to offspring.
- **Maturation** According to Piaget this is the fundamental tendency to organise experience so that it can be assimilated.

Family factors might influence the child's development, for example the number of adults present in the home, parental views concerning child rearing and ways of upbringing, as well as issues such as bonding, control and discipline, child neglect and friendships. These issues will be discussed further in the final chapter.

Housing issues could impact on children's health and well-being, influencing their ability to thrive and develop. The number of siblings, security of relationships and significant happenings in family life, such as a death in the family, can further impact on a child's understandings of their world. A child's health and welfare factors in the wider community could also play a part.

The transition from home to playgroup, nursery, Children's Centre or reception class in a school can have a significant influence on a child's ability to learn and develop. Smooth transition between home and another setting can ease this period in the child's life and could be a positive transition and development for the child. An insecure child might need further reassurance to support the settling-in time, before feeling sufficiently confident to access activities in the early years setting or make friends. The child might be dependent on an adult and increasingly become independent, depending on previous experience and personality. The Early Years Foundation Stage suggests a key person supports this transition and helps the child to enjoy new experiences.

The socialisation process enables the child to take his/her place in the adult world. This is a complex process which involves the child acquiring the cultural rules, attitudes, values and social skills necessary for integration into a wide range of institutions, like the play-group, the school, the place of worship or other people's homes. The socialisation process involves the child in social learning, play, imitation and identification through interaction with parents, adults and other children and in assimilating the experiences gained.

EARLY LEARNING

Research into child development has continued to question and explore new ideas and ways of thinking about how children progress and what supports them. According to Nutbrown and Page (2008: 16) 'modern visual and audio recording techniques have enabled researchers and practitioners to create a fuller knowledge base about young children'. This amazing research demonstrates how little we previously knew of the development of babies and how aware even the youngest baby is of their surroundings and those closest to them. Recent research in neuroscience has encouraged people to reflect on their perceptions about babies' abilities and understandings. Nutbrown and Page (2008: 17) contest that 'studies in neuroscience (Greenfield 1997; Greenough et al. 1987) the scientific study of the nervous system, have shed new light on how the brain develops, and so have challenged some long accepted beliefs about babies'.

Babies can hear and recognise familiar sounds, such as the whistle dad makes as he is busy in the house. Newborn babies can copy facial expressions demonstrated by a proud father. However, studies also show that babies need security and affection to thrive.

BOWLBY'S ATTACHMENT THEORY

The findings from Bowlby's research in 1953, *Child Care and the Growth of Love*, suggested that babies and young children needed to be at home with their mothers. He claimed that if this bond was broken in the first six months of a young baby's life then irreparable damage would occur which could not be redressed. This 'Attachment Theory' proved thought-provoking at the time and arouses strong feelings today. Questions about the validity of the research have been considered, for example whether the inclusion of children who were in hospital was appropriate, and it has also been criticised as disregarding other crucial factors, for example the role of the father, grandparents or siblings. It is also considered that Bowlby's findings were used to dissuade mothers from returning to work after the war as employment was needed for men returning from the battle lines.

PLAY

According to Froebel, play is the purest, most spiritual activity of man at any stage. There are many interpretations and discussions regarding play and the importance it has on children's learning and development. Play covers a variety of aspects, such as physical activities, manipulative tasks, verbal games, humour and shared interactions about the world, and making sense of our surroundings.

The motives for play have intrigued practitioners and academics and there are a number of explanations. Classical theories of play include:

- The surplus energy theory where the release of excess energy takes the form of aimless play activity.
- The relaxation theory where play becomes a means through which energy can be replenished, for example a short break where children can run and exercise after sitting at formal tasks to enable them to renew their energy for work.
- The practice theory identified by Karl Groos, where children play to practise the skills they will need in adulthood, for example a mother caring for a child, or a visit to the doctor's.
- Recapitulation theory where children rehearse the activities of our ancestors, thus ridding themselves of the need to express such primitive behaviour in adulthood, for example when play fighting or chasing.

A CULTURAL VIEW OF PLAY

Culture is always invented in the playful mind, for example law and order or science are all arenas of playful enquiry. Special rules apply in a variety of social areas of play such as at the tennis court, at home or in a setting. Culture grows as play and play is informed by the culture the child is part of. A child's toy in one culture is part of a ritual and could be a serious object in another. The fun of kitchen tools can be a rich source of play. Children create novel realms to play in. Children construct social worlds. By signs and symbols children create worlds of cops and robbers or mothers and non-mothers. Children set up and direct created worlds in which a leader and followers emerge. There can be a politics of play with specific rule setting, for example children know the rules of the playground. This consists of a private system between friends and may differ from a public system of rules. We live in a world of social systems. This is further discussed in Chapter 14 which looks at the social context of learning.

PLAY AND PHYSICAL DEVELOPMENT

Physical development is often broken down into two types:

- **Gross Motor Skills**   The use of large muscles through activities such as climbing, running, balancing and pulling. Children involve their whole body and we see evidence of this in play such as swinging, climbing, riding bikes or moving pieces of equipment.
- **Fine Motor Skills**   These relate to the co-ordination of hand and eye movements through activities such as cutting and pasting, working puzzles, table games, drawing and painting, water play and so on. Precision grows through constant experience. These activities are persistent and repetitive, and play is an ideal medium for them.

Clearly appropriate opportunities and materials are necessary for both types of development to take place. Play of this nature helps to increase self-confidence and autonomy as well as promoting physical health.

PHYSICAL DEVELOPMENT

Consideration should be given to: height and weight gained during childhood; mobility and movement: crawling, sitting, standing, walking, climbing and the use of gross motor skills and fine motor skills. Note the child's ability to dress/undress. How does the child learn to walk, run, catch, climb, throw, roll, fall, swim? These developments are often tracked to ensure a child is progressing healthily, for example through records, observations, charts and diagrams.

COGNITIVE DEVELOPMENT

Recent studies of the brain have led to further consideration of child development, with an awareness that very young children and babies develop at a much faster rate than previously thought.

Cognitive development is concerned with the child as 'knower', how the child thinks, learns, acquires concepts, remembers, understands relationships, solves problems. The child is actively trying to 'make sense of the world' or construct a meaningful picture of the world through the senses of sight, touch, smell, taste and hearing.

🗁 Case Study

A group of 17 early years children were sitting waiting for a communal snack with their teacher. A parent had brought in a melon as a treat for them and they had talked about the melon and thanked the child whose parent had brought it, for the kind thought. The adult cut it in half and the children were struck with wonder at the red, bright, mouthwatering fruit inside the green case. 'Now I need to cut it into smaller pieces for us. How many pieces shall I cut each half into?' asked the teacher. The teacher became distracted with another child, forgetting the question for a while, but then she turned and was about to cut the fruit into pieces when a girl said 'You'll need nine for each half – there are 18 of us'. She had watched her mother cut cakes into pieces and counted them with her. She had observed the teacher and worked out the problem.

JEAN PIAGET (1896–1980)

Piaget was born in Switzerland and studied at the University of Neuchatel. He was interested in the qualitative development of knowledge.

Piaget suggested there were stages of development. These consist of the following.

0–2 Years Sensorimotor

The child uses extensive trial and error movements and develops bodily control and hand-eye co-ordination. Perceptual field is organised into objects having permanent identity under varying conditions (being hidden). The child learns to differentiate him/herself from and relate to an external world of objects and events. This stage marks the beginning of symbolic thought (mental operations), for example remembering, anticipating, pretending. Motor actions show reversibility (hiding and retrieving an object).

2–4 Years Preconceptual Thought

This stage is marked by the development of mental imagery – through play the child is able to represent and organise experience(s). Language gradually takes over mental operations from motor and visual imagery – especially during social play and when communicating. Verbal concepts are very simple as the child cannot grasp class relationships (e.g. seeing an object as a member of a class). Language and thinking emphasise egocentricity. Thought is irrational, inconsistent and closely linked to the child's own needs and feelings. Reality is seen from the child's point of view and he/she has little appreciation of other view points.

4–7 Years Intuitive Thought

The child's perceptions dominate thinking which shows a lack of reversibility as a result. Judgements lack 'conservation', for example changes in the appearance of an object mean changes in quantity/number. Judgements are intuitive and global, based upon superficial impressions and the overall appearance of a situation. Complex situations are reacted to as an unanalysable whole. Children take account of only one relationship at a time and cannot co-ordinate relationships – (failure to understand part/whole relationships or serial relationships). Thinking slowly moves towards stability and reversibility and there is a transitional stage where judgements are correct in some cases.

7–11 Years Concrete Operational Thought

This stage is concerned with concrete materials (e.g. classifying, forming a series). These systematic logical structures (operations) gradually replace the global inconsistent actions of the previous stage. Concepts are organised into classificatory systems (e.g. dogs/cats, adults). Temporal relationships are merged into notions of unitary space and time. Operations with concrete materials present can be imagined (carried out mentally) and results may be anticipated (e.g. in forming a series). Thinking in concrete situations shows important logical properties (e.g. reversibility) – judgements become rational and consistent. Children can co-ordinate relationships and grasp the principle of conservation (of quantity, space, time, etc). These operations are confined to concrete situations with tangible materials and do not extend to abstract and purely verbal situations. This limits the amount of transfer from one situation to another, since the child cannot abstract and formulate general laws and principles.

11–16 Formal Operational Thought

Operations on symbols and ideas can be carried out mentally. The child no longer needs to deal with objects directly. The child can move away from the actual and consider the possible. Accurate comparisons and deductions can be made from verbally presented information and data. The form of an argument can be followed disregarding the content. Formal operations involve propositions, hypotheses, logical relationships and contradictions. The child can formulate and test out hypotheses. The child is capable of considering variables and discovering general laws and principles.

Piaget's ideas influenced many educationalists and became popular in the 1970s with the development of the child-centred approach.

LEV VYGOTSKY (1896–1934)

Vygotsky was born in Russia (Belarus today) in 1896. Vygotsky investigated child development and how this was influenced by culture and context of the provision. 'Vygotsky's perspective on development is often referred to as a socio-cultural view because of his emphasis on the child's culture and the social environment as forces which shape development' (Keenan 2002: 132). Vygotsky believed that an individual's cognitive development was a social process.

Vygotsky proposed the notion of the Zone of Proximal Development (ZPD). Children's progress could be supported by interactions with knowledgeable others, capable peers or adults. He described the Zone of Proximal Development as the difference between children's actual developmental level and their potential level when guided by others. Vygotsky's contention was that interactions suported the child's learning and development. Development is considered in terms of a child's potential, rather than a point which they reach.

ERIK ERIKSON (1902–1994)

Erikson proposed a theory of development which considered social and cultural factors. It consisted of a series of stages which contained conflicts to be resolved at each stage. He felt there were eight stages which individuals passed through from birth to the end of their lives.

Erikson's psychosocial life-stages consisted of:

1. Basic trust versus mistrust from birth to one year/eighteen months
2. Autonomy versus shame and doubt from twelve/eighteen months to three years
3. Initiative versus guilt from three to six years
4. Industry versus inferiority from six to twelve years
5. Identity versus identity confusion at the adolescence stage
6. Intimacy versus isolation in young adulthood
7. Generativity versus stagnation in middle adulthood
8. Ego Integrity versus despair in late adulthood

'How successfully an individual resolves each crisis determines the nature of further development: successful resolutions lead to healthier developmental outcomes while unsuccessful or incomplete resolutions lead to less optimal outcomes' (Keenen 2002: 22). These crises are resolved through the interactions of three systems relevant to the individual, that is somatic, ego and societal.

JEROME BRUNER (1915–)

Bruner was born in America. He was awarded his PhD at Harvard University in 1941. He points to the ability of humans to learn without any accompanying observable behaviour, that is we can manipulate the world by vicarious mental actions rather than by trial and error. He recognised that cognitive growth resulted from both environmental impact, or 'culture', and the internal action that occurred to process this information. He considered the evolution of the mind was dramatically affected by three waves of inventions, or amplifiers, that were culturally transmitted:

- Devices that could amplify motor capacities (e.g. wheels, levers, pulleys)
- Devices that could amplify sensory capacities (e.g. glasses, hearing aids, radio, TV)
- Devices that could amplify ratiocinative (intellectual) capacities (e.g. language, number systems, computers).

Bruner further identified three modes of representation, corresponding to these developmental stages, that we use to make meaning:

- Enactive representation: when things get 'represented in the muscles' (cf. motor amplification)
- Iconic representation: using mental images to stand for objects/events (cf. sensory amplification)
- Symbolic representation: using symbol systems (cf. intellectual amplification).

Johnston (Johnston and Nahmad-Williams 2009: 118) highlights Bruner's thoughts on elements which need to be considered when educating children. She notes 'Bruner (1960) identified a number of important factors affecting children's cognitive development' and which successful cognitive support or teaching needs to consider:

- Structure in learning
- Readiness for learning
- The spiral curriculum
- Intuitive and analytical thinking
- Motivation.

Bruner argues that the mind structures its sense of reality through cultural mediation, including others, the cultural context and experiences of situations.

SOCIAL AND EMOTIONAL DEVELOPMENT

Social and emotional development are inextricably linked. The word 'emotion' in psychology refers to the 'feeling' or 'affective' component of behaviour. The term incorporates such emotions as fear, anger, rage, liking, love, desire. They may be divided into two broad groups, those that are pleasant and those that are unpleasant. Emotional states involve physiological reactions – pounding heart, 'butterflies', muscle tension, sickness etc. Observed emotions include facial expressions, body posture, speech and action, for example the impulse to run away or to fight. Emotions influence the way babies and children can learn. From a secure emotional base children can learn to meet new experiences positively, and be resilient when faced with difficulties. Practitioners can devise strategies to promote this aspect of their practice through careful reflections of experiences the children have when accessing the provision. Social development can also be carefully structured if a child is experiencing difficulties in this area. From caring adults in the setting and an appropriate 'buddy' system children can expand their social circle gradually if need be. Children often observe a child who is struggling and kindly support them. For example if a child comes to the provision who does not speak English, children use signs and other non-verbal communication to support the child, along with the adults concerned, and help them to find out what is happening around them.

📁 **Case Study**

A boy entered an early years setting very unhappy. He was living with a foster carer and had experienced a difficult time at his previous home. Support was to be given to the practitioners but as yet had not arrived due to the urgency of the case for the boy to be moved. He was isolated and alone in the setting and would only respond to a few adults after a number of days there. One of his particular dislikes was to go through doors. He had had unpleasant experiences of going to other places and did not want it to happen

(Continued)

(Continued)

again. Practitioners needed to coax him through any doors in the building, including going in and out at the beginning and end of sessions. He did not want to play with others and watched them or played silently with the toys available. After a number of weeks it started to get sunny and summer was on its way. He daily took up his place watching the children play outdoors while he was sitting on a chair in the indoor area. Then at last, when one of the children called him over to play with them, he went! He ran up the grassy hill with them and they sat on the slope drinking and eating a snack.

Whenever he experienced a difficulty with others or with an aspect of his activities he became anxious and lost, for a while, the ability to go through the open doors in the setting.

Social and emotional development will be discussed further in Chapter 5 on self-esteem and motivation and in Chapter 14 on the social context.

 Questions for Discussion

How are children's needs catered for in your setting?
Is there a range of provisions to ensure children's individual needs are met?

LAWRENCE KOHLBERG (1927–1987)

Kohlberg was born in New York. He worked as a professor at the University of Chicago and Harvard University. Having specialised in research on moral education and reasoning, he is best known for his theory of stages of moral development.

Moral Development

This refers to the development of ethical behaviour in the child and is linked to the child's growing awareness of what is acceptable and what is unacceptable behaviour. The way that ethical issues are dealt with may have consequences for the individual's conscience. Consider the child's acquisition of notions of good-ness and evil; right and wrong; deceit and truthfulness. Kohlberg suggested stages in the development of moral behaviour which a child and later the adult pass through and achieve, depending on their personal reflectivity.

Kohlberg's six stages can be more generally grouped into three levels of two stages each: pre-conventional, conventional and post-conventional. Stages cannot be skipped; each provides a new and necessary perspective, more comprehensive and differentiated than its predecessors but integrated with them.

Level	Stage
Level 1 Pre-Conventional	1. *Obedience and punishment orientation* A child would behave in this way in order to avoid punishment.
	2. *Self-interest orientation* Children think about what they can get from a situation.
Level 2 Conventional	3. *Interpersonal accord and conformity* Children try to win approval from others by following social norms.
	4. *Authority and social-order maintaining orientation* Children follow rules and insist they should be followed.
Level 3 Post-Conventional	5. *Social contract orientation* There is an awareness of the needs of others in the community which may be greater than personal needs.
	6. *Universal ethical principles* These concern deep moral principles held, which the person would want to follow. Few reach this stage.

Children learn and develop in a variety of ways. This is explored in Chapter 11 which focuses on learning and teaching styles and discusses different learning styles.

📁 **Case Study**

The different ways children learn was emphasised in a Key Stage One class which favoured formal learning and organised the children in the class to reflect this. The children were put into ability groups and were well aware which were the higher or lower ability groups, although they had not been told. Groups were changed for specific subject areas, such as mathematics or English. One boy was perpetually in the lower group for all the subjects. He listened, sometimes attentively, at other times perhaps not so, to others giving answers or recording results. In the summer it was decided to re-design the

(Continued)

(Continued)

outdoor area and the children went outdoors and discussed the space and possibilities for it. He had found his strength! He knew the possibilities and, while he led the group his peers followed his instructions. They sometimes had difficulties with the tools and implements required but he willingly showed them how things worked and what was to be done. The quiet, shy boy in the classroom had become a confident learner and leader.

Further Reading

Alexander, R. (ed.) (2010) *Children, their World, their Education: Final Report and Recommendations of the Cambridge Review*. London: Routledge.

Gopnik, A., Meltzoff, A. and Kuhl, P. (1999a) *How Babies Think*. London: Weidenfeld and Nicholson.

Gopnik, A.N., Meltzoff, A. and Kuhl, P. (1999b) *The Scientist in the Crib: Minds, Brains and How Children Learn*. New York: William Morrow.

Illeris, K. (ed.) (2009) *Contemporary Theories of Learning: Learning Theorists … In Their Own Words*. London: Routledge.

Keenan, T. and Evans, S. (2002) *An Introduction to Child Development* (2nd edn). London: Sage.

Morrison, G. S. (2009) *Early Childhood Education Today*. London: Pearson Education Limited.

Woolfolk, A., Hughes, M. and Walkup, V. (2008) *Psychology in Education*. Harlow: Pearson Education Limited.

Useful Websites

www.learning-theories.com
www.learningandteaching.info

References

Bowlby, J. (1953) *Child Care and the Growth of Love*. London: Penguin.

Greenfield, S. (1997) *The Human Brain*. London: Weidenfeld and Nicolson.

Greenough, W.T., Black, J.E. and Wallace, C.S. (1987) 'Experience and Brain Development', *Child Development* 58: 569–82.

Keenan, T. (2002) *An Introduction to Child Development*. London: Sage.

Johnston, J. and Nahmad-Williams, L. (2009) *Early Childhood Studies*. Harlow: Pearson Education Limited.

Nutbrown, C. and Page, J. (2008) *Working with Babies and Children: From Birth to Three*. London: Sage.

3 PARTNERSHIPS WITH PARENTS/CARERS

Pat Beckley

Learning objectives

- Knowledge of recent findings concerning effective partnerships with parents
- Strategies for collaboration between practitioners and parents/carers
- Understanding of means to provide an inclusive, welcoming environment
- Liaison with the wider community

As parents/carers are a child's first and possibly most significant influence, discussion includes recent findings which highlight the importance of effective partnerships with parents/carers, such as the Parents as Partners in Early Learning (PEEP 2005, Sylva et al. 2005) project, and ways in which successful relationships can be promoted in early years practice. Reflections are made on strategies to foster shared practice, such as assessment strategies, booklets, family learning groups, home/school projects, open days and celebration events. Attention is given to ways of developing harder-to-reach groups such as fathers, working parents or those who do not speak or understand English. Strategies are discussed which address ways of working with the wider community.

PARTNERSHIPS WITH PARENTS

Statutory documents in England have mentioned the importance of creating partnerships with parents. In 2000 the Foundation Stage curriculum guidelines stated 'parents are central partners in their child's education and practitioners need to work effectively with them.' Between 1920 and 1930 involvement with parents in early years provision was deemed as compensatory, addressing deprivation to prepare young children for future schooling. Wolfendale (1983: 9) contends that:

> the terms parental involvement and parental participation have tended to be used synonymously and interchangeably. Involvement can range from a parent being a member of a

school's parent–teacher association, to turning up to parents' evenings, to representation as a parent governor, to direct collaboration in the learning process and the curriculum.

Working with our youngest children can involve a whole range of activities and commitments, which do vary from a response to a newsletter to becoming a valued member of the partnership team. A true partnership recognises a sharing of practice on equal terms. This is emphasised by Whalley, working with the team at the Pen Green Centre.

According to Whalley (2007: 8) 'the concept of a "triangle of care" was developed in the *Start Right* report (Ball 1994), which described a new kind of partnership between parents and professionals'. Through this equal and active partnership, a secure, warm and stimulating environment could be created for children. Parents, for the first time, were described as having their own proper competence, and parents' deep commitment to their children's learning was finally acknowledged.

The General Teaching Council in a statement of Professional Values and Practice for Teachers (2006) declared that 'Teachers should respond sensitively to the differences in the home background and circumstances of young people recognising the key role that parents and carers play in children's education.' The statement continued that they should seek to 'work in partnership with parents and carers respecting their views and promoting understanding and cooperation to support the young person's learning and well being in and out of school.' The Parents as Partners in Early Learning (PPEL, Young 2007) in 2007 considered projects which looked at ways to work in partnership with parents. The focus was on two crucial areas of learning, personal, social and emotional and communication, language and literacy. Some parents may struggle to cope with the demands of parenting and benefit from further help in learning the skills needed for effective parenting.

The Early Years Foundation Stage framework clearly states that 'parents are children's first and most enduring educators. When parents and practitioners work together in early years settings, the results have positive impact on children's development and learning.'

Shared discussions between parents and staff can lead to beneficial outcomes devised as part of an action plan and given a timescale for implementation. This can include such aspects as:

- Arrange times for meetings to discuss partnership arrangements
- Times to celebrate – arrange events such as Summer Fayres and Open Days to work together to organise
- Think about the requirements of parents/children, for example Family Literacy or Mathematics Days
- Visits – what are the timings of visits planned and when will they take place?
- Visitors – who can visit the setting to enhance the children's learning?

- What aspects do the children specifically need? This might be such things as help to prepare an outdoor area for planting
- What elements of provision can be shared, for example making and sharing Storysacks?
- Consider strategies in place where information is shared on a daily basis – could this be improved?
- Share understandings of children's development to enable parents to participate in activities at home and record keeping of a child's progress
- Share understandings of children's progress at home and consider ways this can be developed in the setting.

Parents have long been recognised as a crucial part of children's learning and development. Children's lives outside school have a significant impact upon their learning. They need support and encouragement from both home and early years settings. There are many ways informal communication through daily liaison can be fostered. This includes discussions before and after sessions, home visits and visits by parents to the setting prior to the child's start. Formal communication can be incorporated into routines through planned meetings with parents/carers, celebration days such as harvest festival, and specified meetings to discuss their child. This is particularly effective when it includes a celebration of work achieved.

INVOLVING PARENTS

Sometimes in our busy lives it is hard for parents to meet early years staff and participate in shared dialogue with them. Early years practitioners are busy at their own settings and parents are often unable to meet those who care for their children at school-based times. A key person who liaises with both parties is particularly welcome at such times. However, it is useful to maintain a dialogue despite being unable to meet in person. This can be achieved by keeping records of the child's interests, activities, learning and development at home and at the setting. It is important to involve fathers in this way too. Fathers may dislike coming into a setting where there might appear to be only female adults. The links through newsletters and records can help to keep fathers in touch and enable them to participate when they can. Having a young family can be one of the most rewarding parts of a person's life. It can also be one of the most stressful, especially if there are other worries, such as financial or housing concerns. Trying to sort out these issues can be daunting, but attempting to do this while caring for young children can sometimes prove too much. Having a supportive network for parents can make huge differences to the well-being of the local community; for instance in providing a setting where parents can come and meet other parents, worries can be aired and solutions found. Some parents might feel uneasy about entering a situation they were not happy with themselves. These feelings might include 'anger fear and anxiety; not fitting in; feeling undervalued; feeling numb; isolation; tendency to run away, avoid authority; and inadequacy' (Whalley 2007: 99). If a parent is harbouring any of these feelings it is easy to see why a repeat of the situation which brought it about, would not be welcome. This quickly can be resolved if practitioners are aware of the issues and open dialogues about their children. This in turn can only help to support the children's happiness. New parents can be welcomed in similar ways, particularly if English is not their first language. Parents who are gay and lesbian may have experienced some form of prejudice. Procedures in the early years setting can be reviewed to ensure stereotypes are not perpetuated in documentation or photographs. Practitioners must be honest with themselves and address any negative feelings they might have about any of the parents coming to the setting. Fitzgerald (2004: 71) stresses 'It is important for practitioners to take time to build a trusting relationship with all parents and recognise their role within the partnership'.

This can be enhanced through careful reflections on practice by the team. For example, does documentation used in the setting promote the vision of a welcoming, dynamic setting within a multi-cultural, diverse society; are displays and notices reflecting the vision we want to promote; are staff good role models to demonstrate respectful relationships where all are valued and accepted; are children able to follow the role models set; are children expected to show respect for others; are parents and families supported when necessary?

PARENTAL SUPPORT

Parents can be wonderfully generous with their time and commitment to the setting. This can be channelled into productive partnerships which can lead to their personal development. Whalley (2007: 23) concurs, stating that parents 'had shown us that it was possible for parents who had everything stacked against them in terms of socio-economic status, lack of educational achievement and low levels of family support to become very effective advocates for their children'. Home visits or welcome mornings or afternoons for new children and their parents provide a golden opportunity to get to know parents and help them to become part of the team. These can be organised to facilitate higher than usual levels of staffing to enable practitioners to spend time talking to them and getting to know them and their child. It enables them to express any concerns they might have. These can be discussed over a snack to make them feel welcome. A crèche could be arranged with an understanding that young children will be returned to them if they do not settle in the crèche. Booklets, suitable for a diverse group, can contain pictures as well as written text to aid understanding for any parents who have difficulties reading or have English as an additional language so that they are not excluded. If differences do arise they can be resolved and relationships can remain amicable, when based on firm foundations such as trust and honesty. Parents and practitioners should question and reflect on changes to keep the partnership dynamic and responsive to necessary changes that might occur.

> ### Case Study
>
> An afternoon was arranged for an open afternoon at a setting. Parents and their children who were about to start the provision were welcomed into the setting. The new children could access the resources available. During this time parents and practitioners were able to discuss the children's activities and interests – whether they had similar interests at home, what they were, what made the child happy and whether there was anything the practitioner should know about. Parents were at ease and able to talk to the practitioners, getting to know the child's key person, while feeling reassured that their child was safe. The child's achievements at home were discussed and a record started. A record was also kept of relevant information, for example whether the child was known to be allergic to anything or the name of the child's doctor. Parents were given a booklet describing the main routines of the day and the setting, with the incorporation of contact details that might be needed in the future, for example what to do if a parent was late picking up the child or if the child could not attend the provision due to illness. The child took home a book and a treasured painting or model made during the visit.

It is a big leap of faith for parents as well as the child to trust that their baby or young child will be given the security and love that they, hopefully, experience at home. It can be an anxious time for the parents when a child leaves the home environment for the first time, away from those closest to him or her. The parents' anxiety could feed into the child's feelings of well-being and cause the child to be anxious about the parents. They may think there is a reason why a parent is anxious although not knowing what it is. Meeting a parent and getting to know them in advance can dispel many of their fears but practitioners can also reassure parents that they too will manage without the company of their child. Routines and procedures that were familiar in the home environment might be missing in the setting, where management of a larger number of children means that individual routines could be changed. Nutbrown and Page (2008: 144) remind us that 'all human beings handle parting and separation differently, and this must be borne in mind in the context of the family, their culture and the place of the child in the family'. They continue 'separation anxiety will undoubtedly be more problematic for the child who has experienced insecure attachments in the past or many separations'. A child who separates happily from his parents may be secure and confident, have a positive self-esteem and be ready for a new challenge. A child who is insecure with low self-esteem may cling to a parent for reassurance and comfort. These scenarios are only possibilities, but each child enters the setting with his or her own history, personality and interests and the practitioner welcomes and includes them all.

In a daycare setting it is useful to keep a record of activities for practitioners to share with parents to reassure them of the activities the baby or child enjoys and the variety of experiences utilised.

PRINCIPLES

Strong partnerships between parents and carers can only prove to be advantageous for the children concerned. These help the children feel secure in a strange environment so that experiences can build on experiences gained at home and in the community. 'Positiveness, sensitivity, responsiveness and friendliness can all be demonstrated through effective communication and form a central element of establishing and maintaining effective partnerships' (Fitzgerald 2004: 13). When parents are supporting their children and the child is thriving in the learning environment, the practitioner or teacher is inclined to believe that the child is capable of more and has higher expectations. Trodd and Goodliff (2008: 4) suggest 'Parents seem to be motivated by the success of their children and feel encouraged to continue and increase their involvement in their children's learning and development. In addition to this motivational influence, parental participation has a positive effect on how teachers see the child.'

STRATEGIES FOR COLLABORATION BETWEEN PRACTITIONERS AND PARENTS/CARERS

Settings can devise their own routines and procedures relevant to the community they serve. These can include home visits, informative booklets about the provision, pictorial and bilingual booklets, open days, children's individual achievements files and any shared resources.

Discussions about children's work during open days can cover aspects such as information about their child in the setting, learning, discussion of any problems, opportunities to look around the setting and see what is happening, sharing the new experience with their child, possible help with a CRB check if they come to help in the setting and information on the parents'/carers' notice board.

Questions for Discussion

What strategies can be used to promote a welcoming, inclusive environment for parents, carers and their children?
If you are working in an early years setting how do you promote positive relationships with parents and carers?
Do you feel this can be developed? If so, is there an action plan in place to organise the implementation of strategies for developing partnership?
How are parents and carers new to the setting or locality encouraged to feel part of the provision community?
Do the links include events each term and on-going collaboration and liaison?

MODELS OF PARTNERSHIP

Epstein and Saunders's (2002) continuum of partnership models comprises the following:

- Protective model – this operates along the lines of a business and requires parents to delegate responsibility for education to the setting, as the aims of home and the setting and the roles of practitioners and parents are different.
- School-to-home transmission model – this model recognises the importance of the family but only places an emphasis on one-directional communication – from the setting to the home – and assumes a level of parental agreement with decisions taken by the setting. In this model there is likely to be little sharing of ideas between the setting and community.
- Curriculum enrichment model – this model recognises the benefits of collaborative learning between practitioners, parents and children and integrates knowledge from families and the community into the curriculum and learning. There is a focus on the curriculum as this is seen as an important vehicle for impacting on learning.
- Partnership model – this model is built on long-term commitment, mutual respect and widespread involvement of families and practitioners at different levels, such as joint planning and shared decision-making. It reflects the fact the children are embedded in and influenced by the home, the setting and the community.

The model is cited in Fitzgerald (2004: 24).

IDEAS FOR PROVIDING A WARM, WELCOMING ENVIRONMENT

A notice board can be used to keep parents/carers informed of events in the provision, key aspects that happened during the week and planning for the forthcoming week. Parents/carers can be shown around the provision to ascertain the routines and learn about the ethos and vision of the setting. If parents do help in the setting, care could be taken to ensure their strengths are used and that the activities supported are not only 'messy' areas such as crafts, rather than areas such as the reading corner.

Parents supporting the provision can benefit relationships in many ways:

- The child enjoys parental involvement in his/her setting
- Parents and practitioners get to know each other better and have more informal relations, where information about their child can be more readily shared
- Children enjoy a better adult:child ratio
- Parents can use the skills they learn in the setting when they seek employment
- Parents enjoy the setting's network and share ideas and activities
- The children appreciate kind acts of helping others
- The relationships in the setting forge a sense of community and a positive shared vision.

LIAISON WITH THE WIDER COMMUNITY

An Early Years Adviser reflected on strategies devised as successful attempts to work in partnerships with parents:

> We are looking at sustaining the development with parents' involvement, modelling and providing resources, having sessions that are seen as fun for parents and children, not challenging them or making them feel uncomfortable about their own skills and that threads through the Children's Centres activities. The aim is to help parents help their children. We are trying to engage carers/parents in the early literacy of their children and offer training to them to assist in this. At age three there is an excellent 'treasure box' that goes out to parents and children. This goes out through Children's Centres or the pre-schools that we work with. Finally there is a pack that goes out when the children start school. This is an area we are developing.

According to Trodd and Goodliff (2008: 45) 'the Pre-school Learning Alliance suggests a parent forum that includes staff members as well as parents, while some Sure Start Local Programmes have been working with parent forums entirely made up of parents with a facilitator as the only staff member attending'. They continue: 'In many Children's Centres and Sure Start Local Programmes parent forum members elect representatives who will speak for the forum and parents in general at partnership board and governors' meetings.'

INVOLVEMENT OF PRACTITIONERS/PARENTS

Practitioners often have a wealth of ideas for engaging and welcoming parents to share in the work with their children. Some might live in a setting's locality and have insights into its needs and any local plans. Others may be expert at using ICT and be able to devise websites, blogs or e-newsletters to keep parents informed. There are numerous ways parents can become involved but it is through the expertise of the staff that the planned programmes become successful. Such activities could include:

- Children's home/setting liaison activities
- Shared resources, such as a resource bank of toys for loan
- Daily informal meetings at the beginning and end of sessions
- Specific events, for example open days/mornings/afternoons, Summer Fayres
- Children's performances
- Weekly family days
- Baby and toddler groups
- Home visits
- Meeting a new teacher
- Visiting a playgroup/Children's Centre/Nursery/Early Years in school/Key Stage 1 teacher
- Home/link diary
- Open evenings
- Workshop sessions, for example based on literacy or mathematics or ICT
- Supporting children when visiting different communities, for example a farm.

📁 Case Study

A group of parents agreed to visit the setting on a Saturday, when it was usually closed, to make a start on improving the outdoor area. This had been a long-term project involving children, parents and the local community. The children had been invited to design the outdoor area and incorporate aspects they would like to see in it, for example a grassy area, a hill or shrubs and trees. Older children heard of the project and also expressed a desire to support the younger children. The class teacher in the secondary school felt this could be achieved as part of her students' end of key stage exams in Art and Design.

When the younger children completed their designs they were taken to the older children. They adapted the designs on a one-to-one basis, sharing their ideas with the younger children. A small group from the local community chose a design to be constructed and developed. The ground had been prepared and the grass was growing. The Saturday morning came and parents, staff and children met to paint the fence (rainbow colours had been chosen) and paint pictures on the concrete area (a ship, shapes, a snail, giant footprints and a crossing across a 'road').

Those participating were proud of their achievements and the maintenance of the work was assured by the many people who had taken part. The older children kept a record of the project, using a video, written diary, posters of designs and photographs of the work in progress. This was used as a resource by the younger children to discuss their plans and the work they had achieved.

ON-GOING LIAISON

It is a requirement to have a key worker in the provision who has responsibility for the care and well-being of individual children. This person can provide liaison and work in partnership with the parent/carer through a thorough knowledge of the child. This will also be the person the child seeks for reassurance and security in the setting and who can provide a strong link between the child, the home and the setting.

Further Reading

Crozier, G. and Reay, D. (2005) *Activating Participation: Parents and Teachers Working Towards Partnerships.* London: Trentham Books.

Pugh, G. and Duffy, B. (2010) *Contemporary Issues in the Early Years.* London: Sage.

Sandow, S., Stafford, D. and Stafford, P. (1987) *An Agreed Understanding? Parent–Professional Communication and the 1981 Education Act.* Windsor: NFER-Nelson Publishing.

Ward, U. (2009) *Working with Parents in Early Years Settings.* Exeter: Learning Matters.

Whalley, M. (2001) *Involving Parents in their Children's Learning.* London: Paul Chapman.

Useful Websites

www.teachingexpertise.com
www.teachernet.gov.uk

References

Ball, C. (1994) *Start Right: The Importance of Early Learning.* London: Royal Society for the Arts.

DfEE (2000) Curriculum Guidance for the Foundation Stage. London: QCA.

DfES (2008) The Early Years Foundation Stage: Setting Standards for Learning, Development and Care for Children from Birth to Five. Nottingham: DfES Publications.

Fitzgerald, D. (2004) *Parent Partnerships in the Early Years.* London: Continuum.

Goodliff, G. and Trodd, L. (2008) *Achieving EYP Status*: Exeter: Learning Matters.

GTC (2006) *Professional Values for Teachers.* London: GTC Whittington House.

Nutbrown, C. and Page, J. (2008) *Working with Babies and Children.* London: Sage.

OECD (2006) *Starting Strong II*: Early Childhood Education and Care. Paris: OECD.

Sylva, K., Evangelou, M. and Brooks, G. (2005) *Enabling Parents: An Evaluation of Parent Early Education Programme (PEEP).* Learning and Skills Council, 2002–2004.

Whalley, M. (2007) *Involving Parents in their Children's Learning.* London: Paul Chapman.

Wolfendale, S. (1983) *Parental Participation in Children's Development and Education.* London: Gordon and Breach Science Publishers.

Young, K. (2007) *Parents as Partners in Early Learning Case Studies.* Derbyshire: The National Strategies/Early Years.

4 PEDAGOGY IN PRACTICE

Pat Beckley

Learning objectives

- To consider perspectives of pedagogy
- To gain an understanding of prominent thinkers in early years provision
- To acknowledge the challenges faced when implementing an appropriate learning environment for young children
- To provide suggestions for practical applications

This chapter seeks to describe some of the achievements of key figures in early childhood provision. This will be considered for practical applications of strategies. The chapter will incorporate suggestions for ways to implement appropriate strategies for young children.

PEDAGOGY

There are a number of perspectives concerning the meaning of the term pedagogy. It could be viewed as the instruction of teachers, or the science of education or the philosophical beliefs underpinning the rationale for education. The pedagogical views of the practitioners working in the settings have a profound influence on how they are organised, what is taught and the way it is delivered, and concern the rationale and aims underpinning the philosophy of the provision.

KEY THINKERS FOR EARLY YEARS PROVISION

Leaders of early years settings have, of necessity, to devise, organise and implement their own views and pedagogy as to what constitutes quality provision for young children. The notion of quality is value laden and depends on the views of those seeking quality provision. What might be deemed highly desirable practice by one person might appear inappropriate to another. Some of these notable thinkers and educators have been mentioned in Chapter 2 on theories of learning.

The following section describes some of the achievements of influential key practitioners and leaders of early years pedagogy and thinking. Their pedagogical approaches can be seen in the contemporary world, as modern day practitioners who agree with the ways in which certain individuals organised and led their provision run their settings along similar lines today.

FRIEDRICH FROEBEL (1782–1852)

Froebel was born in Germany. His mother died shortly after his birth. He was mainly brought up by his uncle, who nurtured his nephew's love of nature. At the age of 15 Froebel became the apprentice to a forester. In 1799, he decided to leave his apprenticeship and studied in Jena. From 1802 to 1805, he worked as a land surveyor.

Froebel was a student of Pestalozzi (an educator discussed in Chapter 2), working with him in Switzerland where his ideas about education further developed. In 1831 he founded an educational institute in Lucerne and from 1835 to 1836 he was the head of an orphanage in Berne. He returned to Germany, dedicated himself almost exclusively to preschool child education and began manufacturing playing materials for children. Activities in the first kindergarten included singing, dancing and gardening, and featured self-directed play.

Froebel recognised the importance of children's active learning. He is believed to have laid the foundation for modern education based on the recognition that children have unique needs and capabilities. He developed the concept of the kindergarten or children's garden and designed the educational play materials, which included geometric building blocks and pattern activity blocks. These are used in modern settings as part of on-going resources. Kindergartens were banned in Prussia between 1851 and 1860 as it was thought they were too radical, but later his ideas started to flourish. In 1908 and 1911, kindergarten teacher training was recognised in Germany through state regulatory laws. Froebel's ideas have continued to develop throughout the world.

MARIA MONTESSORI (1870–1952)

Montessori was an Italian physician and educator known for her philosophy of education. Her educational method is still in use today throughout the world.

She studied at the University of Rome Medical School, becoming the first female doctor in Italy. She worked with children who had special needs and because of her success in helping them she was asked to start a school for children in a housing project in Rome in 1907. Her success led to international recognition.

Montessori's pedagogy consisted of:

- Learning in three-year groupings of children, for example three–six-year-olds
- Child-sized furniture and environment
- Children as competent beings
- Observations of the child as part of on-going assessments for ways forward to help support the child through planning an appropriate curriculum
- Stimulating and motivating periods of development, for example for language
- The ability of the child to achieve competence
- Self-correcting materials
- Activities are child-centred but not child-led.

She had to leave Italy after refusing to allow her charges to become soldiers in the war. In 1939 she was invited to India to lead courses for teachers. These courses laid a strong foundation for the Montessori Movement in India. After the war Montessori lived out the remainder of her life in the Netherlands, which now hosts the headquarters of the AMI, or Association Montessori Internationale.

RACHEL (1859–1917) AND MARGARET MCMILLAN (1860–1931)

In 1908 Rachel opened a school clinic, followed in 1911 by an open air nursery in Deptford. Margaret agitated for reforms to improve the health of young children, wrote several books on nursery education and pioneered a play-centred approach. She was interested in how children could learn in an outdoor environment and emphasised the importance of children's health. She felt children could not learn properly if they were under-nourished. The Rachel McMillan College was founded in 1930. This remains today, along with numerous nursery schools and establishments bearing their name.

RUDOLPH STEINER (1861–1925)

Steiner was born in a part of Austria which is now in Croatia. He developed anthroposophy, which is a philosophical doctrine based on the importance of thinking. He believed thoughts were as relevant as hearing or seeing. He advocated the importance of spiritual growth and an holistic education. He founded the Anthroposophical Society. His views led to threats to his well-being, including from Hitler.

Steiner believed young children should follow schedules and cycles for activities to reinforce their feelings of safety in their learning. Children completed their age phase cycle at the end of their seventh year and they should not be forced into formal learning before that.

The following sections discuss two settings, one in England and another in Norway, where different pedagogies underpin practice and foster challenges in their implementation.

CHALLENGES TO PRACTITIONERS

The introduction of the Early Years Foundation Stage framework (2008) appears to have brought challenges to practice.

Two approaches to the provision, play-based and formal, were observed by one headteacher, who commented that 'It is now very much play-based provision with planned activities taken from the child and their experiences. The introduction of Letters and Sounds is made more formal in the way we teach phonics'. Practitioners note the emphasis on child-initiated aspects of provision and some have made changes in the setting to accommodate this more fully. One practitioner stated: 'children self select a lot more. They used to sit down and get on with their work. We introduced outdoor learning in the last year. The EYFS [Early Years Foundation Stage] was different from what we had been doing'. For early years teachers organising Letters and Sounds and having rooms to allow for differentiation could have changed practice. It leads to decisions for practice into Year 1. Closer links need to be forged between the Early Years Foundation Stage and Year 1. Planning can be tailored in the first term of Year 1 to be freer and gradually bring in more formal elements to children who are expected to sit and concentrate for longer periods. Weekly planning meetings support these moves which help seamless transition for children.

 Case Study

Children were observed choosing their own activities from the variety of resources provided. These included role play of the three little pigs, word mats with letters and making pig puppets. Alongside these activities children devised their own tasks through the resources, for example large construction models, playing with 'eggmen', using wheeled toys and the climbing frame outdoors.

Figure 4.1   Children can add to the display when they make their shape models

DOCUMENTATION

The EYFS (2008) is underpinned by four key principles: a unique child; an enabling environment; positive relationships; and learning and development. These emphasise the importance of starting with the child and building on the achievements attained. This is facilitated in a stimulating, enabling environment, both indoors and outdoors. The framework covers six areas of learning, including communication, language and literacy development which is arranged in sections: language for communication, language for thinking, linking sounds and letters, reading, writing and handwriting. These are described as a progressive awareness of aspects of the area of learning in sections called Developmental Matters. They culminate in the Early Learning Goals which children are expected to reach at the end of the year in which they are five years old.

APPROACHES TO LEARNING

Constructive and instructive approaches are evident. 'The overarching aim of the EYFS is to help young children achieve the five Every Child Matters outcomes of staying safe, being healthy, enjoying and achieving, making a positive contribution and achieving economic well-being' (EYFS 2008: 7). These aims are used alongside specific skills to be taught, for example 'Use a pencil and hold it effectively to form recognisable letters, most of which are correctly formed' (Early Learning Goal, EYFS 2008: 60).

Practitioners suggest that planning is changing. In some ways planning was more structured and there has been a move towards a freer structure where the children's ideas are drawn upon. There could be a move towards child-initiated learning away from a cycle of planning. This could be daunting at first. It is difficult to plan in advance but the children appear to be more motivated when this approach is used. Planning is from the children's interests. There are different learning areas to encourage the children to develop their own ideas and be motivated by their surroundings, for example when developing a role play area and home corner. Practitioners can resource and implement the Letters and Sounds and organise the room so that children can be grouped in their different phases. The furniture should be organised to allow for the changing emphasis on child-initiated play while incorporating phonics every day. The layout of the classroom and some changes in the order of the school day can be implemented. There is less formality and structure to the day, with outdoor provision an inclusive part of ongoing practice. For those with younger children, EYFS planning is not topic based any more. The child is leading the exploration and play. Each area can be adapted to allow for independent activities to develop. Natural materials can be used which support child-initiated tasks. According to an early years teacher working in one setting, there were 'massive changes' with the 2008 EYFS. 'We are not just planning a term at a time but having the child as the focus of the planning, from their interests'. She continued 'concern for children's interests has formed better bonds with them'.

Case Study

Children's phonics groups were observed. High attaining children went to the Year 1 class, the average attainers joined the early years teacher's group, while those deemed to be struggling with their phonological awareness worked on practical activities with the early years practitioner.

Figure 4.2   Children and adults devise the role play area

TRANSITION ISSUES

Changes to the approach to learning have resulted in many settings needing to collaborate further with colleagues taking young children and those in Key Stage 1, and challenges for those working in early years to liaise and provide a smooth transition for the children. The ethos has changed in favour of more personalised learning and an independent learning environment. Practitioners have evolved independent learning for children rather than more formal teaching. Yet, there are always pressures about standards and children's achievements.

One practitioner taking younger children was concerned about differing approaches:

> Our links are mostly with out of school clubs. We have children who move into the school but the staff do not ask for information from us and we do not get feedback about how the children are doing. There is no particular sharing of information. The

sudden change from one regime to another is difficult for many children. Teachers at school have many more children to deal with. They have introduced a 'Link Diary' which is good.

Another early years teacher was concerned about the child-centred approach and preparing children for their next stage of schooling. She was concerned about 'transition to KS1, tracking continuity of schemes, working hard to develop areas of learning [in the setting] for personalised learning'. She explained that 'later in the year Foundation children "buddy" with Y1. The classes are next to each other and at playtimes they are together'. She was aware of the needs of the children in her age phase who 'need specific skills different from KS1 and 2'. Awareness is cited regarding the formal aspects of the provision.

> Phonics and letter formation prepares them. Without these they would struggle in Y1. There is a formal environment, sitting and working in Y1 so they must have these skills. It is also dictated by the seating arrangements. There are some concerns about the amount of phonics work needed in the FS and learning words.

A child deemed a high attainer worked with the Y1 class looking at texts including poems, poetry and rhymes. She attempted to answer questions and listened to others' responses. The Year 1 teacher helped children to sound out words. The girl read a book in a group and enjoyed participating in guided reading and writing sessions with the older group. Early years providers can use an organisation which responds to the needs of individual children. Links with multi-agency working, discussed in Chapter 15, can further promote children's individual well-being.

ACCOUNTABILITY

The EYFS (2008: 20) states 'Providers must maintain records, policies and procedures required for the safe and efficient management of the settings and to meet the needs of the children.' They must 'plan and organise their systems to ensure that every child receives a challenging learning and development experience'. The adult needs to be proactive in devising strategies to support children's learning and ensure adequate records are kept to provide evidence for regulators to acknowledge this.

The importance of assessments and the adults' accountability to provide evidence of children's progress is important to maintain an understanding of aspects of practice a child might benefit from, tracking their progress and development. A KS1 teacher noted 'observations of activities are used for the EYFS profile. These are recorded in booklets with goals, points'. An early years practitioner agreed, claiming:

The early years teacher does most of the assessments but we can look at them to have some input. The assessments help us to gauge where the children are when they get to us. We do an on entry assessment. In some years the children might be good at phonics already.

The emphasis is on objectives rather than activities but evidence is needed to show colleagues and explain why aspects of practice are delivered in certain ways. When children are tracked and assessed all the time, dips in development can be noted and ways devised to rectify them.

An early years practitioner highlighted the desire for ease of transition between key stages:

The observations for the EYFS profile can be carried out during activities, such as through observations. They are recorded in a booklet with all the goals listed. Observations, where they come from, where they go, what they do, how they talk, how they speak, how they interact and what they do while they are learning. Such observations can move the children on from what we see them doing.

As the children develop at different rates groupings can be changed to reflect the dynamics of the group. Information to help with assessment can be shared. Assessments can be used as an ongoing process with specific goals identified in planning. Children's work can form a Record of Achievement to share with others; staff members, children, parents, carers or as a reflective activity to look through their personal achievements quietly by themselves.

THE EARLY YEARS FOUNDATION STAGE PROFILES

The EYFS profiles (introduced in 2003 by DfES) mirror the sections for Communication, Language and Literacy from the EYFS framework, namely language for communication and thinking, linking sounds and letters, reading and writing. These include the Early Learning Goals to be reached approximately towards the end of the Foundation Stage:

- Speaks clearly with confidence and control, showing awareness of the listener
- Attempts to read more complex words using phonic knowledge
- Shows an understanding of how information can be found in non-fiction texts to answer questions about where, who, why and how
- Begins to form captions and simple sentences, sometimes using punctuation.

Local authorities 'have a duty to monitor and moderate the EYFS Profile judgements' (EYFS 2008: 17). Local authorities are under a duty to return the data from settings to the DE. Records need to be kept for scrutiny by the Office for Standards in Education, Children's Services and Skills (Ofsted) who provide a regulation of standards for early years provision and whose findings are published and widely available.

Parents/carers can be involved with staff to support children's progress and literacy learning development. According to one early years practitioner:

> Parents come in to the classroom when children first start. We have parents' evenings and open days. Last year I set up a Link Diary after seeing something in the EYFS document. It encourages links with parents, home, school, grandparents, nursery. Anybody can write in the diary which is kept in the children's book bag. It is a good way of communicating.

She explained that on Fridays she formulated a record of what the children had done that week, which the children took home. Parents were also informed of what the children would be doing the following week. The emphasis on sharing skills towards reading was apparent. Another practitioner described the routines for liaison. 'Before the children start school they will come with their parents for an introduction to school. They do literacy sessions in preparation for school such as swapping over reading books and flash cards.' The early years teacher listed the many ways the focused liaison on literacy was achieved. 'Parents share reading books, phonic sounds, home/school diary, story sacks. We open at 8.45am for the children in the first two or three weeks then parents leave the children in the playground. Parents bring in reading books.' The headteacher confirmed the links with parents/carers.

> Book bags are taken home and we have a home/school diary. Practitioners write in them and we encourage parents to write in them as well. There has always been an open door policy where people can come in to chat about things. They also make an appointment to see us if necessary. Home visits are made before they start. Practitioners can get a background picture of the child. We also encourage parents to come in and help in school.

The Year 1 teacher at the setting identified a broader view, incorporating literacy and a child's personal, social and emotional development. 'We have an open door policy and have parents' evenings.'

The purpose and aims of the EYFS state: 'Every child deserves the best possible start in life and support to fulfil their potential. A child's experience in the early years has a major impact on their future life chances' (EYFS 2008: 7).

 Questions for Discussion

How do you draw on the strengths of children as individuals?
Are there international links to other settings in the early years provision you collaborate with?
Can these be developed and celebrated?

A SCANDINAVIAN APPROACH

Rui highlighted the research which revealed: 'Practitioners interpret policy with their own histories, values, and purposes' (Rui in Bray et al. 2007: 250). We now turn to an examination of the rationale behind early years settings in Norway. This section will discuss care and education in the Barnehager (early years settings), a social constructive development model and how this influences the delivery of frameworks for learning, and key aspects of early years provision.

There are many interpretations of the term care, including care as a business or as an approach. Kamerman (2000) suggests that 'Historically "child care" and "pre-school" have evolved as separate systems' (cited in Neuman 2005: 132). Nordic early years settings developed from a basis of care, while English settings had a strong educational element where education was seen as serving intellectual needs, and care as serving physical and emotional needs. Recently, this has appeared to be an unnatural divide and both elements are incorporated into settings. According to Mooney and Munton (1997) 'it is now widely acknowledged that education begins at birth and separating education and care is no longer sensible' (cited in McQuail et al. 2003: 14).

However, this distinction remains the basis of provision. Theories of child development underpin the rationale of practice. The accepted importance of care plays a crucial part in the formulation of early years provision in Norway. Dahlberg et al. suggest 'care, as an ethic, has an important influence on how the project of education is conceptualised and practised' (1999: 39). This is reflected in the broad, developmental approach used in Norway, where care for the child as an holistic strategy is accepted. Clarke and Waller (2007: 7) identify key features of the provision including:

- An holistic approach to caring, upbringing and learning
- A resistance to sequential discipline-based learning, cognitive skills and school readiness
- A disapproval of testing and assessments that rank young children
- The primacy of play.

Moser (in Clarke and Waller 2007: 7) stresses 'the fear common amongst Early Years practitioners in the Nordic countries that the pedagogical curricula currently being introduced might change the focus from social learning and play … with children as the active creators of their culture and as actors of their own development and learning'. A more formal approach could be promoted by legislators, away from a social construct theoretical basis.

Key features of Nordic provision are listed in a Report for the OECD, including:

Figure 4.3   Children play outdoors, devising their own activities

- The child as a subject of rights with autonomy and well-being
- The child is a member of a caring community
- The concept of an outdoors child of pleasure and freedom is stressed – childhood is a time that can never be repeated
- Community and parental interests with no pressure placed on children
- A broad national guideline
- Focus on working with the whole child
- Confidence is placed in the child's own learning strategies and centres of interest
- Growing confidence in the national language
- Broad orientations rather than prescribed outcomes
- The environment and its protection is an important theme
- Formal assessment not required
- Quality control based on educator and team responsibility.

(*Starting Strong II* 2006: 141).

These aspects of provision were also reflected in strategies in school, evident in the ethos of the schools. For elementary (6–9 years) children:

> The learning process must put emphasis on strengthening pupils to cooperate and work together in both formal and informal contexts ... By expressing their ideas and opinions, discussing them and listening to the views of others, pupils learn to communicate. Through cooperation they learn to plan and allocate tasks, find solutions to problems and evaluate results of their efforts. Cooperation between pupils must therefore have a prominent place in school activities. (Royal Ministry of Education, Research and Church Affairs 1999: 69 in Broadhead 2001).

The broad aims based on co-operation and local values were apparent in preschool provision. Moss (2003: 6) argued 'The Nordic countries ... have decentralised much responsibility for services to local authorities. In practice this means no national standards for services, few "earmarked" funds and broad curricular frameworks which leave much scope for interpretation to individual local authorities, schools and other institutions.'

Norwegian early years provision is based on a social constructivist approach where early childhood is a stage in its own right. Children are seen as competent and agents of their own learning, co-constructing knowledge through dialogue with practitioners. This goes alongside an approach integrating age groups of children from birth to six with groupings across ages for at least part of the time. Well trained adults scaffold children's learning, while 'appropriate interventions are various and require discrimination and professional discretion' (McQuail et al. 2003: 15). Practitioners use their professional judgement to organise and manage the facility, to work as part of a team to devise access to an appropriate environment to promote children's development and construction of learning.

🗀 Case Study

After welcoming children into the Norwegian kindergarten in the morning adults and children put on their warm clothes and walk to the woodland area behind the barneharge [early years setting] buildings. There is a clearing in the woods, surrounded by pine trees. The children choose activities they devise themselves, climbing trees, building with branches and twigs in small groups, looking for small creatures in the undergrowth.

The Norwegian practice is underpinned by developmentalist theories such as those of Vygotsky who claimed that the learner is a social constructor of knowledge through their own experiences. This knowledge is scaffolded and developed through appropriate interactions with others. The scaffolding builds on what the learner can do and was described by Vygotsky as the Zone of Proximal Development (ZPD). Jordan (2004) discusses a significant difference between expert–child interaction and that of an equal partnership where the child is the significant partner in the dialogue (cited in Waller 2009: 38). The emphasis in Norway appears to favour the latter approach where the child is, at least, an equal partner, driving interactions. The approach draws on children's interests and development through interaction with others, yet it could disadvantage children if Norwegian is not their first language or there are difficulties with verbalising thoughts, because of speech and language problems or lack of confidence. James and Prout (2002: 1) suggest 'The ideology of the child-centred society gives the child and the interests of the child a prominent place in the policy and practices of legal, welfare, medical and educational institutions'. The importance of the child is located in the care of the community. Rogoff (1993) argues 'developmental processes are not just within individuals but also within group and community processes. Learning and development are therefore inseparable from the concerns of interpersonal and community processes' (1993: 91, 93). The child as a member of the community is stressed.

Mooney et al. (2003: 9) provide an overview of the provision, stating:

> Nordic countries have: generous leave entitlements; no school-based early years services … ; extensive non-school and age-integrated services; entitlement to service; supply subsidy funding mechanisms; and a well trained workforce. This is consistent with welfare regimes, which emphasise generous benefits and universal entitlements and a strong public sector role in provision and/or funding.

AN HOLISTIC APPROACH TO EARLY YEARS LITERACY IN NORWAY

There are different interpretations of what an holistic approach entails. For some it is a cross-curricular approach to learning, while for others it includes the whole range of aspects for the child including social, emotional, physical and intellectual development. In Norway an holistic approach concerns the whole child in the broadest sense, perhaps to reflect and compensate for family life. As early as 1982 Van der Eyken observed family structures were changing in Norway where 'the child must prepare itself for being able to master a future with great challenges and changes in family life, economic life and societal conditions' (1982: 136).

An holistic approach as perceived in Norway is evident through the policies to promote such provision. 'ECEC (Early Childhood Education and Care) in Norway has long been regarded as part of the general family policy, and establishing ECEC institutions was seen as an important tool in order to enable women to participate in the work force' (Eknes 2000: 9). The provision was based on a notion of care for the child. Esping-Andersen (1999) cites the development of defamilialisation welfare regimes where policies were developed, especially in childcare, that enabled women to reduce their family responsibilities particularly for caring. 'So far the Nordic welfare regimes stand apart for the extent to which they have pursued and achieved this aim' (Moss et al. 2003: 6). In a study of 15 European countries women's employment was found to be 'highest in the Nordic countries' (Mooney et al. 2003: 4). However, Qvortrup questions the rationale for the provision: 'The demand for more kindergartens … is unequivocally understood as a positive children family policy by parents who both want to work. Can we be so sure it is also a positive children's policy?' (quoted in James and Prout 2002: 102). Solberg considers the quality of the care provided in the fast growth of the ECEC institutions, claiming 'the situation constitutes an important background for political claims for better day-care facilities' (James and Prout 2002: 102).

Guidelines from the national government were broad and open to local interpretation. The 1997 guidelines included four areas of child development to be encouraged in early years settings:

- Community, religion and ethnic dimension
- Culture, music and practical activities
- Language and communication
- Physical techniques, nature and health.

The importance of local geographical resources as a crucial learning environment was emphasised. Assessment is by observation and used to inform the school of achievements made by the children. There is no external reporting of children's progress in the wider community.

📁 Case Study

Children and adults gathered around the camp fire lit by the staff to keep warm and share the lunchtime food. Some helped to stir the ingredients, while others prepared the site for sitting and eating the meal. Children helpers gave out pieces of bread and drinks to the others.

Figure 4.4   Children and adults enjoy a shared time while they eat their lunch

Children experience a coherent provision where services have an integrated structure, for example a setting which provides access from one to five, including flexible hours and timings to suit working parents. This approach should be readily interpreted within settings as it forms part of the existing practice. Neuman states 'Municipalities in parts of Norway have integrated kindergartens, leisure-time activities, schools and children's welfare services into a Department for Growing Up, with a responsibility for a child's total environment (2005: 136).

Further Reading

Keenan, T. and Evans, S. (2009) *An Introduction to Child Development* (2nd edn). London: Sage.
The book considers different approaches to child development.

Miller, L. and Pound, L. (2011) *Theories and Approaches to Learning in the Early Years.* London: Sage.
This book explores contemporary and historical perspectives of the theories of early years learning and development.

Useful Websites

www.nationalcollege.org.uk
This website contains resources that explore the professional practice relating to the learning and development of babies, toddlers and young children.

www.ttrb.ac.uk
This website considers researching effective pedagogy in the early years.

References

Bray, M., Adamson, B. and Mason, M. (eds) (2007) *Comparative Education Research: Approaches and Methods.* Hong Kong: Comparative Education Research Centre and Springer.

Broadhead, P. (2001) *Curriculum Change in Norway.* York: University of York.

Clarke, M. M. and Waller, T. (2007) *Early Childhood Education and Care.* London: Sage.

Dahlberg, G., Moss, P. and Pence, A. (1999) *Beyond Quality in Early Childhood Education and Care.* London: RoutledgeFalmer.

Eknes, K.G. (2000) *Financing Early Childhood Education and Care in Norway.* Ottawa: Lifelong Learning as an Affordable Investment Conference.

EYFS (2003) *The Early Years Foundation Stage Profiles.* Nottingham: DfES.

EYFS (2008) *The Early Years Foundation Stage.* Nottingham: DfES.

Framework Plan for the Content and Tasks of Kindergartens (2006) Norway: Ministry of Education and Research.

HM Government (2004) *Every Child Matters: Change for Children.* London: Department for Education and Skills.

James, A. and Prout, A. (2002) *Constructing and Reconstructing Childhood.* London: RoutledgeFalmer.

McQuail, S. Mooney, A., Cameron, C., Candappa, M., Moss, P. and Petrie, P. (2003) *Early Years and Childcare International Evidence Project.* London: Thomas Coram Research Unit, Institute of Education.

Mooney, A., Moss, P., Cameron, C., Candappa, M., McQuail, S. and Petrie, P. (2003) *Early Years and Childcare International Evidence Project Summary.* University of London: Thomas Coram Research Unit.

Moss, P., Cameron, C., Candappa, M., McQuail, S., Petrie, P. and Mooney, A. (2003) *Early Years and Childcare International Evidence Project.* University of London: Thomas Coram Research Unit.

Neuman, M.J. (2005) *Governance of Early Childhood Education and Care: Recent Developments in OECD Countries*. TACTYC, Colchester: Taylor and Francis.

Quality in Kindergartens (2008) report nor. no. 41. Norway: Ministry of Education.

Rogoff, B. (1993) *The Cultural Nature of Human Development*. Oxford: Oxford University Press.

Van der Eyken, W. (1982) *The Education of Three to Eight Year Olds in Europe in the Eighties*. Windsor: NFER-Nelson Publishing Company.

Waller, T. (ed.) (2009) *An Introduction to Early Childhood: A Multidisciplinary Approach* (2nd edn). London: Sage.

PART 2

SUPPORTING YOUNG CHILDREN'S LEARNING

Part 2 seeks to consider aspects of provision that underpin an holistic approach to children's learning and development. It includes discussion of children's motivation and self-esteem, inclusion and 'educating' the whole child, issues regarding diversity and the promotion of children's thinking skills.

Chapter 5, focused on children's motivation and self-esteem, aims to promote an awareness of a range of communication strategies to aid interactions and dialogue between children and adults, gives suggestions to enhance perseverance and provides ideas to support planning for personalised learning and to celebrate children's achievements. This chapter considers communication strategies for different ages, abilities and needs. Ways to encourage children's perseverance while responding to their particular interests are addressed. Links are made to planning and personalised learning based on individual interests and experiences. Consideration is given to sharing children's achievements while encouraging them to understand the next steps in their learning. Through such strategies children are able to take considered risks, make mistakes and be given time for them to become engrossed in tasks in planned sessions. In this way, they can make links in their learning and try out new ideas in a variety of ways, for example acting out personal or devised experiences or using newly acquired language. Children respond well to set boundaries of behaviour and show self-discipline and consideration for all others in the setting. These life skills can enhance their learning in social communication for their on-going development and while providing them with the means to cope with challenges posed in the future.

Chapter 6, written by Sue Lambert, further explores children's individuality and development through issues regarding inclusion. She highlights the view that few would argue with the key principles which aim to ensure all children have the opportunities to reach their full potential, that their well-being should be central to the process, that services should be responsive to children, young people and families, not designed around professional boundaries, and that it is better to prevent failure than tackle crisis later (DCSF 2007a). She feels that to be inclusive, education needs to include achievement and attainment in a much broader sense than has sometimes been the case historically and politically where the emphasis has been on measurable 'standards'. Consideration is given to what inclusion actually means and differing interpretations of what it entails. Special Educational Needs provision is described with useful case studies given to support her views. The importance of children's voice is emphasised. This is supported by documentation such as the publication *Working Together. Listening to the Voices of Children and Young People* (DCSF 2008b: 7), which illustrates the importance of giving children a voice. She states that children feel included when their views are recognised and considered, not just in the devised learning environment but in the wider community. The examples of two vulnerable groups, looked after children and child carers, are given to highlight the challenges of ensuring inclusive practice and the importance of being aware of how our own values, beliefs and experiences could lead to assumptions being made that may exclude rather than include.

Chapter 7, written by Helen Hendry, provides an awareness of a range of diversity issues that can affect early learning. It considers the influence of our own assumptions about children and families and offers practical suggestions to encourage positive and inclusive learning experiences for children and those involved with their care and education. Ensuring that children feel valued, included and that they respect others' ideas and opinions is arguably one of the most important aspects of their learning to develop. Each child is influenced in a unique way by their experiences at home, the wider community and in the setting. The chapter explores how areas of diversity can be influenced by the needs and expectations of the child, their families and carers and the values and philosophy held in the setting. Practical examples of suggestions for resources and the learning environment are given to support the promotion of an inclusive atmosphere. The emphasis in the chapter is that we are all different but we all belong. Helen feels that providers must act upon individual circumstances with specific support and intervention but can also support all the children in their care through careful choices of inclusive policy, practice and procedure, and perhaps even more importantly through their own personal level of understanding. This laudable philosophy, discussed throughout the chapter, is linked to practical suggestions that can be implemented, and these are described to ensure this ethos can be incorporated as the underpinning philosophy in provision for young children.

The final chapter in this section was written by Sharon Marsden, who uses her experience as a headteacher to describe the journey she took with colleagues and children at her school to successfully implement strategies to promote thinking skills and enhance the notion of listening to children's voices, as introduced in Chapter 6. She highlights the views of Costello (2000: 85) who believes that 'teaching thinking skills in schools is about bringing children to an understanding that they have the ability to advance ideas, views and arguments in ways and contexts which are frequently not exploited by the traditional curriculum'. This viewpoint can be promoted from children's earliest interactions. Sharon suggests that using thinking skills with children allows for a more balanced approach of knowing *how* rather than knowing *what*. It creates opportunities for enthusiasm and motivation which enable creativity and individuality to emerge in the children and leads to them wanting to learn more and be an active part of their development rather than a passive, bored observer. The case studies described encouraged the children to develop the three elements which Davis (2008) saw as making up deeper learning. These elements involved hearing the child's voice, empowering the learner so that they were learning to learn and using assessment for learning. It draws on previous chapters in this section which promote children as individuals whose views are valued and respected.

References

Costello, P. (2000) *Thinking Skills and Early Childhood Education*. London: David Fulton Publishing.

DCSF (2007a) *The National Children's Plan: Building Brighter Futures*. Nottingham: DfES Publications.

DCSF (2008b) *Working Together: Listening to the Voices of Children and Young People*. London: DCSF.

5

MOTIVATION AND SELF-ESTEEM

Pat Beckley

Learning objectives

- Awareness of a range of communication strategies for children and adults
- Knowledge of ways to promote children's perseverance
- Understanding of planning for personalised learning
- Ideas to celebrate children's achievements

This chapter considers what motivation and self-esteem are. It describes communication strategies for different ages and needs. Ways to encourage children's perseverance while responding to their particular interests are addressed. Links are made to planning and personalised learning based on individual interests and experiences. Consideration is given to sharing children's achievements while encouraging them to understand the next steps in their learning.

SELF-ESTEEM

Self-esteem considers the value the child places on his or her own worth. It covers the child's self-image, the stage the child feels they are at and the ideal self, what the child would like to be. If the child is happy with their progress then positive self-esteem will be evident.

MOTIVATION

Motivation stems from emotions and the feeling that we want to do something, we are motivated to do it. There are intrinsic and extrinsic motivators. Intrinsic motivation comes from inside the person. It is a personal desire to achieve the goal the person has set themselves. It is meaningful to them and gives them pleasure in doing it. This is evident in children's pastimes at playtimes in school when they carefully work on a project that has relevance to them. Extrinsic motivation comes from others. It is to please them or gain some reward for achieving something. In an early years setting or classroom this can take the form of a school reward or form part of a progression of rewards, gradually building in perceived worth.

 Case Study

Tom was a well-loved child whose parents had full time employment. He attended day-care daily. This provision was also attended by four girls and the practitioner's son. Tom was popular with all the children and they played well together and enjoyed each other's company. After a summer break one of the girls left to go to school and her place was taken by a young boy, Toby, who was bright and easily made friends with Tom. Surprisingly Tom's motivation began to wane and he did not want to go to the daycare. When asked about his feelings he said that everyone was very kind there but that Toby was obviously much brighter than he was and he felt he could not do anything anymore. Toby could run faster, write, read and was learning to count. Tom's self-esteem had plummeted because he was comparing himself unfavourably to what he perceived he would like to be. He needed to be reminded of the qualities and strengths he possessed to help him come to terms with differences of ability and achievements and be aware of his own self worth.

There needs to be the right amount of challenge for children to be motivated and feel they can succeed. The goal cannot be out of their reach or too easy or they give up, feel it is not worth trying or become upset. A child might try to avoid an activity rather than be faced with a challenge where others might think them silly for being unable to do it.

A child's previous experience might influence the response given in a particular situation. If a child has been brought up in a household with adults he/she might have difficulties making social relationships or be motivated to participate with peers. Conversely a child may be at ease with his/her peers but feel nervous and uncomfortable when speaking to an adult. A child with a low self-esteem may not give of his/her best because it is felt it is already decided that the outcome would not be good.

To support children develop a positive self-esteem it is beneficial to help them have an awareness of their personal achievements and of themselves. In this way they can have a realistic view of their ideal self, one that is achievable and that they can work towards.

BABIES AND YOUNG CHILDREN

Babies respond to those around them and closest to them. They develop their concept of themselves from birth as they respond to how others see them. Bowlby's attachment theory recognised the importance of contact between a child and his or her mother to develop an attachment bond. This was felt to be particularly important in the first six months of a child's life. Failure to achieve this was felt to possibly lead to irreparable damage. These conclusions, which Bowlby later considered did not completely reflect the nature of his research, did however, raise an awareness of the importance of a young child's first experiences and relationships. Bowlby's work is further discussed in Chapter 2 which looks at theories of learning. 'Positive and close relationships with adults are crucial for all children – indeed for all human beings' assert Nutbrown and Page (2008: 21).

📁 Case Study

A baby accessing daycare is observed and records kept of his development and progress. This provides an excellent means of sharing his activities during the day and milestones in his personal development with his parents who can talk about it to grandparents and friends.

Wednesday 12 January, Cameron 1 year 2 months
Arrive: 7.45am, Depart: 5pm
Nappies: 11am, 4pm; sleep: 10.30am–10.55am, 2pm–3pm; milk: 11.05am; dinner: 12.15pm

Cameron settled straight away at the daycare provision and played with the transport toys until it was time to go to take the older children to school. When we got back we had a music session and Cameron used the shakers. He then played with stickle bricks and building blocks. After a sleep Cameron played with another boy and used inset trays. Cameron pointed to the pictures and said cat and dog. He played with the shape sorter until his mother came to pick him up.

Thursday 13 January
Arrive: 7.45am, Depart: 12 noon
Sleeps 9am–9.30am

Cameron played with the transport toys and the wooden train track set. After going to the school we went to the childminders' meeting. Cameron and his friend made some painting prints. He liked the feeling of the paint on his fingers. He also played with stickle bricks, cars and garage and looked at some books. He joined in the group music session and clapped his hands when the others did.

(Continued)

(Continued)

Figure 5.1 Cameron enjoys painting and feeling the paint on his fingers

Friday 28 January
Arrive: 7.45am, Depart: 2.15pm
Nappies: 10.10am, 2pm; sleep: 12.15–12.50pm; milk: 10.30am; lunch: 11.45am

Cameron settled straight away and went into the tent with his friend until it was time to go to school. After walking to school Cameron enjoyed playing in the soft play area, musical instruments and playing outside at his playgroup. He had lunch with his friends at the playgroup. In the afternoon he played with wooden stackers and transport toys.

The childminder keeps an account of Cameron's activities and interests to provide a record of his achievements and development and a means of sharing his progress with his parents. His routines are established. From this safe base he is able to be sociable with his friends and he enjoys new experiences. His interests are evident. He likes the transport toys, but has also started to look at books on his own. From these records Cameron's parents and the practitioner can share in his interests and build on them to support him in his next steps.

Children become aware of the effects of their presence on those around them. Children who feel safe and secure and have a positive self-esteem are prepared to take risks and explore their surroundings. They are able to communicate through non-verbal expressions and make known their wants and fears. When children are in their second year they recognise themselves in pictures and photographs. There world is peopled with adults they are familiar with and they will refer to themselves as 'me'. The term daddy could be a generic term used for anyone's daddy and they progress through a stage of calling any man 'daddy' until they learn to differentiate individuals and the specific concepts that are appropriate. Through language children have a growing awareness of the world around them and increasingly distinguish elements, forming new concepts as they learn them. They enjoy make-believe and role play events that might happen in life or imaginary scenarios, where hopes and fears can be acted out in a safe environment.

THE KEY PERSON

This secure and safe relationship with an adult can be continued in early years provision. According to Nutbrown and Page (2008: 21) 'the development of close and safe relationships is never more important than for young children who spend time in day care – away from their own homes and parents'. A key person in a setting can provide a crucial link between home and the provider for the child. Records can be kept, like the one described above in the case study, to provide a record of progress and a point of reference for discussion when sharing views on the activities and interests of the child. This can provide invaluable information to help parents and practitioners plan the next experiences for the baby or young child and enhance the relationship formed between those concerned for the benefit of the child. In this way planning continues to be appropriate, relevant and sufficiently challenging for the child, stimulating interest and motivation to explore and investigate. A range of ways of sharing information can be used, such as photographs, written observations, paintings, drawings or models, and could take the form of shared experiences, for example when growing plants.

CHILDREN AS INDIVIDUALS

Practitioners are responsible for devising an appropriate setting for the children in their care. Consideration of factors to support this can include provision of opportunities for children to investigate, create, practise, repeat, revise and consolidate their learning in enjoyable ways. Children show their involvement with the tasks they or an adult have devised by looking and listening intently, asking questions and taking part enthusiastically in the range of activities in the setting. They can feel sufficiently confident in their own abilities and the responses received in the setting to initiate their own activities that promote learning and help them to learn from each other. They are able to take considered risks, make mistakes and time is available for them to become engrossed in tasks through periods of time in sessions. In this way, they can make links in their learning and try out new ideas in a variety of ways, for example acting out personal or devised experiences or using newly acquired language. They respond well to the boundaries of behaviour set, and show self-discipline and consideration for all others in the setting.

To foster this approach to the setting practitioners should show a good knowledge and understanding of the principles underpinning national guidelines, for example the Early Years Foundation Stage framework and the rationale for it. They should be technically competent in teaching phonics and other basic skills, especially using language work to promote children's thinking and understanding. However, these aspects can be greatly influenced by the emotions and feelings of the children and adults working in the setting.

Children can be encouraged to develop a positive self-image through activities to celebrate the individual strengths and achievements of each person in the setting. Children's self-esteem can become low after feelings of security at home change. Divorce, separation or changes in circumstances can affect all family members but could influence a young child through low self-esteem. Lawrence (2006: 43) states that:

> whatever changes occur in a family's circumstances or its structure, it is the way that the whole family reacts to the changes, the emotional support they give one another and their expectancies for the future that are the prime influences on the child's developing self-concept.

MASLOW'S HIERARCHY OF NEEDS

Maslow's hierarchy of needs is a theory in psychology, proposed in his 1943 paper 'A Theory of Human Motivation'.

Maslow identified a series of needs, starting at the foundations of the pyramid, which can be met (see Figure 5.2). It starts with physiological needs, where factors for human survival are apparent, such as food and breathing. These need to be met before other forms of needs can be considered:

- *Safety* – With their physical needs relatively satisfied, the individual's safety needs take precedence and dominate behaviour.
- *Love/belonging* – This concerns a human need to belong to groups such as family or friends. If these supportive networks are absent anxiety and depression can arise.
- *Esteem* – Esteem presents the normal human desire to be accepted and valued by others. People need to engage themselves to gain recognition and have an activity or activities that give them a sense of contribution, to feel accepted and self-valued. Maslow noted two versions of esteem needs, a lower one and a higher one. The lower one is the need for the respect of others, the need for status, recognition, fame, prestige and attention. The higher one is the need for self-respect, the need for strength, competence, mastery, self-confidence, independence and freedom.

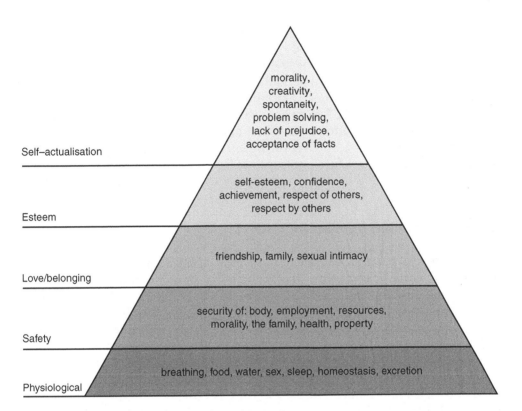

Figure 5.2   Maslow's hierarchy of needs (Maslow 1943)

- *Self-actualisation* – This level of need pertains to what a person's full potential is and realising that potential. Maslow describes this desire as the desire to become more and more what one is, to become everything that one is capable of becoming.

According to Woolfolk et al. (2008: 108):

> over 100 years ago, William James (1890) suggested that self-esteem is determined by how successful we are in accomplishing tasks or reaching goals we value. If a skill or accomplishment is not important, incompetence in that area doesn't threaten self-esteem. Learners must have legitimate success with tasks that matter to them.

GENDER

Gender identity comes from birth and is apparent when a baby is born. Gender is affected by gender stereotypes, which are commonly held beliefs about males and females in society. These beliefs are affected by cultural values. Gender issues might arise when a person does not 'fit' into the gender stereotype of the culture he/she belongs to. Culture can affect self-esteem. The culture in a child's locality could be different from the one where he attends early years provision. Practitioners would need to ensure an inclusive atmosphere was established to negate this factor. Parenting styles could also affect self-esteem. A child might live in a household which is authoritarian or laissez-faire. If they attend provision which requires independent thinking of the children or has a structure and routine, the child could find the adjustment difficult.

UNDERSTANDING YOUR EMOTIONS

It is possible to experience a range of numerous emotions. It is how we deal with them in the early years setting that matters, in order to promote a positive, empowering environment for children and adults within it. Children might be experiencing positive feelings, such as enthusiasm or friendliness, or negative feelings, for example anger, unhappiness or a desire to withdraw from the environment. These emotions can be recognised by the practitioner and accommodated and supported in an appropriate way. Assessment of a child's state of well-being can be noted at the beginning of the session and consideration made of whether it is important to intervene, or simply observe the situation to channel or celebrate reasons for positive behaviour or outlook, or whether, and what type of, further support is needed if the child is experiencing a negative emotion. It might be that the child can be observed to see whether coming to the setting changes the emotion and whether when they have seen their friends their negative emotion disappears. It might be that a child requires a more proactive approach and a few well chosen words are needed to encourage the child to participate in the atmosphere of the setting. Negative emotions might be understandable when the circumstances are known, for example the death of a pet, and can be acknowledged and the child supported. Negative emotions might be too deep seated and more support for the child might be needed, for example in cases where they are an indication of abuse.

Some emotions can be positive or negative, for example contentment. A child could be content and happily develop their learning, whereas another might be content to do nothing or get into trouble with another child!

Both children and adults need to be engaged in a setting which values all in the setting and incorporates an appropriate ethos, where occasional happenings which result in negative emotions can be seen to be supported, and children helped through difficult times.

THE EMOTIONAL LEARNING ENVIRONMENT

Adults and children need to feel emotionally safe in order to learn and achieve. There are times when emotionally stressed or anxious people tend to behave in a different way than they would normally. This could include such behaviour as talking too much or too little, having an inability to 'take in' instructions or listen carefully to others. It is extremely unpleasant to be anxious and can result in conditions such as panic attacks for the child or adult, if the anxiety is severe. Again, if the condition is too severe the child or adult may need further help to address a debilitating and overwhelming emotion and find out why it is occurring.

Practitioners should be aware of possible events or happenings which might trigger negative emotions in some children and consider controlling the situation before it becomes one where a child might be anxious.

 Case Study

A child who had previously had an unhappy home situation had recently changed schools to live with a new foster carer. He entered the classroom at his new school quietly and had difficulty concentrating on any of his work. When there was any change from the movements to or from the classroom he could not contain his emotions and screamed, kicked and shouted. This happened in a number of situations during the day, such as playtimes or a lesson change to the next lesson. He found school assemblies particularly challenging and would suddenly scream, kick and shout in the middle of the quiet communal time. The teacher could not cope with him in her large, busy class so he was sent to another class which was less formal. Here the child was emotionally supported and allowed to come to the teacher if he felt anxious. He was aided during the change of sessions and his outbursts declined, then ceased. He was taken to the assembly hall and shown there was nothing to fear in the large open area. Eventually, he successfully participated in assemblies and was helped to gain sufficient confidence to return to the class where the rest of his age phase were.

Questions for Discussion

In the early years setting how can children's self-esteem be promoted?
Are strategies clearly in place to do this?
Can the provision for this aspect be improved? If so, in what ways?
Is the importance of this aspect of provision appreciated by all adults working in the setting?

Some situations could be challenging for a child, yet sufficiently so to provide a welcome experience for the child to positively achieve, for example a problem-solving activity in which the child or a group of children feel challenged in a safe learning environment where they know they will be accepted whatever the outcome of their deliberations. It is important to plan for situations that might be emotionally challenging for a baby or young child. This could include moving from hospital to home, home to daycare or nursery provision, nursery class to reception class, Foundation Stage to Key Stage 1, and so on. Events happening during this time can also be challenging, for example the change of a key worker, assistant or teacher or a move to a different area in the setting. Emotional challenges can occur throughout the day, such as the absence of a friend or a change in routine or an unexpected event when things happen, for example the roof leaks or the boiler breaks.

Events at home can be challenging too. They might be serious, such as divorce or changes in financial circumstances, or minor, for example the car breaking down. The child observes and responds to emotions the adults around them are experiencing and reacts accordingly. They may well be upset because a parent is upset and not know why!

CIRCLE TIME

Strategies can be devised in an early years setting to promote self-awareness, the needs of others and positive self-esteem. With babies a calm, kind, reassuring voice can sometimes be sufficient to soothe a child. Discussions with young children can be enlightening and they will invariably tell the listener the truth about how they perceive a situation, what happened and what might happen. Further reflections from the child can be encouraged with such activities as circle time. Children sit in a circle with adults present and take turns to talk on a specific subject. This can begin with themes such as:

> I am happy when …
> I am sad when …
> I am frightened when …
> I enjoyed going to …

This can be developed to promote empathy with others in the group. For example, starting points such as those listed can be used but the child talks to a partner about it. He/she then feeds back to the group what the partner thought. Children can sometimes disclose child protection issues during such times. These need to be reported to others in the hierarchy of the provision.

If a child is reluctant to speak in the circle you can tell them to tell you if there was anything they want to say later. This usually only occurs once or twice before the child gains sufficient confidence to speak in the group. The circle time can be used to enhance self-esteem with such themes as:

I like [name] because …
[Name] can …

To promote a child's self-esteem they need to become aware of themselves and others. Goleman categorises Emotional Intelligence as:

- Self-motivation
- Empathy
- Reflection
- Impulse control
- Optimism
- Understanding relationships
- Self-awareness

This spells the word SERIOUS (cited in Burnett 2002: 57).

Children may continually choose the same area of the provision. This is useful to develop their understanding of the resources available in this area and scenarios for play. However, it may become a comfort zone and children can be encouraged to explore all areas to try out different experiences.

STORIES

Careful use of selected stories can promote discussions of valuing individual strengths and supporting others. These can be used within the framework of the provision to enhance the areas of learning and development. They can cover all areas of the framework and provide a stimulating focal point for shared consideration between children and adults. Such books are plentiful and can be picture books or contain written text. Books from Neil Griffiths' Storysack collection are useful.

Other forms of expression can be useful if a child is experiencing low self-esteem. Art, music, physical activity can all encourage children to respond in different ways to their emotions.

HOW WE COMMUNICATE

There is much literature on the importance of spoken communication and developing language to interact with others. Alongside this there are other ways of communicating in an early years setting which are just as important, if not more so, in carrying meaning, particularly for very young children. Yet possibly far more attention is given to what we say than to other elements in communication. We can possibly all think of instances where a statement is said, for example 'that's lovely', but the expression and the tone of voice seem to mean the opposite! You may well have noticed such instances occurring in an early years setting, for example when a practitioner says to a child that the work achieved 'looks interesting' while the practitioner has not looked at the work and is not paying attention to the work or the child.

It is thought that we respond to a speaker in the following proportions: to their facial expression 55%, to the tone of voice 35%, and to the words merely 10%. Young babies and children seem to be able to pick up clues from our body language and facial expression particularly readily. Perhaps you have noticed when a parent with a new baby suggests that she does not know what is wrong with the baby – he/she has been changed, fed, kept warm. One of the reasons could be that the mother herself might be experiencing difficulties or have doubts about her own capabilities and the tense way she is holding the baby is being communicated to the young child who is responding appropriately to the anxiety. It is useful occasionally to model managing difficult emotions by explaining how you will cope, for example 'I might look a bit fed up this morning because my car broke down on the way to school, but I am sure when we have read the next part of this brilliant story I will start to feel a little better...'.

Children might demonstrate their body language and communication in three ways.

- *Aggressive* – rude, unpleasant, arrogant
- *Assertive* – polite, pleasant, confident
- *Submissive* – humble, servile, timid (Lawrence 2006: 104).

High self-esteem is shown through confident politeness where children are content with their self-image and have nothing to prove. Low self-esteem could result in timid behaviour or aggression, where a child is covering feelings of low self-worth by being rude. A child might have an inflated perception of themselves and be arrogant towards others. If a child is bullying others it is important, therefore, to find out why as it could be because the child has a low or an inflated self-esteem.

The role of the adults in the setting is crucial to sustain feelings of self-worth with the young children. Interactions can be powerful tools to affirm a child's sense of personal value. As Trevarthen (2002: 17) notes: 'A child's pride in knowing and doing must be recognised and supported too. Shame of not understanding, or of not being understood, is destructive of learning. The child who is proud to learn, and whose pride is recognised with admiration, will learn.' (cited in Nutbrown and Page, 2008: 32).

PRAISE

To receive praise is a motivating experience but what do we praise children for? It is important as early years providers to consider that praise not only concerns the child's achievements but addresses a positive affirmation of the child's worth as a human being, for example, 'thank you for those kind words', 'that was thoughtful of you', 'well done for being such a good friend'. High-achieving children may also believe that they are only worthy when they do something well. They need to feel valued not just for academic success or they might find it hard to cope in the future if they get something wrong.

Sometimes individual children may feel uncomfortable receiving praise from an adult in the setting as they might not be used to praise and not know how to respond, or they might feel it is not 'cool' to receive praise. Praise can be adjusted to respond to their needs, for example a quiet word to them when something is good, a smile or a thumbs up when no one else is particularly paying attention.

Praise plays an important part in a child's self-esteem. Lawrence (2006: 21) states: 'whilst there is a place for genuine praise in self-esteem enhancement, this has to be realistic praise, otherwise the child will be in danger of developing a faulty self-image'. He continues 'sustained high self-esteem in the child is not dependent on internal factors such as feelings of confidence and personal integrity and not on external factors such as praise'.

A negative word or look can be demoralising for any of us and can start a wave of emotions that takes a while or a positive happening to dispel. How often have we felt 'out of sorts' and it is not until we have thought about it and tracked down why we feel that way that it becomes apparent that it began with a frown or a cross word earlier. A simple word of praise or even a smile can make such a difference to a person's emotional outlook and can brighten the start of a day. Imagine what an effect a practitioner has on the feelings of well-being of the children in the setting.

Further Reading

Roberts, R. (2002) *Self-esteem and Early Learning.* London: Paul Chapman.

Useful Website

www.nasonline.org
This website provides useful information about aspects of motivation and self-esteem in young children.

References

Burnett, G. (2002) *Learning to Learn.* Carmarthen: Crown House Publishing Ltd.

Lawrence, D. (2006) *Enhancing Self-Esteem in the Classroom.* London: Sage.

Maslow, A. (1943) A Theory of Human Motivation. *Psychological Review* 50: 370–96.

Nutbrown, C. and Page, J. (2008) *Working with Babies and Children.* London: Sage.

Woolfolk, A., Hughes, M. and Walkup, V. (2008) *Psychology in Education.* London: Pearson Education Limited.

6

INCLUSION AND 'EDUCATING' THE WHOLE CHILD

Sue Lambert

Learning objectives

- To provide an awareness of inclusion within an holistic approach
- To be able to meet the needs of individuals and groups to promote inclusion
- To demonstrate ways to ensure vulnerable groups are included
- To reflect on personal practice and values

This chapter considers issues and challenges posed when promoting inclusion in an early years setting. It opens with an account of relevant policies and a discussion of the challenges they possibly pose in implementation. Reference to an holistic approach and 'educating' the whole child is used as the basis of reflections. This includes the child as part of the community, involving liaison with parents and carers. The effects of the Children's Plan (DCSF 2007a) and personalised learning are discussed. Differing views of the meaning of what the term inclusion means are used to illustrate the challenges faced when implementing inclusive practice and promoting an holistic approach. The Special Educational Needs (SEN) Code of Practice is described, with an overview given of the different 'waves' within the procedures. Examples of strategies to support children throughout the stages are given. The importance of incorporating awareness of children's voice in the ethos and planning of the setting is described. It is emphasised that children's and young people's participation gives practical expression to children's rights and supports their well-being. Specific examples are given to illustrate how this can be achieved. The chapter continues with a discussion of ways to promote an inclusive environment and ethos for vulnerable groups. Children in care (looked after children) and child carers are identified to support the deliberations. Finally readers are requested to consider personal values and practice and identify ways in which practice might be enhanced.

It has been noted in earlier chapters that the values held by the wider community and society are reflected in our settings. Children learn the values of those around them, therefore it is vital to provide an inclusive society in our learning environments to enable children to learn to respect others and their ideas and thoughts. This supports their moral development and views of social justice and equality. Policies have sought to develop a way of tracking children's progress which in turn benefit children's awareness of others in their company and of society. In an holistic approach support can be given to children as individuals. In this environment all children are valued, supporting their own ability to respond appropriately and with respect to their peers. Relevant legislation has enabled policies to be devised which can be implemented in early years settings.

The reasoning behind the ECM agenda (DfES 2004), 2020 Vision (DfES 2006a), Excellence and Enjoyment (DfES 2003), personalised learning, extended schools, the Early Years Foundation Stage (EYFS) (DCSF 2007a), the Children's Plan (DCSF 2007b) and Sure Start, to name but a few initiatives and reports within the last decade, are now well known. Few would argue with the key principles which aim to ensure all children have the opportunities to reach their full potential, that their well-being should be central to the process, that services should be responsive to children, young people and families, not designed around professional boundaries, and that it is better to prevent failure than tackle crisis later (DCSF 2007b).

The challenge is to consider what this looks like in practice and who it should involve. To be inclusive, education needs to include achievement and attainment in a much broader sense than has sometimes been the case historically and politically where the emphasis is on measurable 'standards'. Despite challenges in balancing the accountability agenda within education with a more holistic approach, the emphasis on the child at the centre of the process should continue to be the goal. Although education is about learning and academic achievement it is also about enabling children to explore and develop a wider range of skills, and if they do not enjoy 'education' they will not engage with it (Knowles 2009: 25, 96). There are arguably challenges in how settings and schools can do this effectively when the standards agenda has moved us away from an interconnection between enjoying education and achieving and attaining within education (Barker 2009: 47), and there are also some contradictions in a school system that at present is politically driven with an emphasis on accountability and measures of narrow 'academic' attainment as the indicator of success, but where there is also an emphasis on well-being, personalised learning, creating world-class citizens and the wider role of the community. League tables may lead schools to focus on standards over well-being, but the perception that well-being is at odds with standards is not necessarily the case. There are many schools and settings where focusing on the wider well-being of children has maintained and enhanced academic performance.

The emphasis on the school's importance to and responsibility for children's holistic development needs family, community and children's services to work in collaboration with the fundamental aims of school or setting to be truly inclusive.

For supporting children in reaching their full potential, a broad approach is needed involving all those who work with children from home, school, health, social care, the wider community and many more. But working together and sharing information should be driven by the needs of the children and young people as well as by the ECM outcomes (Barker 2009: 40). It should ensure enjoyment and engagement with learning, celebrate diversity, embrace community and meet the needs of individuals. For teachers and all those involved in helping children have the opportunities to reach their full potential the challenge is how do we address a wide range of diverse needs, interests, values and beliefs about what successful education is and how do we know we are being genuinely inclusive.

As previously mentioned, there have been many initiatives and changes in early years settings and schools and perhaps teachers should be encouraged and cautiously optimistic about the changes that have been implemented and recommended for education since the Children's Act 2004 and the ECM agenda, as the key messages recognised that schools alone cannot solve the problems of society and that they need support from others who have a direct interest in the well-being of children. However, recent media coverage, political statements and discussions with organisations who have an interest in the education and well-being of children, still show there is a tendency to put schools and teachers at the forefront of addressing the wider issues of society, such as SRE (Sex and Relationships Education), drugs awareness, being healthy and safe use of the internet, when perhaps a more interlinked approach with all those involved with children's education would be more appropriate. West-Burnham et al. (2007) suggest schools are only one component of education across a locality and cannot and should not ignore the influence of context and environmental issues on educational achievement, but equally others should not ignore this wider influence on the education of children and young people when addressing societal issues. Learning is shaped not only by institutions, teacher and learners, but also by contextual and external factors (Pollard and James 2004).

INCLUDING PARENTS AND CARERS

Particularly in early years settings, the interconnectedness of home, school and community can help develop strategies that foster social and emotional development as a precursor to learning (West-Burnham et al. 2007). The quality of the relationship between home and the setting is a key determining factor in how well a child achieves and enjoys learning. While school is a central feature of the lives of the vast majority of children and young people from the age of five, it is not their first experience of learning. The skills and attitudes they need to become expert learners are shaped from birth (DfES 2006a: 23). The Birth to Three Matters materials and the EYFS both recognise that every child is a unique child and is 'a competent learner from birth' (DfES 2007a: 5). Although some argue that the emphasis in the EYFS on areas of learning that closely match the KS1 and KS2 curriculum rather than on the skills was an opportunity missed (Rich 2006). What is clear is that the influence of parents and carers is significant in children's progress. Whatever changes occur politically, hopefully the wider view of who educates children and ensures their inclusion in school and society will recognise the importance of a joined-up approach, as it is clear from research that when parents and carers and the wider community are seen as part of the process, children make better progress.

Schools and early years settings are a major part of the education of children but cannot work in isolation from the education children experience in other parts of their lives through the impact of their families, communities and the wider environment. *2020 Vision: Report of the Teaching and Learning in 2020 Review Group* (DfES 2006a) suggests that schools draw in parents as their child's co-educators, engaging them and increasing their capacity to support their child's learning. Parents have a disproportionate effect on children's attainment, particularly in the early years of schooling (West-Burnham et al. 2007: 66) and it is important to engage in partnership with parents to help children have the best opportunities they can to reach their full potential. For parents and carers, access to services such as health and social services and childcare, providing information and advice and engaging them in supporting their child's development, are also important. Targeted and specialist support to parents of children requiring additional support is also valuable. Schools and EY settings have a key role in signposting parents and carers to relevant services and people who can help, not necessarily all on one site, and this puts the onus on schools and settings to have good relationships with a broad spectrum of professionals from other fields, strong community links and other contacts with specialists. For inclusion to be successful it needs to not just include children in their own education but parents and carers too.

There are many examples of good practice in engaging parents in the education of their children and sometimes schools may see parents and carers as hard to reach, but perhaps it is the setting or school that is hard for parents and carers to access. Creating a welcoming school has challenges but also reaps rewards. Parents' own experiences of schooling and education can impact on parental confidence in engaging with staff and supporting their children. 'School speak' and specific language such as SATs, partitioning, chunking, Foundation Stage profiles, may all seem like another language and can alienate if not approached appropriately. Successful initiatives in schools break down the myths and jargon barriers and make schools less threatening or unnerving for those who perhaps did not have positive school experiences themselves. Activities such as, inviting parents and carers in to work alongside children or to come and see their work following a topic week, practical sessions to introduce new ways of working in mathematics, newsletters in easy to read and understandable language, rooms for parents to meet and have coffee and a chat, a Mother's Day picnic, and open door policies at particular times of the day or week, are just a few examples. Several schools also involve parents and carers in Strengths, Weaknesses, Opportunities and Threats (SWOT) analyses and they are invited to contribute to discussing the school vision and values (usually in language that avoids education jargon). There may always be some parents and carers who do not engage in the process of supporting the education of their children in a way that schools and EY settings would like and the reasons may be many and varied, but the more lines of communication schools can open, the more likely parents and carers are to engage with what goes on, particularly if the children are involved in their learning and enthusiastic about it too.

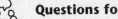 **Questions for Discussion**

From your experiences in school and early years' settings can you think of successful examples that involve parents and carers in supporting their children? Why were they successful?

MEETING THE NEEDS OF INDIVIDUALS AND GROUPS TO PROMOTE INCLUSION

The Children's Plan (DCSF 2007b) aimed for a world-class education system for all, and personalised teaching and learning are at the heart of making this aim a reality (DCSF 2008a). There have been a number of definitions of personalised learning, which can cause confusion, but here is an example that perhaps summarises personalised learning quite well.

> Personalised learning and teaching is about taking a highly structured and responsive approach to each child's and young person's learning, so that all are able to progress, achieve and participate. It means strengthening the link between learning and teaching by engaging pupils – and their parents – as partners in learning. (DfES 2006a)

Although personalised learning is for all children and it is good practice to ensure they are fully involved in reflecting on their learning and have ownership of it, the following sections will focus on groups with specific needs who may need additional or further differentiated support to ensure they are included.

There are many differing views about what the term 'inclusion' means and about whether, for example, withdrawing groups or individuals to support children helps to include or exclude them, or whether without targeted support they could be fully included. Corbett (2001: 2) argues that inclusion has two levels, both the ideological and structural. The ideological level is shared values and beliefs. The structural level is strategic planning and coherent delivery, which requires a solid analysis of pedagogy. Our own values and beliefs and experiences may also influence how we plan and approach inclusive practice and we may, although unintentionally, not have sufficient experience or expertise to be able to ensure inclusion for all (Knowles 2006: 20), especially if we have not encountered the particular needs before. It is also important not to make assumptions about groups or individuals who may have particular labels as will be discussed in the following sections.

For some children the things that are going on in their lives outside of the school environment are things they bring to school with them and they can have a noticeable impact on their ability to learn. If, for example, they are tired, emotionally unsettled, are the main carer for siblings or parents, have not had breakfast, are suffering a bereavement, have family circumstances that are changing, or are 'at risk' in some way, it is understandable that they may find learning challenging at times but may not be able or willing to articulate this. What is seen in the classroom or early years setting are the behaviours they use to cope with the situation and this may hinder their ability to learn but equally their ability to interact with adults and their peers and be included. Despite this and the child appearing to almost want to push people away and be excluded, school may be the one environment that provides consistency and stability in their life at challenging times. Communication within school, with parents and carers and others with expertise to help is vital in supporting children and their families so they develop resilience to cope with their situation, feel supported and hopefully included.

The SEN Code of Practice (DfES 2001) describes a 'graduated response' to identifying and meeting special educational needs which were identified in materials to support the Primary National Strategy (DfES 2006b) as three waves of support. Although the Primary National Strategies may no longer reflect the current government's agenda, the definitions of the waves of intervention are helpful for considering ways to promote inclusive practice.

Wave 1 is the effective inclusion of all children through high quality teaching (quality first teaching). This includes such areas as effective planning and differentiation for ability and interest, ensuring a range of approaches are used to meet children's learning preferences and using Assessment for Learning to engage children in their learning and identify next steps to move learning forward.

Wave 2 is about small group interventions such as Early Literacy Support, Additional Literacy Support, Springboard or phonics programmes for those children that will be able to be on a par with their peers once the interventions are completed. These may not be SEN interventions although sometimes children on these programmes will have SEN in terms of emotional or behavioural needs that may have impeded their progress, or perhaps communication difficulties or physical or sensory impairments for which they are on IEPs (Individual Education Plans) for other support they receive. Wave 2 is seen as relating specifically to needs in maths and English but, as the case study below illustrates, when Wave 2 is viewed in a broader perspective to include small group interventions to target a range of needs it can be very effective.

Wave 3 is targeted interventions for individual children which may relate to specific subjects but also to other needs that are barriers to learning. In most cases Wave 3 support will be for children on the SEN register and may include those where external agencies are involved.

Below is a case study of support systems in place to promote effective inclusion for children in a large urban primary school in an area of social deprivation. It uses the waves approach but not just for maths and English support. It has a number of children with a broad range of social, emotional, behavioural and language needs too.

📁 Case Study

A large urban primary school has a nursery and reception unit with parallel classes of mixed reception and nursery aged children. The classes in KS1 and KS2 are mixed age Y1/2, Y3/4 and Y5/6.

The school works closely with a wide range of other agencies and voluntary groups and targets interventions at groups and individuals as appropriate as well as promoting inclusion by effective use of strategies mentioned within Wave 1. Some practices are ongoing, some are blocked and others are introduced when a specific need is identified.

The teaching staff and support staff work closely together and the support is carefully timetabled and planned to meet the needs of the children. The school also works closely with family support services, education psychologists, social services and the police. Below are just a few examples of the sorts of support provided.

Learning Support (Wave 2 small groups with support staff)

Baking (sequential learning)
Speaking and listening groups such as talk time
Head to Head and Fuzz Buzz (reading)
Social skills group activities
Wide range of booster groups for maths and English e.g. ELS, Springboard
SEN programmes
Self-esteem activities e.g. fun club
Learning mentors supporting building positive peer relationships

(Continued)

(Continued)

Working with Others (Waves 2 and 3)

Speech and language blocks of therapy for referred children with school staff and those from Speech and Language Therapy
EAL support for children so they gain confidence in their use of English but also in social interactions and settling in through buddying with older children with the same language
Gifts counselling addressing grief and loss
Relate counselling addressing challenging behaviour
Women's aid for supporting emotional well-being
Barnados inclusion programme

Working with the Pupil Referral Unit for smooth transitions to Y7

Parent partner reading throughout the school
Sports coaching support
Fire and rescue fire prevention programmes
Breakfast and lunchtime clubs

Learning Support (Wave 3 individual with support staff)

Health and hygiene
Dyslexia programmes
Anger management
IEP programmes for all aspects of SEN

Although the range and number of groups means that some children are withdrawn from some lessons for short periods of time each day or over the week, the focused support enables them to develop or learn strategies that mean they can cope and interact in class more fully and addresses gaps in learning so they have more confidence and arguably are therefore more included than they would be if the issues that create barriers to learning were not addressed.

PUPIL VOICE

The importance of involving parents and carers, waves of support and close communication with others who can support schools in inclusive practice are important, but for children to feel included they need to have ownership of their learning, not feel it is something that is done to them.

Research led by Rudduck and Flutter (2004) shows that consulting children and involving them in teaching and learning approaches leads to higher pupil engagement and attainment, particularly through assessment for learning. The use of assessment for learning strategies enables all children to have ownership of learning, engage in self reflection and target setting, evaluate and check work/ activities, and use their own initiative. The focus on child-initiated learning within the EYFS is a good example of ensuring that children feel they have ownership of their learning and in the direction (with guidance) in which they want the learning to develop.

The publication *Working Together. Listening to the Voices of Children and Young People* (DCSF 2008b: 7) illustrates the importance of giving children a voice.

Children's and young people's participation gives practical expression to children's rights and supports their well-being. It does this by:

- Sending a powerful message that children and young people of all ages are citizens too
- Recognising children and young people as major stakeholders in society with important contributions to make to their community
- Enabling children and young people to influence decisions and services which affect them in order to make them more sensitive to their needs.

However, inclusion is wider than just involving children in their academic progress and target setting. Children feel included when their views are recognised and considered, not just in what goes on in the classroom but also within the school and community. Below is a case study from a school that shows how this has been addressed.

🗁 Case Study: Importance of Pupil Voice

In a small rural primary school all the children have an opportunity to contribute to the ethos of the school through the School Council. Each class from reception to Year 6 has a representative. Some of the older classes have two representatives so that as an older child leaves someone is still familiar with the role and a new person can be trained alongside the more experienced pupil. They meet regularly with designated staff and the designated governor to discuss issues important to them and the school. This has included: helping to make choices about the music used in assemblies, ideas for play areas and equipment, supporting healthy schools activities, deciding on particular themes for study, suggesting visitors from the community and how they can be involved in school life, and which charities to support. They also write a report for the governors on their activities and further ideas for the school.

The close links between the children, staff, governors and others who come into school ensure that everyone feels valued and included and this in turn has helped all stakeholders to engage in and support children's learning and education. The children feel their opinions are valued and hence have real enthusiasm for what goes on both within and outside the classroom.

VULNERABLE GROUPS

As already discussed, to be inclusive of all children is challenging and it cannot be ignored that, for a broad range of reasons, there are some groups of children that research and data show underachieve when compared with their peers. Below is a discussion of two vulnerable groups that can help to illustrate the challenges of ensuring inclusive practice and the importance of being aware of how our own values, beliefs and experiences could lead to assumptions being made that may exclude rather than include.

Children in Care (Looked After Children)

Schools can be the most important institutions in the lives of children in care. They provide a point of stability when other aspects of a child's life may be in chaos. They have the potential to transform the life chances of children (DCSF 2007c).

There is no evidence to support the point that high academic performing schools have poor pastoral care, but it was often an assumption that these might not be the best places for children in care. However, there is strong evidence that children in care do better in higher performing schools (DCSF 2007d).

As teachers we need to be careful not to make assumptions and use children's previous difficult experiences as an excuse for lack of ambition. There are problems, such as many children moving between care placements and spending significant amounts of time outside education and often children in care do not have an engaged parent or carer who can support them, but, although it is important to recognise this, it is equally important to develop strategies to overcome these possible barriers to learning.

A useful starting point is the Personal Education Plan (PEP). Children in care want to be consulted and involved in their education. The PEP is an excellent opportunity for the child to have input into planning their education, but those consulted were clear about not wanting to be singled out in front of their peers as being in care (DCSF 2007d). As a teacher these are all things to consider carefully in terms of including children. Whether intentionally or not, it would be very easy, through lack of experience or making assumptions, to exclude rather than include a child by emphasising their additional needs or how their situation may differ to that of other children within the class.

A further consideration is that some children may have attachment difficulties, especially if they have carers who are not able or experienced enough at meeting the needs of the child and/or they come from a background where the attachments were not formed when the child was young.

Insecure attachments can prevent a child from learning to form close bonds with other people. These children will often show behaviours which challenge relationships and tests carers' commitment. It then becomes a self-fulfilling prophecy and the same behaviour may be seen in school. Equally, some children who have been in care may not have these issues and again assumptions should not be made that all children in care never go home or have difficulty forming relationships. What is key is for schools and early years settings to work closely with all others involved with the care of the child to ensure everyone is very clear about how to support the child and to access appropriate expertise such as counselling.

As teachers we also need to consider what we do in terms of our teaching and planning. If we are teaching about family, for example, the child may not have that information or experience so is it appropriate or would it exclude the child? Some may be fine, particularly if they have got their life story books and photographs, but this again shows the importance of knowing the individual child and their situation and the vital role of effective communication between all those working with the child.

Child Carers

Young carers may take care of a relative who has a long-term physical illness, mental ill health, disability or substance misuse problem. Data from the 2001 census showed that there are 175,000 young carers in the UK, 13,000 of whom care for more than 50 hours a week, and although the average age is 12, over 5,000 are between five and seven (Barnardos 2009).

A young carer may also care for siblings, where the parent(s) is absent or dead, but a young carer may be acting as the main carer even where another adult is in the household. Being a carer can have a considerable effect on a child's learning and feelings of inclusion, but the school may not be aware that a child is a younger carer. Many young carers are not known to be carers by anyone in their school. Being a young carer can be a hidden cause of poor attendance and/or underachievement and bullying, with many young carers dropping out of school or achieving no qualifications. A fifth of young carers experience educational difficulties as a result of their care responsibilities (SocietyGuardian 2005). The challenge for teachers is that they may see things that are causing barriers to learning but if they are unaware of the child's role as a carer they may unintentionally contribute to the child's feelings of exclusion. Sometimes the child may have few or no peer friendships but may conversely get on well with adults and present as very mature for their age, which may mask some of the issues that can impact on their learning. Sometimes there may be, for example, behavioural problems, as a result of anger, tiredness or frustration expressed inappropriately; they may arrive late or be tired and unable to attend extra-curricular activities. The difficulty is there may be other reasons for this, so it is again important not to make assumptions, as most children affected by family disability, health problems or substance misuse do not become young carers and it is important to be wary of making such assumptions about people with disabilities or other health issues and labelling young people or their parents. The role of the teacher and support staff is to be open, non-judgemental and approachable so as to establish trusting relationships which may encourage a child to discuss issues, but like children in care, carers too may not want to be seen as different.

When considering inclusive practice it is important to recognise possible areas that may prevent the child feeling included, for example late or incomplete homework as they do not have time to do it or someone to help with it, and consider strategies to overcome this. Establishing a homework club for the class may help and as it is not specific to that child it does not make them appear 'different'. For younger carers who do not get opportunities to read at home, use peer reading programmes or parent helpers. There may be difficulties engaging with parents and they may not be able to attend parents' evenings, etc. but it may be possible to organise other means of communication and assumptions should not be made that the parent is not interested in the progress of the child or children. Many feel guilty about the 'burden' they put on the child and are keen to support as much as possible. Seeking advice is important as there may be support available to help that means the child may not be late or has some respite through out-of-school groups and clubs.

 Questions for Discussion

Consider both looked after children and child carers:

What is the role as the class teacher?
What strategies will you need to consider to avoid making the child uncomfortable, especially if they do not want others to know?

CONCLUSIONS

The term inclusion is well used but perhaps not well understood in terms of what it means for teachers in classrooms and early years settings. The challenge for teachers is to reconcile their core role as teachers with meeting the wider needs of the children. The range of specific needs children may have that are barriers to learning and inclusion are many and varied and some are not within a teacher's area of expertise and are outside of their control. This highlights the importance of working closely with others with expertise in supporting the specific needs identified, with information about the child that can help teachers develop inclusive strategies, and the importance of partnership with parents and carers to support the child.

Perhaps one of the most important things to do is to look at ourselves as teachers and ensure we are very aware of our values, beliefs, expertise and limitations, so we do not through ignorance or assumption, however unintentionally, exclude rather than include children.

Questions for Discussion

Consider what you do to ensure children are included in your classroom.

Who could you talk to and get further advice from?
How would you find out more about effective ways to support and include the child?

What would you do if you had a child in your class that you found out was:

- the main carer for a parent
- had suffered a bereavement in the family
- did not get any breakfast before coming to school each day?

Further Reading

Jones, P. (2005) *Inclusion in the Early Years: Stories of Good Practice*. London: David Fulton.
Nutbrown, C. and Clough, P. (2006) *Inclusion in the Early Years: Critical Analyses and Enabling Narratives*. London: Sage.

Useful Websites

www.pre-school.org.uk/practitioners/inclusion

References

Barker., R. (ed.) (2009) *Making Sense of Every Child Matters: Multi-professional Practice*. Bristol: The Policy Press.
Barnardos (2009) *Young Carers*. Available at: http://www.barnardos.org.uk/what_we_do/our_projects/young_carers.htm?gclid=CJKnxMehvqMCFWIA4wodzV4V8w
Corbett, J. (2001) *Supporting Inclusive Education: A Connective Pedagogy*. London: RoutledgeFalmer.
DCSF (2007a) *The Early Years Foundation Stage*. Nottingham: DfES Publications.
DCSF (2007b) *The National Children's Plan: Building Brighter Futures*. Nottingham: DfES Publications.
DCSF (2007c) *Care Matters: Time for Change*. Nottingham: DfES Publications.
DCSF (2007d) *Care Matters: Best Practice in Schools Working Group Report*. Nottingham: DfES Publications.

DCSF (2008a) *The Assessment for Learning Strategy.* London: DCSF.

DCSF (2008b) *Working Together: Listening to the Voices of Children and Young People.* London: DCSF.

DfES (2001) *Special Educational Needs Code of Practice.* London: DfES.

DfES (2003) *Excellence and Enjoyment.* London: DfES.

DfES (2004) *Every Child Matters: Change for Children in Schools.* London: DfES.

DfES (2006a) *2020 Vision: Report of the Teaching and Learning in 2020 Review Group.* London: DfES.

DfES (2006b) DfES *The Primary National Strategy Waves of Intervention Model.* Available at: http://nationalstrategies.standards.dcsf.gov.uk/node/46539.

Knowles, G. (ed.) (2006) *Supporting Inclusive Practice.* London: David Fulton.

Knowles, G. (2009) *Ensuring Every Child Matters.* London: Sage.

SocietyGuardian (2005) *Working with Children 2006–07,* London: NCH/SocietyGuardian.

Pollard, A. and James, M. (2004) *Personalised Learning: A Commentary by the Teaching and Learning Research Programme.* ESRC. Available at: http://www.tlrp.org/documents/personalised_learning.pdf

Rich, D. (2006) Does Birth to Three Matter? *Practical Professional Childcare,* November, p. 10.

Rudduck, J. and Flutter, J. (2004) *How to Improve your School.* London: Continuum.

West-Burnham, J., Farrar, M. and Otero, G. (2007) *Schools and Communities–Working Together to Transform Children's Lives.* London: Network Continuum Education.

7 DIVERSITY IN THE EARLY YEARS

Helen Hendry

Learning objectives

- To be aware of the range of diversity that can affect early learning
- To consider the influence of your own assumptions about children and families
- To be aware of practical ways to offer inclusive learning experiences for children and families

Ensuring that all children are included and learn to value one another is one of the most challenging and important roles that early educators face. In order to learn and thrive in early years environments children must feel comfortable, valued and listened to within a framework of clear boundaries and expectations. When early years educators consider diversity and how they will support young children's learning they must reflect upon the following aspects:

- Young children's concepts of themselves, identity and belonging
- Young children's awareness of others' needs, beliefs and contexts, similarities and differences
- Their own understanding of the possible influence of children's home circumstances and their awareness of assumptions that may act as barriers to learning.

Early years educators must also consider the possible influence of the expectations of other families and parents over their own behaviour.

Each child or adult is influenced in a unique way by the combination of their home and school relationships and experiences. Table 7.1 shows some possible areas of diversity that may influence the needs and expectations of children, families and early years educators. It is important that early years educators approach each child and family's requirements individually and that assumptions are not made about any particular issue. For instance, the needs of a child who has recently arrived in this country and who is learning English as an additional language may be different on every occasion depending on their home

Table 7.1 Some possible diverse influences and needs of the children in our care

Cultural	Linguistic	Social	Familial
Country of origin	Children learning English as an additional language	Parental education and literacy	Looked after children
Gypsy, Roma Traveller heritage	Isolated learners in monolingual schools	Economic status	Adopted children
Experience of education elsewhere	Multilingual or monolingual families	Unemployed parents or on a low income	Same sex parents
Religion	Literate or non-literate family members	Working parents using childcare	Single parents
Dietary requirements	Newly arrived families or established in the UK	Refugees' experience of trauma and living in temporary accommodation	Divorced parents

support network, community, extended family, prior experience of education, their parents' language and literacy and financial situation. Providers must act upon individual circumstances with specific support and intervention but can also support all the children in their care through careful choices of inclusive policy, practice and procedure and perhaps even more importantly through their own personal level of understanding.

INFORMED AND REFLECTIVE PRACTITIONERS

What is your own cultural, linguistic, social and familial experience?
What is your view of a family?
How do you feel in an educational setting?

As early years educators we are required to support all the children in our care to fulfil their potential but we may feel that their experience of family life is so different to our own that we find it difficult to know how best to do this. We may also be carrying with us stereotypes and assumptions that lead us to avoid issues that make us feel uncomfortable. For example, Pearce (2005) writes about her experience as a white teacher in an ethnically diverse school. Her own lack of personal experience of racism meant that she found this difficult to tackle when talking to children and she initially lacked the confidence to discuss racism fully. Richardson and Miles (2008) draw attention to some high profile legal cases where racist abuse between children has been inappropriately likened to other childhood insults such as being called fat or ginger. Such instances show that when adults lack personal experience of being part of a minority group, in this case being the victim of racism, they may not react appropriately. Practitioners may be equally uncomfortable and perhaps unsure of how to react when working with the children of same sex parents, those from Traveller backgrounds or children 'looked after' by social care systems. All professionals need to reflect upon their personal experiences of childhood, education and family life and consider the barriers that their own assumptions may create when trying to meet children's needs (Beckley et al. 2009).

In the early years some practitioners may overlook racist, homophobic or other insulting comments used by young children with the explanation that 'they don't really understand what they are saying'. One experienced teacher, for instance, shared with me the example of children using the word, 'Paki', as an insult for any other child, regardless of their ethnicity. Young children may not always fully realise the implications of the words that they have chosen but they are capable of choosing such vocabulary with the broader intention of hurting others. The early years educator should not ignore such comments but instead enable children to understand what these words really mean and to realise the effect that language like this has. The educator must also intervene and reassure the child who is being insulted. Professionals should be aware that the difference between their own experience and that of the children in their care could lead them to brush such important events aside and shy away from having 'difficult' conversations with children and families about verbal abuse. They must be brave enough to act even when confronted by the ignorance or copied remarks used by children in the early years (Siraj-Blatchford and Clarke 2000; PLA 2001; Beckley et al. 2009). They should also be vigilant to notice and intervene sensitively when they observe the less obvious signs of prejudice in children's play such as teasing, rejection, mocking family members and behaviour or asking certain children to play a stereotypical role in a game (Lane 2008; Richardson and Miles 2008).

Practitioners need to find language that they can use comfortably with children to raise awareness and understanding of family diversity, for example educators may be self-conscious about using terms such as lesbian and gay to describe parents because of implicit links to sex (Casper and Schultz 1999). All children need to hear relevant vocabulary that describes their parents or others' family situations used in a positive way. Practitioner confidence about appropriate language choices is important when discussing aspects of diversity, whether linked to ethnic origin or sexuality. Finding vocabulary that is clear, sensitive and appropriate may require some discussion between parents and carers and early years practitioners. One parent explained to the early years teacher that she described her daughter as, 'having two mummies', this then became the preferred way of referring to their family situation in the classroom. Early years practitioners must also consider how they portray the range of different families, including, gay or lesbian parents, divorced or single parents, adoptive and birth parents or foster families, as well as the ethnic diversity of families, so that all children feel accepted and know about and respect families different to their own (Allen et al. 2009).

The first step to challenging some racist, homophobic or other negative views adopted by children is to acknowledge that they exist in the families that we work with and in our own lives. One way to address this is to share stories of personal experience within the staff as part of staff development (Lane 2008). Staff may also actively encourage children to share examples of unkind remarks and behaviour and talk about why this might happen and how children feel. Often practitioners suggest that this may draw children's attention to differences that they are not yet aware of and cause more problems. In reality this is an idealistic view. Children will begin to be aware of differences and similarities between themselves and others from at least three years of age and a developing awareness of ethnicity is shown in research amongst children in the four- to five-year-old age range (Smith et al. 2003). Consequently it is most useful for practitioners to use this growing awareness positively by equipping children with appropriate language to describe differences, and helping children to understand why prejudice and racism are wrong and what to do if they experience them in the early years setting. Practitioners may also be able to use art or play opportunities to help children to cope with traumatic experiences such as refugees fleeing their home country. Again it is better to talk about and acknowledge difficult experiences than to pretend that if ignored they will go away (Rutter 2003). Early years education also offers an opportunity to emphasise the positive attributes of each individual as well as similarities between children and families, including raising awareness of family diversity through carefully chosen resources. This means planning ways that learning experiences can help all children to feel positively about themselves and each other, including those of white British heritage.

There may be unconscious racism, homophobia or other prejudices affecting the expectations and perceptions of the staff in the setting. The good intentions of early years practitioners can sometimes perpetuate misconceptions and difficulties, which is why being a reflective and informed practitioner is crucial to the promotion of diversity. Early years provision should use direct curriculum opportunities to discuss issues and to teach about different family structures, languages, countries of origin, faiths and cultural practices. However the danger of this in an early years environment is that such learning opportunities can become a token gesture or lead to further stereotyping of a group of people. As a teacher new to an early years setting where many children had Indian, Pakistani, Bangladeshi, Somali or Nigerian heritage, I planned a learning opportunity based around 'exotic' fruit but I was disappointed when my class showed little interest or excitement as we examined and then ate papayas and mangos. It was only when I later asked the children to name apples and pears and discovered that these were unfamiliar to them that I realised my own cultural background had influenced me to plan an activity that did not reflect the children's needs. What was 'exotic' for me was everyday to them. This unfortunate assumption was not strictly racist but it does highlight the importance of cultural awareness for staff so that they are able to make choices relevant to the children in their care and plan meaningful activities.

Practitioners may assume that children of a certain ethnic group, family background or gender, will have particular interests, talents and aptitudes or difficulties. Or they can fail to realise how children's different family experiences impact on their behaviour in the classroom. For example, research shows that some children in the EYFS may be judged to be lacking in initiative and independence in a school situation because of their early experiences helping adults at home and their unfamiliarity with child-initiated play. In some cases such assumptions may lead practitioners to have low expectations of attainment or behaviour for children from certain groups (Siraj-Blatchford and Clarke 2000; Klein and Chen 2001; Brooker 2002; DfES 2006; Beckley et al. 2009). It is important to talk openly about stereotyping like this amongst staff members so that practitioners are more aware of these assumptions and can plan strategies to counteract them.

Such invisible barriers may also be present between early years practitioners and parents from different cultural and socio-economic groups. Early years practitioners may make assumptions about how much or how little parents value education. They may make value judgements about the parenting decisions and capabilities of certain families because they differ from their own choices as parents or their own experiences as children. Equally, parents may be carrying many expectations and assumptions about teachers and schools based on their own upbringing. Such beliefs from both educators and families are often silently held, unacknowledged and unchallenged. Child-rearing practices are also frequently culturally determined, for example the age at which a child might be expected to use the toilet independently or dress themselves can vary a great deal depending on their family background (Lindon 2006). The only way to resolve all the possible misconceptions and anxieties is to open up discussion about them and involve parents and carers with the early years setting through home visits, activities and out-of-hours experiences. It is only when settings and families really work together in varied and regular ways, that they can discover their common goals and understand one another's differences. Practitioners should find ways to meet children's needs in a culturally sensitive way but may also need to talk to parents about what is not possible because of the impact on other children within the setting or the legal and educational frameworks they work within. By fostering an understanding of diverse families amongst early years educators and children we can meet individual needs but also improve relationships between the setting and families and within the community itself (Ouseley and Lane 2006).

 Case Study

In a large urban infant school children were working on a topic about animals. Because the children had little experience of animals, it was decided that they would benefit from a visit by a mobile farm. A large number of families in the school were Muslims and so the staff were concerned about how the families would feel if the children were exposed to pigs, which are regarded as unclean in the Islamic faith. The staff also did not want to disadvantage the non-Muslim children who may have never seen a pig before by asking the farm to only bring other animals. In order to ensure that the visit was successful parents were invited in to discuss their feelings about the animals before the visit was arranged. Most parents were happy for their children to see the pigs but not to touch them, only one child out of 120 was not allowed to be involved and the visit went ahead. Without the forward planning and discussion the teachers might have assumed that Muslim parents would not want their children to see pigs and might have avoided this extremely enjoyable and interesting learning opportunity.

VALUING IDENTITY, CHILDREN LEARNING ABOUT THEMSELVES AND EACH OTHER

How does each child and family in the setting know that they are welcomed and respected?
How do children learn about languages, cultures and ethnic groups that are not represented within the setting?
How do we know that our practice is genuinely inclusive and not reinforcing stereotypes?

The *resources* and *environment* send clear signals to children and families about whether they will be respected and valued in an early years setting. As outlined in the discussion about informed reflective practice, these are key issues which cannot be simply rectified by the introduction of some 'multi-cultural' cooking utensils or dolls with different skin colours. Practitioners need to ensure that all curriculum resources and opportunities throughout the year reflect a wide range of family backgrounds, multiple languages and faiths. Exploration of these should not be limited to 'multi-cultural week' or activities around religious festivals. Whilst focused investigation of the art, music, dance or religious celebrations of different people can be enjoyable and enriching, practitioners need to give greater thought to their choices of learning opportunities, communication strategies and use of the environment as a whole. Early years settings should plan ahead to ensure that their choices of topics and learning opportunities link to relevant home experiences for children in the setting but also introduce new experiences and ideas that build on the familiar. It is important that children are encouraged to make links between their own and others' experiences, to be aware of similarities and to feel a sense of connection and belonging. Early years educators should also try to find ways to share with children the contributions of individuals from minority ethnic backgrounds living in Britain today and in the past. That is not to suggest that early years settings should never mention white English figures from history, composers or artists for example, but they should ensure that a genuine balance of different role models is offered to children, whatever the balance of different languages, faiths and cultures within the setting.

Stories, songs and *rhymes* are at the heart of much early years practice and these are one way to reflect and value the diversity of our society by sharing them with children, using them as a starting point for further work and ensuring that a wide range are available for children to access independently in books or on CD. It is important that stories, rhymes or songs from any country are not portrayed as an isolated example of a particular culture or language, and therefore that children learn about real people in modern Britain and other countries. For example, one student teacher related a story to me of a younger relative who tried to give her charitable donation to a black child in her class following school fund-raising in the aftermath of a natural disaster abroad; another five-year-old suggested to me that all African people lived in rural villages. Such examples highlight the need for practitioners to ensure that teaching about children from different ethnic backgrounds is set in an appropriate context and linked to the children's real-life experiences rather than encouraging them to view other cultures as far away, different and perhaps even inferior. Stories should also reflect different family circumstances and be used as a starting point to discuss them. There are many possible texts to include in your setting but 'The Family Diversities Reading Resource', offers reviews of current picture books linked to different family issues and so is a great place to start improving the inclusivity of your book collection. Another way of helping children to be sensitive to others' different family backgrounds and see them as part of their own lives is through using Persona dolls. A doll with its own 'history' can be introduced to the setting so that children are able to learn positively about the doll's family life and suggest ways to help with issues such as feeling different, not knowing what to do at school, learning a new language or being the victim of racism. Persona dolls might be used to explore the experiences of a refugee or Traveller child, whether or not they are present in the setting (Brown 2001).

> ### 📁 Case Study
>
> An EYFS class in a mainly mono-cultural area spent a term working with a visiting project supported by the local authority. Each week the children worked with the visitors to be introduced to new aspects of Brazilian culture, including listening to stories, learning songs, hearing music, learning playground and clapping games, tasting food and drumming carnival rhythms. During follow-up activities with the class teacher the children researched and made carnival wings using inks and fabric, they shared more fiction and non-fiction texts about Brazil and other South American countries and they included the music, songs and games in their free play. Finally the class worked together to create a performance to share the work with their families. Although no children had South American heritage this learning opportunity allowed all the children to talk about their experience of other languages and countries and therefore positively affirmed the benefits of diversity, whatever their ethnicity.

Role play can be an enjoyable and reassuring way for children to re-create their home experiences using familiar clothes, cooking utensils, play food and dolls and should be resourced with a variety of these to reflect a wide range of cultural and ethnic backgrounds. Daymond (2005) relates how simply purchasing a few domestic items such as baby blankets and clothes from the Appleby horse fair provided children from Traveller families with some familiar play equipment for home-based role play. However, all children must first be helped to treat unfamiliar equipment or clothing with respect and understand that mocking behaviour is insulting towards others' family traditions. Practitioners should also be careful when purchasing dressing-up outfits because of the possibility that they may reinforce stereotyping. A 'traditional' African or Chinese costume may be as unrepresentative of clothing worn on a day-to-day basis as a flamenco dancer's costume would be for a Spanish person and should therefore be avoided in the dressing-up equipment. Early years educators should ensure items of religious significance are treated with respect and do not end up being treated as play objects (Lindon 2006). The same consideration is needed when practitioners select *visual images* and *display* to use in the early years setting. They must ensure that posters or photos are up to date and ideally representative of people from different ethnic and cultural backgrounds living in modern Britain as well as abroad. Where possible it is ideal to involve the real families, children and community of the setting in providing photos and artefacts for use with the children. The DfES report *Excellence and Enjoyment* (2006)

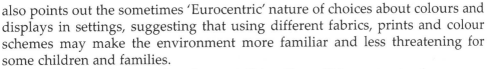

also points out the sometimes 'Eurocentric' nature of choices about colours and displays in settings, suggesting that using different fabrics, prints and colour schemes may make the environment more familiar and less threatening for some children and families.

It is important to remember that not all families will incorporate play opportunities with their children at home. Some parents will not understand the play-based nature of the early years as it differs greatly from their own school experience. Some families may not use books at home because of their own limited literacy (Daymond 2005). Others may have a lack of space in which to play or store games, such as in Traveller trailers or in the temporary accommodation given to refugee families. Lack of money to provide books and toys may be an issue or the children's role in some cultures may be more about helping with adult activities in the home (Daymond 2005; Wild-Smith 2005). It may be useful for the setting to provide activities that can be used at home and returned so that families can see how their children use and enjoy play resources. Some settings are also able to offer stay and play sessions for toddlers or older children around the school day; these can help adults to understand the benefits of play and to become more familiar and relaxed in a school or early years setting. Once again, resources that are used with families need to reflect the diversity of those who are perhaps feeling like 'outsiders' in the educational setting. In particular, sending home books and play resources that reflect the language and culture of travelling or newly arrived families can send a welcoming message. However, this should not mean that these families are only offered a narrow selection of resources and that no other children and families access resources which reflect family diversity. Practitioners may assume that families who have been in the community for longer or Traveller families who are in settled housing will no longer require resources that reflect their culture. In settings where many of the population are British born but with varied ethnic origins, practitioners can assume that special provision, or resourcing is unnecessary. In fact all of these families still need support to be involved in education, the children continue to deserve resources that reflect their identities and many will need help with developing the language needed to be academically successful.

Information and *communication* must be clear and not disadvantage any families if a setting wishes to really value and support children's diverse needs. For instance, settings should make sure that parents with little English or limited literacy can access information easily. Working parents or children who move between the homes of their divorced parents can also be overlooked and miss out on information in the form of notices and letters. Verbal, visual and virtual communication with parents may make information more easily available and understood and a range of these methods should be used. It is not realistic to expect settings to translate all written materials into many different languages but other bilingual adults can be used to help communication and monolingual English-speaking adults can learn key words. Systems should be put in place to help parents understand the expectations, events and routines of the setting. This is of course especially important for families who are newly arrived to the country but Traveller families and those established in the area but with English as an additional language could also benefit. Children will also need support with making relationships and understanding the routines of the setting and the use of visual timetables and labels and buddy systems will be important for them. Other ways to help might include: giving new families a key person to liaise with and a parent buddy to help with language and literacy needs or to go to for reassurance; arranging meetings flexibly to accommodate different family circumstances; making sure that parents realise their first language is an asset for their children and should be maintained; and finding out as much as possible about children's home background and previous education (Dulai 2008; Lindon 2006; DCSF 2007).

In my work with early years settings I have frequently been told that children for whom English is an additional language are 'doing brilliantly', quickly communicating in English, and that 'they have no language needs'. Other misconceptions are that only newly arrived children or children who do not use English at home have language needs. Sadly this shows a lack of understanding about the nature of language and its influence on children's learning in the early years. Home language is not only an issue for communication but much more than this it is part of children's identity. It is simply not good enough to presume that a child who is fluent in English should never use or acknowledge their home language or languages whilst in the setting, as this communicates the message that the language of their family life is redundant and inferior to English. Children who experience this may feel embarrassed or try to hide their home language and can even feel ashamed about being bilingual (Datta 2007; Smidt 2008; Statham 2008). This is one reason why practitioners should make sure that many languages are shown in the setting in books, CDs, notices and labels and that these are actively used in learning experiences. Different adults and children should be encouraged to share their languages by teaching others. In monolingual settings children should be supported to find out more about languages from around the world and to value multilingualism as a skill.

Children who may have less obvious language needs may also need support to develop the 'Standard English' vocabulary and grammar needed for academic success; these include children from Black African and Caribbean families and children from Gypsy Roma Traveller families who may be using their own versions of English and other languages. Practitioners need to learn about the process of language acquisition and be aware of the impact that learning English as an additional language or being bilingual can have on other aspects of the children's learning (Smidt 2008). Practitioners need to notice and value the influence of children's home language such as using home language words or symbols in their writing or the directionality or grammar of their home language applied to English. Parents and children should be encouraged to share and use home language texts, alphabets and video in the setting alongside English resources (Kenner 2000; Ross 2007). Isolated learners in mainly white English-speaking schools should not be expected to learn by immersion; they still need specific provision for their language and cultural needs and are likely to need even more support to feel that their unique identity is recognised and valued (Statham 2008). Practitioners can benefit from using other bilingual adults but should not feel that they are unable to provide for children without this help. They can use visual props, body language, facial expression and gesture to help children to tune into English. They can benefit all the children by using frequent speaking and listening activities, music, stories, songs and rhymes, supported with props and puppets (DfES 2006; Ross 2007; Smidt 2008). During all of these activities the practitioner must be planning opportunities to model language use, to give children a real purpose for using language and to extend children's interactions through sensitive one-to-one dialogue. Ross (2007) suggests offering quiet spaces and props to encourage children to practise, retell and repeat the English language experiences that they have.

Questions for Discussion

Are you challenging your assumptions and reflecting whether they demonstrate an inclusive philosophy?
If you are working in an early years setting does it reflect a diverse society?

PRINCIPLES FOR PRACTICE

There is so much to say about the need to support the diverse families with children in early years settings that it is impossible to do justice to all the possible circumstances of the children in our care. However there are some simple principles that should guide any early years educator in any location. Consider who you are and how your experience and expectations influence your view of the children and families that you work with, acknowledge your assumptions, challenge them and move forward. Ensure your curriculum, environment and communication reflect the diverse society in which we live, but avoid tokenism; listen to the stories of your community, the history and heritage of the families around you. Get to know each child and family as individuals and enter into a genuine dialogue with them about what you each want and expect from each other. Adapt the learning and the language to support the children in your care, observe them closely to find out what they need. It is a hard task but an important one. It is a key responsibility of early years educators to help children and families to understand that we are all different but we all belong.

Further Reading

Beckley, P., Elvidge, K. and Hendry, H. (2009) *Implementing the Early Years Foundation Stage: A Handbook*. Buckingham: Open University Press.

Johnston, J., Nahmad-Williams, L., House, A., Cooper, L. and Smith, C. (2009) *Early Childhood Studies*. Harlow: Pearson Education.

Lane, J. (2008) *Young Children and Racial Justice*. London: National Children's Bureau.

Pearce, S. (2005) *You Wouldn't Understand: White Teachers in Multiethnic Classrooms*. Stoke-on-Trent: Trentham Books.

De Palma, R. and Atkinson, E. (2009) *Interrogating Heteronormativity in Primary Schools: The No Outsiders Project*. Stoke-on-Trent: Trentham Books.

Donovan, J. (2005) 'Still Travellers? Housed Travellers in a London Borough', in C. Tyler (ed.) *Traveller Education: Accounts of Good Practice*. Stoke-on-Trent: Trentham Books.

Siraj-Blatchford, I. and Clarke, P. (2000) *Supporting Identity, Diversity and Language in the Early Years*. Maidenhead: Open University Press.

Wooley, R. and Morris, J. (2008) *Family Diversities Reading Resource*. Bishop Grosseteste University College Lincoln. Available at: http://www.bishopg.ac.uk/docs/Research/Family%20Diversity%20Reading%20Resource.pdf (accessed 11 August 2010).

Useful Websites

Wooley, R. Morris, J. (2008) *Family Diversities Reading Resource*. Bishop Grosseteste University College Lincoln. Available at: http://www.bishopg.ac.uk/docs/Research/Family%20Diversity%20Reading%20Resource.pdf (accessed 11 August 2010)

www.multiverse.ac.uk

www.naldic.org.uk

www.insted.co.uk

www.globaldimension.org.uk

www.pre-school.org.uk

www.tactyc.org.uk

References

Allen, A., Atkinson, E., Bruce, E., De Palma, R. and Hemingway, J. (2009) 'Addressing Lesbian, Gay, Bisexual and Transgender Equality in the Primary School', in R. De Palma and E. Atkinson (2009) *Interrogating Heteronormativity in Primary Schools: The No Outsiders Project*. Stoke-on-Trent: Trentham Books.

Beckley, P., Elvidge, K. and Hendry, H. (2009) *Implementing the Early Years Foundation Stage: A Handbook*. Buckingham: Open University Press.

Brooker, L. (2002) *Starting School: Young Children Learning Cultures*. Buckingham: Open University Press.

Brown, B. (2001) *Combating Discrimination: Persona Dolls in Action*. Stoke-on-Trent: Trentham Books.

Casper, V. and Schultz, S.B. (1999) *Gay Parents/Straight Schools*. New York: Teachers College Press.

Datta, M. (2007) 'My Language Story', in M. Datta, (ed.) *Bilinguality and Literacy Principles and Practice* (2nd edn.) London: Continuum.

Daymond, L. (2005) 'It's All About Me – Resources at Foundation and KS1', in C. Tyler (ed.) *Traveller Education: Accounts of Good Practice*. Stoke-on-Trent: Trentham Books.

Department for Education and Schools (DfES) (2006) *Excellence and Enjoyment: Learning and Teaching for Bilingual Children in the Primary Years*. London: DfES.

Department for Children, Schools and Families (DCSF) (2007) *New Arrivals Excellence Programme Guidance*. London: DCSF.

Dulai, K. (2008) 'Working in Partnership with Parents', in: S. Smidt, (ed.) *Supporting Multilingual Learners in the Early Years*. Abingdon: Routledge.

Kenner, C. (2000) *Home Pages*. Stoke-on-Trent: Trentham Books.

Klein, M.D. and Chen, D. (2001) *Working with Children from Culturally Diverse Backgrounds*. New York: Delmar.

Lane, J. (2008) *Young Children and Racial Justice*. London: National Children's Bureau.

Lindon, J. (2006) *Equality in Early Childhood: Linking Theory and Practice*. Abingdon: Bookpoint.

Ouseley, H. and Lane, J. (2006) 'We've got to start somewhere: What role can early years services and settings play in helping society to be more at ease with itself?' *Race Equality Teaching* 24(2): 39–43.

Pearce, S. (2005) *You Wouldn't Understand: White Teachers in Multiethnic Classrooms*. Stoke-on-Trent: Trentham Books.

Pre-school Learning Alliance (PLA) (2001) *Equal Chances: Eliminating Discrimination and Ensuring Equality in Pre-school Settings*. London: Pre-school Learning Alliance.

Richardson, R. and Miles, B. (2008) *Racist Incidents and Bullying in Schools: How to Prevent Them and How to Respond When They Happen*. Stoke-on-Trent: Trentham.

Ross, M. (2007) 'Bilinguality and Learning in the Early Years' in: M. Datta. (ed.) *Bilinguality and Literacy Principles and Practice* (2nd edn.) London: Continuum.

Rutter, J. (2003) *Supporting Refugee Children in 21st Century Britain: A Compendium of Essential Information* (2nd edn.) Stoke-on-Trent: Trentham Books.

Siraj-Blatchford, I. and Clarke, P. (2000) *Supporting Identity, Diversity and Language in the Early Years*. Maidenhead: Open University Press.

Smith, P. K., Cowie, H. and Blades, M. (2003) *Understanding Children's Development*. Oxford: Blackwell.

Smidt, S. (2008) *Supporting Multilingual Learners in the Early Years*. Abingdon: Routledge.

Statham, L. (2008) *Counting Them In: Isolated Bilingual Learners in Schools*. Stoke-on-Trent: Trentham Books.

Wild-Smith, K. (2005) 'Improving Access to Early Educational Opportunities for Traveller Children', in C. Tyler (ed.) *Traveller Education: Accounts of Good Practice*. Stoke-on-Trent: Trentham Books.

8 THINKING SKILLS

Sharon Marsden

Learning objectives

- To examine how thinking skills can become an integral part of planning for children's learning
- To further awareness of differing views of thinking skills
- To consider a research project promoting creativity and thinking skills

This chapter explores how children's learning can be enhanced and extended by using thinking skills, whether they be taught in stand-alone or cross-curricular activities. According to Costello (2000: 85): 'Teaching thinking skills in schools is about bringing children to an understanding that they have the ability to advance ideas, views and arguments in ways and contexts which are frequently not exploited by the traditional curriculum'. Thinking skills have been studied by a variety of researchers throughout the twentieth and twenty-first centuries but it is only recently that they have been developed extensively within the British school system. This chapter also considers how thinking skills can develop the opportunity for more creativity within lessons and encourage the move away from an overemphasis on knowledge.

What then do we mean exactly by the term thinking skills? There are many different interpretations as to this with researchers like Quinn (1997), Baron and Sternberg (1987) and Lipman (1991) supporting the idea of thinking as a skill. Others like De Bono (1976), Smith (1992) and Adey (1994) question whether thinking could be referred to as a skill or a mental process. Whichever meaning is taken, all agree that 'people of any age can be taught to think more clearly, to express themselves and their thoughts … and grow in self-esteem as a result' (Rockett and Percival 2002: 39). As research has progressed throughout the twenty-first century, thinking skills have become more specific. The National Curriculum (DfES/QCA 1999) made reference to the five specific thinking skills of information processing, reasoning, enquiry, creative thinking and evaluation, and in 2001, Wallace furthered the research on intelligence through the publication of TASC: Thinking Actively in a Social Context. The TASC wheel went on to become a popular tool used for identifying and developing thinking skills, particularly within schools. It allowed teachers and pupils to develop their own capacities to use thinking and problem-solving skills in a formalised format which could be developed and reviewed each term. There has now been a move '… away from the idea of thinking being a thought process hidden in people's heads to the idea that it is a specific set of skills to be learned and taught.' (Smith 2006: 14). Smith reflected Bloom's Taxonomy when breaking down the thinking skills into six levels of: knowledge, comprehension, application, analysis, evaluation and synthesis, or to put it simply, to know something, understand it, use it, examine it, judge it and create it. There is still a large amount of disagreement, however, as to precisely which skills develop thinking to the greatest extent.

ENGAGEMENT AND MOTIVATION

One thing which most people do agree on is that in order for thinking to flourish there is a need for engagement and motivation. Thinkers need to be interested and use their thinking skills for a positive outcome. Moon (2008) identified the importance of questioning in order to develop and challenge thinking. Children need to be encouraged to enquire and reflect on as many opportunities as they can. They should listen not only to their teacher but also to other children's views which could then be used to aid discussion, reasoning and an awareness of others' attitudes. The teachers need to listen, understand different opinions, promote correct questioning and know where to go next in order to use the children's thinking skills to their full.

The National Curriculum for England and Wales (DfES/QCA 1999) made reference to six Key Skills and five Thinking Skills which were clarified and renamed as the key aspects. The new primary curriculum (DfES/QCA 2010) made reference to the essentials for learning and life where children would focus on Literacy, Numeracy, ICT, personal learning, thinking and social skills. 'By enabling them to secure these essential skills in the primary phase we are giving children the capacity to learn, to collaborate and to reflect' (DfES/QCA 2010: 14). More opportunities for thinking skills are now being offered in schools as the emphasis for learning moves towards thinking and the use of everyday skills rather than facts. Schools however are still '… places where children receive rather than give information and thought' (Fisher 1990: ix). There is little opportunity for the children to control the learning or move it in a direction which interests them. Smith (2006: 33) said that our curriculum still 'focuses too much on know-what and not enough on know-how'.

Although we would like to believe that the National Curriculum (DfES/QCA 1999) promotes the teaching of thinking skills the evidence by researchers suggests that there are still restraints which prevent the direct teaching of thinking skills within the classroom.

Kelly (2005) agreed by saying that children would say things which they thought the teacher wanted them to say. Guessing answers, pursuing their own interests and thinking out of the box were not favoured because they were not linked to the school curriculum. He questioned whether children really approached any of their learning in a deep manner or if they just scratched the surface and did enough to get by. In the end Kelly related classroom learning to that of a production line, which is quite a worrying notion. Rockett and Percival (2002) felt that the National Curriculum was beginning to offer more opportunities for teachers to move away from the traditional subjects and look at learning, thinking and creativity, but this required motivation and enthusiasm from the teachers rather than being guided by descriptive documents. Yet the National Curriculum continued to promote the key skills through each subject. Thinking skills were not made explicit within schemes of work or planning and this is where the old curriculum fell short in promoting the use and development of these skills. Many of the studies conducted on thinking skills, like Instrumental Enrichment, Somerset Thinking, CoRT and Philosophy for Children, were all based on teaching thinking skills through single subjects. McPeck (1981) also supported this single subject approach which would match well with the curriculum set up in Britain as it moved away from topic work and identified a subject specific timetable with the Literacy Hour and the Numeracy Hour. Within these strategies there is reference to the key skills, but they are not identified in the context of actually teaching each subject, and this again is where the National Curriculum does not encourage the use of thinking skills effectively. It may also suggest why teachers have felt unable to let children explore and question more for themselves, as the materials were quite descriptive.

A CROSS-CURRICULAR APPROACH

Baron and Sternberg (1987) argued against the single subject approach and advocated the mixed model of subject-discrete infusions to continue, or as it is more commonly known, the topic approach. This was supported by the ACT's thinking skills programme which also used the infused approach. The HighScope approach to learning has been promoted heavily, particularly in the Early Years Curriculum, to encourage children to think more for themselves. The Plan, Do, Review system gives the children the capacity to think, reason and argue while the teachers have time to question and observe. The Early Years Framework

(DfES/QCA 2007) encourages this approach, through which both children and teachers are able to bring more thinking opportunities into everyday activities in the school.

 Case Study

A small group of four children decided to attempt to make a bridge as part of their play. They discussed the challenge of building a suitable structure which spanned the building blocks created. After careful building and a number of changes to the design they were able to build a structure which could support the weight of the vehicles they were playing with. They tested the strength of the structure, revising it to increase its strength and discussing together ways to improve it.

Both single subject and infused thinking skills programmes have been successful and both agree that even though the thinking skills have been taught, they are not successful unless they are transferred to situations and used. The curriculum today is promoting a return to a more integrated timetable with topics becoming more popular again. The new curriculum which was proposed for 2011 joined subjects like history and geography together, again moving towards a more integrated approach rather than the single-subject approach we have become used to. The evidence shows that it does not matter how we choose to teach thinking skills but that we use these skills in our teaching.

ACTION RESEARCH

A review was undertaken in a primary school to see how children could be encouraged to become better thinkers and more enthusiastic learners. Action research was used to gather data over a five-month period from a target group of nine mixed aged children. Action research allowed for the freedom to try out ideas, collate and analyse data and evaluate the results. It could then be used to '... improve practice rather than produce knowledge' (Elliott 1991: 49). The research was based around whether thinking skills could be integrated into today's classroom and how a link between thinking skills and the development of a child's creativity could be made. In order to gain the teacher's and the children's point of view the methods chosen were classroom observation, individual interviews and classroom artefacts. One of the first activities undertaken by the nine focus group children was the alternative thinking skill method in a stand-alone lesson. The children were given a scarf and they had to think of as many alternative uses for it as they could within one minute. This task was carried out in October and then revisited five months later in March, after thinking skills had been used every day in the classroom. Results showed that five out of the nine children were able to think of at least twice as many uses for the scarf than before. The children had overcome the panic of the time restriction and felt more at ease when coming up with new ideas. The children were interviewed and five out of nine said that when the task was carried out in October they were unsure what was expected of them but now they clearly understood the task and knew there were no right or wrong answers. This clearly links back to the argument against schools only providing facts rather than encouraging children to think. They had felt at the beginning that there were right and wrong answers to the task set but had learned over the five months that as long as they could justify their ideas, their answers would be considered as acceptable.

The second activity which was introduced was the odd-one-out method which built on the skills from the alternative task. This was carried out in a variety of subjects, often as quick starters to cross-curricular lessons, and involved the children identifying from a group of objects the odd one out. Children were again told that there were no right or wrong answers but that they only needed to be able to justify their responses. Results from the same five-month period showed how all the children improved on their ability to give justified answers. It was also clear that some children found it easier to give answers in some areas of the curriculum than others. Research also found that topic work odd-ones-out, where children had to identify one odd picture, gave more variety and responses than the maths odd-ones-out. On average there was an increase of seven answers per child for topic work compared to maths odd-ones-out where there was an average increase of only two. Interviews with the children found that they could think of answers for topic work but were not always as confident about mathematical concepts. They were uneasy about being too adventurous and felt that the factual knowledge they needed in order to justify their answers was holding them back. It was only the children who were very confident in maths who could express creative links to mathematical solutions.

Over the five-month period it became clear that the two activities encouraged the children to think for themselves and were improving their ability to make connections between what they knew and their own characters. The results were achieved through both isolated and cross-curricular lessons and the outcomes showed that by encouraging opportunities for thinking skills, children were becoming active participants in the lessons and not passive observers.

CREATIVITY

Cowley (2004) wanted to harness the talents which people already had by giving them more opportunities for creativity and this use of thinking skills might just be the way forward to develop the creativity in children which the National Curriculum (DfES/QCA 1999) referred to. Jeffries and Hancock (2002) felt individuals should have the opportunity to generate and extend ideas, hypothesise, apply imagination and look for alternative and innovative outcomes. Kelly (2005) supported this view, adding how important it was to also see multiple perspectives and value others' points of view. With a return to a creative curriculum based around topic work, children would be allowed to discover things for themselves, adapt work to their own interests and raise their self-steem. The use of thinking skills would surely aid in this venture.

A final method used for developing thinking skills and looking at their impact on creativity within the school was the construction task. As part of a thinking skills day the children's success criteria was to build anything they liked using any materials which they could think of. Boxes, tubes, tubs and other materials had been collected by the school and the children over the previous weeks to ensure that there was a wide selection of choice. Observation and the use of photographs along with interviews were used to record the responses of the class. The children were asked to create a model and then explain what they had done and how it worked. All the children were very excited by this task and the variety of resources which were available to them. They immediately dived in, grabbing as many boxes, tins and tubes as they could carry. Five out of the nine children when asked knew exactly what they wanted to make and how they planned to do it. Two out of the nine said they had not decided what to make but they wanted these resources so had to grab them before anyone else did.

The children worked on their models, adding to and developing them as the morning progressed. Analysis of the photographs showed the children were engrossed in their tasks and were enjoying the freedom of exploring resources and making decisions. Even during the task one child used a rolled up piece of wallpaper as an alternative thinking skill, saying, 'Hey it's a telescope or a trumpet or a walking stick!' This was now a natural response and greeted with laughter by the other children. As the activity progressed the children questioned each other within their conversations and were constantly changing their constructions. Analysis of one photograph showed how the children worked together, discussing and challenging each others' ideas. They were not looking for direction from the teacher but were in control of their own learning and working in a way that suited them in order to reach the goals they had set themselves. The range of models produced extended from robots, dogs, cars, a chair, a scissor holder, a magic switch which changes what people do and where you can travel to, and even a fish in a fish tank. The photographs again showed how proud and happy the children were with their models and how the range of objects created was far greater than if the children had been restricted to set objectives by the teacher following some scheme of work. The different resources the children had used for their creations were tremendous and showed how they were thinking creatively and were not being restricted by only having paper, cardboard and glue at their disposal. They were using lampshades, carrier bags and egg boxes in as many different ways as they could think of. This approach had allowed the children to learn a number of social and construction skills by exploring their own learning paths.

When the teacher was interviewed she commented on how the children were highly motivated. The only comment she had received was 'What? We can do what we like? Cool!' When the children were asked to discuss their work they could explain what they had used and why and what each component did. Seven out of the nine children were also able to say what they would have liked to have done if they had had more time. Five out of the nine were able to reflect on their chosen materials and expressed an opinion as to alternatives they would have liked to have used. One boy remarked,

> We tried to glue the legs first but it wouldn't work so we tried masking tape and the Sellotape and it's kind of OK but if we did it again we said we would cut holes in the box first and then we would stick the tubes in the holes. We could have glued them or we could have cut around the top to make a better anchor.

The teacher was impressed by the language and thought which the children showed throughout the task and in their presentations. Even the quieter children had something to say about their models because they were all different, so no one had said all the so-called right answers. The children were using their existing knowledge to solve the problems which they were being faced with. They were also developing their independence and taking responsibility for the direction of their own creative learning.

From these three tasks it was clear that the children were motivated and excited by the learning processes which they were now being faced with. Throughout the school there was a new buzz about topics, what they knew and where they might take their learning next. There was a real ownership of the curriculum and the learning opportunities by the children. The data seemed to emphasise how the pupils' attitudes had changed throughout these tasks which had allowed them to give clearer and a wider variety of answers. The third task, the construction method, would help clarify if the pupils were also being more creative or if it was simply a rise in self confidence which had resulted in the changes in their attitudes and answers. Cropley (1992: 7) noted how children would '… branch out … only when they had the confidence to do so'. Self confidence is an important element of the creativity strand but are these thinking skills activities only allowing the opportunity for pupils to build their confidence or are they encouraging creative skills as well? The construction task was planned to show this, as it was a move away from the design technology lessons previously offered, and, again, it built on the skills already embedded through the use of the alternatives and the odd-ones-out.

Wilson (2005) noted how design technology was the perfect subject to develop a child's creativity. 'D & T is a hands-on activity in which children make real, tangible objects. It is, however, also "minds-on", involving a balance between doing and thinking, action and reflection' (Davies and Howe 2003: 172).

The method used for this thinking skill was different from previous design technology activities because the pupils were given complete freedom to make anything. Usually a task would be set within guidelines, like being asked to design a vehicle or the well-known slipper/shoe. This time the activity was giving the pupils the freedom to make absolutely anything, encouraging them to think everything through from the start. According to Fisher and Williams (2004) this method was providing creative opportunities for the pupils as it offered a stimulus, had a context, and allowed for reflection and the use of their own knowledge and skill. It also had that risk factor which created the butterfly in the tummy air of excitement as to whether it would be successful and if it wasn't it allowed the opportunity to manage and then review the process. Evidence showed how engrossed the pupils were with their designs and the enjoyment which was seen through the experimentation with the resources. The response of 'Cool!' by the children when they could do what they wanted without any boundaries showed how they could often feel frustrated by the limitations and the constraints of the National Curriculum. Seven out of nine children were able to talk fluently about their designs, showing clearly how their imaginations had taken over. All the children completed the task set which cannot always be said about work set in the classroom normally and every piece of work was individual.

The three thinking skills methods used for this research were easy to integrate into the curriculum as it stood and they helped introduce the children to a new way of learning, where they, the pupils, had more control over the activities and the outcomes. They were the right activities to develop the children's confidence, build self-esteem and encourage them to use their imaginations. This in turn led them to change from passive listeners to active thinkers and move away from, as Kelly (2005) identified, saying what they thought the teacher wanted them to say.

The impact which this research on thinking skills has had on the school is that because of the positive reaction by the children more investment has been made in resources and thinking skills activities. The staff agree that the changes in the children are noticeable across the school and it is worth investing more in a thinking skills curriculum. Extending on from this the staff have revised the curriculum to incorporate more creative topics and more thinking skills activities and this has led to the planning also becoming directed by the thinking skills rather than trying to fit the thinking skills into the present planning and curriculum. It has also led to teachers changing their learning environments to what Fogarty and Opeka (1988) refer to as a thinking classroom. They have thought about the opportunities which they are offering for thinking, such as the climate of the room, areas for children to interact with each other and with the resources, and also the timings given for questioning and reflection.

Teachers have, however, felt the tension described by Wilson (2005: 27) when it comes to promoting creativity within the political and economic restraints of the curriculum. Although the government introduced 'Creativity, Find it! Promote it!' in 2000 it is seen by many staff as an additional, separate initiative to the National Curriculum, not something which works together, building on each other's strengths. The staff are slowly changing their approach to practice and are happier to leave their QCA documents and books and take the learning to the child where they have more choices and control, but as with any initiative it takes time to consolidate. The staff also felt, like Fisher and Williams (2004: 2), that what is '... needed is the confidence to adapt and innovate the basic curriculum ... and build creative thinking skills into all aspects of teaching'. This is not to say that all the tension has been eliminated from the staff. There are still some very cautious changes being made, but the positive, supportive networks are in place to develop this together.

Looking back over the research it was clear how constrained the school staff had become to following QCA documents, how mundane the lessons were and how the children were being held back. The changes in the amount of information gained from the children and staff in the second interviews compared to the first were astounding, and if this could be achieved in five months through just three methods what could be raised in the future if we extended this?

Clive Davies (2008) made references to the need for deep rather than shallow learning within the school curriculum. It was apparent from the beginning of the research that the children were very much used to short, directed activities which basically kept them occupied rather than challenged their thinking. Through the three thinking skills activities carried out for this research, the children were being introduced to more challenging tasks, which were more individual to each child and required them to direct their own learning. Each method built on the previous skills and encouraged the children to develop the three elements which Davies (2008) saw as making up this deeper learning. These elements involved hearing the pupils' voice, empowering the learner so that they were learning to learn and using assessment for learning.

In the alternative task the pupil's voice was heard as they gave clear answers for what the scarf could be used for. The improvement in the answers given the second time around showed how the children had become more confident in expressing their own ideas and thoughts. The improvement in the number of responses also showed how the children now felt more in control of the task. They were directing the task because the scarf could be anything that they wanted it to be. The discussion held afterwards allowed the children to reflect on the task and again use their voice to assess the activity and how it had helped them. Developing these skills through the odd-one-out activity gave the children the chance to discuss their choices, take the learning in the direction that they wanted, because it did not matter which picture or number they chose to be the odd one out, and justify their answers through their own assessment of the task. The construction activity also required the children to use all three of the deeper learning elements. The children talked with each other and the teachers, discussing their ideas and the resources they were going to use. They were in charge of their own tasks, choosing for themselves what to make and how to make it and assessing their models all of the time. If one tack did not work they changed resources, like the glue to masking tape on the dog's legs, reviewed their techniques and tried different scenarios in order to solve the problems they encountered for themselves. The whole activity was then reviewed by the children who extended the task by not only recognising what they had achieved and how they had achieved it but also by saying where they would like to move on to if they were given the opportunity.

All three thinking skills activities used in this research laid the foundations for developing a new and more enlivened curriculum within the school. The children had become much more independent and were beginning to take responsibility for their own learning needs. Staff were also seeing the effects on the children and the lessons they were offering. Although these three activities had been introduced as isolated initiatives in the beginning, by the end of the five-month period they had become integrated into maths, literacy and topic lessons. Using the thinking skills effectively meant that in the beginning the staff had to teach the activities as specific skills through isolated tasks and then apply these skills through more integrated tasks.

Questions for Discussion

Why do you feel incorporating thinking skills in a framework for young children's learning is important?
How can these skills help children in their future lives?

CONCLUSION

Whether it be through isolated lessons or through cross-curricular activities, using thinking skills with children allows for a more balanced approach of knowing how rather than knowing what. It creates opportunities for enthusiasm and motivation which enable creativity and individuality to emerge in the children and leads to them wanting to learn more and be an active part of their development rather than a passive, bored observer. When using thinking skills the children in the study owned more of the learning and responded to the opportunities offered to them. According to Rockett and Percival (2002: 185) 'Education... is about providing the best for our children'. The thinking skills approach definitely meets with approval from the children and became much more prominent in the context of the new primary curriculum as it offered opportunities for teachers to 'design engaging, challenging and coherent experiences ... [and] provides deeper and richer learning to improve progression and achievement for all children' (DfES/QCA 2010: 10). The biggest challenge is now down to the teachers to incorporate these skills when designing exciting and inspiring daily lessons.

Further Reading

Robson, S. (2006) *Developing Thinking and Understanding in Young Children*. Abingdon: Routledge.
Shapiro, S. (2002) *Thinking Skills: Ages 6–8*. London: A and C Black.
Wallace, B. Beverley, N. and McClure, L. (2002) *Teaching Thinking Skills across the Early Years: A Practical Approach for Children Aged 4–7*. London: David Fulton.

Useful Websites

www.nicurriculum.org.uk/ThinkingSkillsintheEarlyYears
This website contains a report from 2007 reviewing practice in the early years with a focus on thinking skills.

References

Adey, P. (1994) *Really Raising Standards: Cognitive Intervention and Academic Achievement*. London: Routledge.
Baron, J.B. and Sternberg, R.J. (1987) *Teaching Thinking Skills: Theory and Practice*. Freeman: New York.
Costello, P. (2000) *Thinking Skills and Early Childhood Education*. London: David Fulton.
Cowley, S. (2004) *Getting the Buggers to Think*. London: Continuum.
Cropley, A. (1992) *More Ways Than One: Fostering Creativity in the Classroom*. Greenwich, CT: Ablex Publishing.
Davies, C. (2008) *A Curriculum that Matters*. Saddleworth: Focus Education.
Davies, D. and Howe, A. (2003) *Teaching Science, Design and Technology in the Early Years*. London: David Fulton.
De Bono, E. (1976) *Teaching Thinking*. London: Maurice Temple Smith.

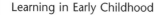

Department for Education and Employment and Qualifications and Curriculum Authority (DfES/QCA) (1999) *The National Curriculum: Handbook for Primary Teachers in England*. London: DfES.

Department for Education and Employment and Qualifications and Curriculum Authority (DfES/QCA) (2007) *The Early Years Foundation Stage*. London: DfES.

Department for Education and Employment and Qualifications and Curriculum Authority (DfES/QCA) (2010) *Introducing the New Primary Curriculum: Guidance for Primary Schools*. London: DfES.

Elliot, J. (1991) *Action Research for Educational Change*. Milton Keynes: Open University Press.

Fisher, R. (1990) *Teaching Children to Think*. Oxford: Basil Blackwell.

Fisher, R. and Williams, M. (2004) *Unlocking Creativity: Teaching Across the Curriculum*. London: David Fulton.

Fogarty, R. and Opeka, K. (1988) *Start Them Thinking: A Handbook of Classroom Strategies for the Early Years*. Arlington Heights, IL: IRI/Skylight Training and Publishing.

Jeffries, M. and Hancock, T. (2002) *Thinking Skills: A Teacher's Guide*. Leamington Spa: Hopscotch.

Kelly, P. (2005) *Using Thinking Skills in the Primary Classroom*. London: Paul Chapman.

Lipman, M. (1991) *Thinking in Education*. Cambridge: Cambridge University Press.

McPeck, J. (1981) *Critical Thinking in Education*. Oxford: Martin Robertson.

Moon, J. (2008) *Critical Thinking: An Exploration of Theory and Practice*. Abingdon: Routledge.

Quinn, V. (1997) *Critical Thinking in Young Minds*. London: David Fulton.

Rockett, M. and Percival, S. (2002) *Teaching Thinking: Thinking Skills: Learning Environment*. Stafford: Network Educational Press.

Smith, F. (1992) *To Think: In Language, Learning and Education*. London: Routledge.

Smith, I. (2006) *Learning to Think: From Teaching Skills to Developing Minds*. Norwich: The Stationery Office.

Wallace, B. (2001) *Teaching Thinking Skills Across the Primary Curriculum: A Practical Approach for All Abilities*. London: David Fulton.

Wilson, A. (2005) *Creativity in Primary Education*. Exeter: Learning Matters.

PART 3

ORGANISING THE LEARNING ENVIRONMENT

Part 3 builds on the pedagogical stance of the first section and the philosophy underpinning the principles in Part 2, to provide practical suggestions of how an holistic approach can be implemented in practice. The chapters cover play as a means to promote an holistic approach, enabling environments, learning and teaching styles, and leadership and management.

Chapter 9, by Lindy Nahmad-Williams, concerns approaches to play. The significance of play on children's learning and development has been recognised for many years and was brought into prominence by philosophers such as Rousseau (1712) and Froebel (1826) who believed that play is the purest, highest and most natural form of learning, and by the theories of Piaget (1976) and Vygotsky (1962) who highlighted the importance of play in children's cognitive and social development. Their views, among those of other prominent thinkers, have influenced the development of early years practice and the recognition that play should be central to any early years curriculum and setting. Lindy refers to the Early Years Foundation Stage (DCSF, 2008: 7) which states that 'play underpins the delivery of the EYFS' and 'underpins all development and learning for young children'. Few child development experts would disagree with this, but for this to happen in practice the adults working with children need to have a good understanding of the nature of play and how to support in-depth play. Lindy explores this knowledge and understanding through a discussion of the significance of play in a child's world. Consideration is given to the different roles adults take in approaches to play and practical ways to promote children's play through space, time and resources. Discussions are underpinned by relevant research findings such as Siraj-Blatchford et al. (2002), which clearly indicate the significance of adults' understanding children's play in order to give them opportunities to practise, consolidate and extend their learning during play.

Chapter 10, written by Jane Johnston, explores enabling environments to support children's learning and development. Enabling Environments is one of four complementary themes of the Early Years Foundation Stage (DCSF, 2008). In the EYFS the environment is recognised as of key importance for children as it supports learning in all main areas of development. The environment that supports learning can be both the physical (indoors and outdoors) and the ethos or ambience of the setting. The enabling environment is one that encourages individuality (DfES, 2003) supports children through transitions, providing continuity in their lives, and where adults (parents, carers and professionals from a range of backgrounds) work together in an effective way that sees the child at the centre of the environment (Alexander, 2009). The chapter aims to provide an understanding of what an enabling environment entails, how this can be achieved through appropriate planning and ways to support co-operation and collaboration to enhance the progress and development of children.

Chapter 11, written by Alison Jakins, aims to provide an awareness of the breadth of teaching and learning styles to accommodate the development of different skills and give an overview of teaching and learning strategies that will help to strengthen the provision for all learners and promote independent thinking. It includes theories such as accelerated learning, which is described by Hughes (2001: 11) as an umbrella term that 'encompasses approaches to learning that are compatible with the way in which the brain operates and learns most effectively'. Consideration is also given to Gardner's Theory of Multiple Intelligences. Gardner (2004) suggests that intelligence is not fixed and can change throughout our lifetimes. The multiple intelligences model recognises different types of intelligence which we all possess but in different proportions. Bloom's Taxonomy of Educational Objectives, which considers the existence of distinct levels of cognitive ability in relation to thinking, is discussed. Implications for practice when implementing different learning and teaching styles are explored, with the challenges this poses to practitioners working in the settings.

Chapter 12 completes this section with a discussion of leadership and management styles which seek to enable an holistic approach to be effectively implemented as a shared vision benefiting every child in the setting. Differences between leadership and management are described, with case studies incorporated into discussions. The significance of a positive role model is considered in fostering an holistic approach, including the importance emotional intelligence plays. According to Goleman (2002), emotional intelligence is the capacity for recognising our own feelings and those of others, for motivating ourselves and others, and for managing emotions well, both in ourselves and our relationships with others. The chapter seeks to demonstrate that good role models have a positive impact on us and can influence our practice at the time and in the future. The importance of reflections of practice are noted. According to Schön (1983: 63) the study of reflection-in-action is critically important. Reflection can greatly enhance teaching and learning by identifying areas of strength and considering possible means to improve aspects where appropriate. This can be beneficial to everyone in the team and those involved with the setting. To be an effective leader and manager reflections form an essential part of the sustainability of the successful environment.

This section seeks to consider aspects of practice – approaches to play, an enabling environment, learning and teaching styles, and leadership and management – which have a significant impact on the effective implementation and success of an holistic approach in early years practice.

References

Alexander, R. (ed.) (2009) *Children, their World, their Education: Final Report and Recommendations of the Cambridge Review*. London: Routledge.

DCSF (2008) *The Early Years Foundation Stage: Setting the Standard for Learning, Development and Care for Children from Birth to Five: Practice Guidance*. London: DCSF.

DfES (2003) *Every Child Matters*. London: DfES.

Gardner, H. (2004) *Frames of Mind: The Theory of Multiple Intelligences* (20th anniversary edition). New York: Basic Books.

Goleman, D. (2002) *Emotional Intelligence*. New York: Bantam Books.

Hughes, M. (2001) *Strategies for Closing the Learning Gap* (3rd edn). Stafford: Network Educational Press Ltd.

Schön, D. (1983) *The Reflective Practitioner*. New York: Basic Books.

Siraj-Blatchford, I., Sylva, K., Muttock, S., Gilden, R. and Bell, D. (2002) *Researching Effective Pedagogy in the Early Years*. Nottingham: DfES.

9 APPROACHES TO PLAY

Lindy Nahmad-Williams

Learning objectives

- To understand the nature of play and the significance of play in a child's world
- To consider the differing roles of the adult in children's play
- To know different ways to facilitate children's play through space, time and resources

This chapter explores the nature of play in early childhood and considers the different ways settings can support children's play. The Early Years Foundation Stage (DCSF 2008: 7) states that 'play underpins the delivery of the EYFS' and 'underpins all development and learning for young children'. Few child development experts would disagree with this, but for this to happen in practice the adults working with children need to have a good understanding of what play is and how to support in-depth play. The phrase 'delivery of the EYFS' is perhaps unfortunate because it creates a picture of the adult imposing a prescribed curriculum, rather than adults providing for the needs of children based on understanding, observation, partnership and collaboration to develop play opportunities that are enriching and valued as central to learning. Siraj-Blatchford et al. (2002) found that the highest qualified practitioners were most effective in promoting children's learning and providing the richest play experiences. Their research clearly indicates the significance of adults understanding children's play in order to give children opportunities to practise, consolidate and extend their learning during play. This chapter examines the ways adults can provide for play through a consideration of their role in different types of play, the use and variety of resources and the creation of an enabling environment that encourages and sustains play opportunities.

THE NATURE OF PLAY

The significance of play on children's learning and development has been recognised for many years and brought into prominence by philosophers such as Rousseau (1911) and Froebel (1826) who believed that play is the purest, highest and most natural form of learning, and the theories of Piaget (1976) and Vygotsky (1962) who highlighted the importance of play in children's cognitive and social development. Their views, among those of other prominent thinkers, have influenced the development of early years practice and the recognition that play should be central to any early years curriculum and setting.

As a result of these philosophies and theories, play is a word that is used constantly by early years researchers, policy-makers and professionals, as can be seen in the EYFS (DCSF 2008), but it is very hard to define what we actually mean by play (Bruce 2004; Johnston and Nahmad-Williams 2009). Bruce refers to play as an 'umbrella word' (2004: 129) and it is true that there are many different types of play and words associated with play. When I did some small-scale research (Johnston and Nahmad-Williams 2009) into the words professionals use to describe play, such as free play, structured play and outdoor play, there were many differing interpretations of the same words, which of course would impact upon practice. Rather than trying to define what the word play means, it is perhaps more helpful to consider what the nature of play is and define the characteristics and essences of play.

 Questions for Discussion

What does play mean to you?

Remember times you played as a child; think about what you see when you watch children play and think about any activities you do now which you would refer to as play. Discuss the characteristics that have made you define these activities as play.
Consider issues such as feelings and emotions, level of involvement, autonomy, flexibility and the influence of others or solitary activities.
Rather than trying to define the word 'play', try to come to some agreement about the nature of play in terms of characteristics and essences.

Feeling and Emotions

In the task above, you may have used words such as fun, enjoyment, excitement, concentration, imagination, freedom. You may also have considered games with rules and included competition, determination, frustration, nervousness, disappointment, fulfilment, confidence. Play with others might have included friendship, companionship, laughing, sharing, arguing, falling out, whereas solitary play might have included concentration, immersion, focus, independence, lost in own world, satisfaction, contentment, control, loneliness. Whatever words you discussed, these feelings are central to who we are and how we deal with events in our lives and it is through play that children learn to make sense of their world, their relationships and their feelings to support their development as individuals and as members of their community (David et al. 2003; Bruce 2004; Lindon 2005).

Cognitive Development

When discussing the characteristics and essences of play, you may also have considered occasions when your play led to risk-taking, pushing boundaries, making choices, negotiating, changing direction, creative ideas, having control and taking responsibility. These are all central to learning and develop independence, self-esteem, motivation and confidence. When I watched four children building a bridge with wooden bricks there was some arguing, trial and error as bricks were selected which then caused the bridge to topple over, re-building with new ideas, and eventually the anticipation and nervousness as the last brick was placed successfully with the resulting excitement and pleasure as they surveyed their efforts. Vygotsky (1978) studied children's play and came to the conclusion that it was fundamental for cognitive development as well as emotional development. He also believed that social interaction, particularly with skilled adults but also with other children, could extend children's learning beyond that which could be achieved alone, known as the Zone of Proximal Development. This 'zone' is what the child is capable of and has not yet reached but is supported in getting there by interactions with expert others. These cognitive skills need to be recognised by the adults observing the play so that opportunities can be provided to develop these further in future planning.

Physical Development

Some of the play activities you thought about may have involved physical skills. These could be playground games such as chasing games, skipping, throwing and catching, making dens, or more organised games such as football or cricket. Even play that you might not have identified as physical may have involved fine motor skills such as dressing dolls, playing with small objects or building things. Physical play is an important part of child development in which children not only develop physically but also develop other skills such as spatial awareness and estimation. You might have discussed playing outside as something you enjoyed. The fresh air, space, different smells and sights and the sense of freedom are all important aspects of being out of doors. There is something innately pleasurable about feeling fresh air on your face, seeing the sky and being able to touch the natural environment, for instance, running your fingers through the grass. Rachel and Margaret McMillan (1911) pioneered the need for nursery schools to nurture a healthy body as well as a healthy mind and in reaction to the strict school methods being used at the time, opened an open-air nursery. Children need to play outdoors as well as indoors to provide for all their developmental needs and outdoors should be seen as a place to play *and* learn, rather than as a place to take a break from learning (Johnston and Nahmad-Williams 2009).

Cultural Development

You may have remembered playing games that imitated the real world such as pretending dolls were your babies or your class of children in school, playing with tea sets or pretending to be a doctor or vet. Other games might have involved re-enacting your favourite television programme or being a character from a film. This type of play helps children to understand their culture and the different roles people have in society. Play that involves real life is dependent on children's experiences, both real and from books or films, and through this play children enjoy becoming, by pretending, the adults they know or would like to be. Popular culture is a feature of our lives and is particularly prominent in children's lives. The advance of technology is constantly changing the way we live and communicate and this will impact on children's play. Although the notion of toxic childhood (Palmer 2007) can provide a negative view of popular culture, research by others, such as Marsh and Hallet (1999), indicates that popular culture provides a rich stimulus for imaginative play, particularly for boys. I would suggest that we ensure children are media literate in the sense that we teach them to be critical and evaluative of what they see and hear in the media so that they learn how to recognise bias, manipulation and sensationalism. It is important that we also recognise that the media is a part of modern culture and therefore is of cultural significance to children and will impact on their play and development.

Social Development

When thinking about your play in childhood, it might also have brought back memories of the friends with whom you shared those play experiences. Friends are very important and most of us can remember a time a child has come up and said 'I haven't anybody to play with' or naming another child 'who won't be my friend' or 'who won't let me play'. Friendships are complex and children gradually learn about what friendship means through play. Sometimes people assume that children make friends effortlessly but, as with adults, some find the process easier than others. Broadhead (2010) states that friendships are integral to the learning process and this can be observed in their play. When children play together they learn how to be friends and how to communicate their needs and feelings through facial expressions, body language and tone of voice as well as the words they use (Nahmad-Williams 2010). They also learn about tolerance, cooperation, consideration of others, give and take, compromise, empathy and social values.

Questions for Discussion

Consider the different types of learning discussed in the sub-headed sections above.

Are there any other types of learning that you would add to this?
What day-to-day activities can be done in a setting that would help children to apply these skills in different situations?
How would you recognise when some of the learning discussed above is taking place? What might you see or hear?

Corrine and John Hutt (Hutt et al. 1988) define two different types of play: epistemic play and ludic play. Epistemic play is about learning new skills or knowledge through play, for example 'What does this object do?' and ludic play is about fantasy or practice play, changing the question to 'What can I do with this object?'. Macintyre (2001: 6) uses a similar distinction referring to 'play as learning and play as practice'. In her definitions play as learning includes constructive play (building things), explorative play (discovering new objects), problem-solving (puzzles), games with rules and play on apparatus. Play as practice includes sensorimotor play (exploring objects with the senses), symbolic play (pretending objects are living things), fantasy and socio-dramatic play (role play and imaginative play) and rough and tumble play. These definitions tend to view learning as an intellectual activity whereas the types of learning discussed in the previous sub-sections view learning as a more holistic activity which encompasses personal, social and emotional aspects of learning. Hutt (1988) and Macintyre (2001) believe both their definitions of play are essential and that there should not be over-reliance on one type. If we view learning as holistic then all types of play impact on learning and children should be provided with opportunities to engage in different types of play at their own level.

The phrase 'learning through play' can sometimes be interpreted to mean activities that are planned by adults and directed by adults to ensure it is 'purposeful' or 'well-planned' (Lindon, 2005: 237). Hopefully by outlining the different types of learning above, it is clear that children will learn through play through their own direction and with their own purpose. Interactions with other children or with adults enrich the potential of the play to promote learning but this does not mean the play should be determined by adults within an adult remit. The next section of the chapter explores the different roles the adult can take to support children's play which involves having an understanding of the different types of learning discussed in the first section of the chapter.

THE ROLE OF THE ADULT

There is a need for a balance between child-initiated and adult-directed activities in early years settings (Siraj-Blatchford et al. 2002; DCSF 2008) and that has created some misunderstandings about the nature of play. At one end of the scale there is formal teaching with play happening after 'work' has been completed, and at the other it is all play activities with some activities overseen by adults. Bruce (2004) believes that both adults and children can initiate play but adults must allow the children to take the play in their own direction. Moyles (1989) views play as a spiral in which the adult observes free play, then directs the play based on the children's free exploration to extend learning and then encourages the children to involve themselves in free play again to practise the skills learnt during the directed play.

It could be argued that any activity that is directed by an adult is no longer play in the truest sense, even if play-based resources are being used to support the activity. If we take the view that play has to be directed by children to be defined as play then we need to consider the role of the adult. I would suggest that adult-*directed* activities, as distinct from adult-*initiated*, are mainly related to the development of skills. For example, children need to be taught how to decode words for reading or how to form letters for writing and these activities would be directed by an adult. However, children also need to apply these newly learnt skills in their play to give them a meaningful purpose for the activity such as reading the menu in the café or writing the patient's symptoms in the doctor's surgery. This play would be directed by children but include independently applying the skills that had been taught through a directed approach by an adult in a previous session. As this chapter is about approaches to play we will not discuss adult-directed activities but will now consider the different roles adults can take during child-directed play.

Partner in Play

Adults can play alongside the child but should avoid attempting to lead the play. They can join in the pretend world and become a character in that world.

Model

Sometimes it can be useful for an adult to model behaviour, for example, role playing being the waiter in the café to introduce children to the vocabulary and style of speech, such as 'May I take your order?'

Listener and Responder

Adults should have conversations with children during their play which are not based on a question and answer approach but which value the child's views and allow a meaningful discussion to develop. These conversations can develop children's thinking and promote their learning in a natural way.

Mediator

Adults can support conflict resolution through sensitive questioning to develop children's negotiating skills rather than making decisions for them.

Observer

Observation is a vital part of an early years practitioner's role. Through observation we learn about the children's likes, dislikes, skills, attitudes, knowledge, personalities and abilities to relate to others. Observation should be planned for in exactly the same way as all other activities are planned, otherwise it will never happen in a busy early years setting. Early years professionals may often feel under pressure to be 'doing' something with the children and may feel uncomfortable standing back and watching, but watching and noticing are finely tuned and necessary skills. Boud (2001: 12) refers to the importance of 'noticing' which is where the practitioner is aware of what is happening when they see any incident, however irrelevant it might appear to others, and why it could be significant. This is a skill which develops with experience. I have worked with trainee early years teachers who feel anxious because when they observe they don't know what they are looking for. Devereux (2003: 182) cites Stierer et al.'s four main purposes for observation as 'gaining knowledge of children's strengths and areas for development, reviewing provision, forward planning and for summative reporting'. I would suggest there are three main purposes and I have broken these down into different headings:

- *Observer* – to learn about the child
- *Assessor* – to learn about learning and development
- *Evaluator* – to reflect on use of time, space and resources

The result of all of these is that they should impact on future practice both in terms of planning and providing for the individual child's needs and planning provision for the setting as a whole.

When observing to learn about the child, it is more holistic in approach. Focusing on one specific child in different contexts can be very illuminating. I remember observing Emma, whom I had always thought of as quite quiet and submissive. During play in the sand she did follow others and stood back to let others dominate. In the home corner, however, she was a different person. She issued orders, subtly dominated the space and resources and showed an assured and confident approach that I had not noticed before.

 Questions for Discussion

Consider the following questions when you observe:

Do you look at the child's facial expressions and body language?
Do you observe the child alone and with others?
Do you note how other children or adults impact on the child's behaviour?
Do you observe the child in different contexts?
When does the child appear happy, contented, focused, confident, immersed?
What makes the child smile or laugh?

Now consider these questions:

How much of what you observe needs to be recorded?
How do you record?
What do you do with these records? (Consider this question carefully – how much is used for 'evidence' for assessment folders and accountability and how much informs your planning and the way you interact with the child?)

Assessor

In addition to the more general observations, practitioners also observe to assess children's learning, particularly in relation to the EYFS (DCSF 2008). Here the observations are explicitly linked to learning areas and profile indicators. The general observations may become assessments if incidents are seen that show a child has developed in their learning or the observations may have a specific focus on assessment (Clarke 2008). Many early years settings have display boards where Post-it notes are placed throughout the week as staff note down significant incidents that are evidence of learning. Others have sticky labels that are put into individuals' folders or profiles. Strategies for assessment include both participant and non-participant observation, talking and, more importantly, listening to children and assessing things they produce such as pictures, mark-making, constructions and models. Evidence of learning is not only visible in planned observations but also in incidental observations which is why a quick and easy recording system is vital.

'Learning stories' (Podmore and Carr, 1999), based on the New Zealand Early Childhood Curriculum *Te Whāriki*, are a good way of recording observations which allow reflection on learning after the event. This is particularly useful for less experienced observers. As with any story they can be a recording of a child's experiences over a long period, such as weeks or months, and added to as appropriate or they can be a detailed story of a particular experience.

📁 **Case Study**

Jeannie was a student teacher who was learning to use observation as assessment. She was not sure what to look for so her mentor suggested she observed one child over a five-minute period and wrote down everything he did as a learning story. This is an extract from Jeannie's learning story.

Alfie was very interested in the trike that was on its side. He spun the wheels round using his hand and watched as they turned. Each time they slowed down he spun them again. He got hold of the trike and tried to turn it upright but he could only just lift it off the ground. He then moved to the back of the trike and tried to push it but it just moved along the ground. He did this twice more but then stopped. He went back to his original position and tried to lift it again but couldn't. He then started to rock it back and forth and in doing so noticed the wheels again. He spun them but did not seem as interested as before. He stepped back and looked at the trike and then ran to the scooters.

Jeannie and her mentor had a discussion about what they could learn about Alfie from this observation. With sensitive questioning from her mentor, Jeannie noticed his independence; that he persevered even though unsuccessful; he tried different ways of trying to solve the problem, showing knowledge of lifting, turning, rocking and pushing; he repeated the action of spinning the wheel, understanding that it would slow down and stop unless he spun it again. They then turned to the EYFS (DCSF 2008) to reference some of what had been discussed. Jeannie was able to identify aspects of Personal, Social and Emotional Development, Knowledge and Understanding of the World and Physical Development. She annotated the learning story with references from the EYFS. They then went on to discuss what steps Jeannie might take to extend Alfie's learning.

Clarke (2008) and Blaiklock (2008) provide examples of frameworks for learning stories. These can include references to the areas of learning down the left-hand side of the page as a prompt and a space at the end for a review of the learning that appears to have taken place and next steps for that child. Blaiklock (2008) does have reservations about the usefulness of learning stories, particularly if they are the main form of assessment, but he does acknowledge their potential for prompting discussions about a child's learning between practitioners and also with parents. I would suggest that as one form of assessment they add to the child's profile and are also particularly useful for inexperienced observers if they are followed up with an in-depth discussion with a more experienced practitioner. The final role of the adult during observation, as an assessor, will be explored in the final part of this chapter which focuses on resources, space and time.

RESOURCES AND SPACE

Evaluator

When we observe we should be evaluating the effectiveness of our provision and practice. There are several questions that we can ask:

- Is there a good range of resources with a balance between different types of resource?
- Can the resources be used in different ways?
- Are they easily accessible for children?
- Are they in good condition?
- Are there some that seem to be played with more than others and if so, why?
- Is there sufficient space for the children to play in the way they want to play?
- Can children use the space in different ways depending on their needs?
- Do children have sufficient time to become fully absorbed in their play?
- What strategies do we use to bring children's play to an end and how do the children respond?

It is useful to do an audit of the resources and then to consider how these are stored; how they are presented to children; how they are used by the children and how frequently they are used. It can then be decided if changes need to be made. I bought some large building bricks and was disappointed that the children rarely played with them. When I observed them being used and talked to the children it was apparent that there were not enough of them to build anything substantial and therefore the children were not interested in them. Observing the children also allows the practitioner to learn what the children are interested in, in order to provide an appropriate range of resources (Bruce 2004).

Resources

Resources can enhance children's play but some resources are so specific that it could be argued that they might restrict children's play. I was once in a setting that had recently bought a play cooker that made all sorts of different noises such as sizzling when certain buttons were pressed. The children were initially very interested but soon became bored and stopped playing with it. In fact the adults were more interested in it than the children. The children did use their imagination, however, and its main use became the central controls of a spaceship rather than a cooker frying sausages. This experience demonstrates the importance of providing resources that facilitate children's imagination. Broadhead (2010) has conducted research which indicates that children's problem-solving and cooperation is far more evident in role play areas with more open-ended resources, such as a clothes horse with blankets and cardboard boxes, than those set up as a specific place with associated resources, such as a shop with goods and a till. I developed role play boxes that contained different resources that children could take into the role play space so that they could turn it into whatever environment they wanted. These included items such as scarves, lengths of material, stones, shells and a variety of different types of containers. Helen Bromley (2009) has developed small world story boxes that fit into a box about the size of a shoe box. An example would be a box which has shiny material, shiny stones, beads, shiny or glittery paper and reflective materials. The children could then create whatever imaginary or real world they wanted.

Objects should be open and flexible so that the children can transform them into whatever their ideas, experiences and imagination want them to be (Nutbrown 1994).

Questions for Discussion

What are the advantages and disadvantages of using play-based resources that have a specific function (e.g. a cooker, a stethoscope, a hairdryer)?
What are the advantages and disadvantages of using more open-ended resources (e.g. strips of fabric, boxes)?
Observe children playing with each type of resource and consider their level of engagement, imagination, creativity, problem-solving and collaboration with others.

Space

Space is very important and it should allow for children to move freely within their play and from play area to play area. The Reggio Emilia approach, pioneered in Italy, places high priority on the space in which children learn and is seen as a vital part of the learning process. Bishop (2001) states that Reggio Emilia preschools' internal and external spaces have symbolic and educational significance. There should be space to come together as a class, space to be quiet, space to build, space to be active, space to be creative, space in which to explore and experiment and space to be imaginative. Some settings have zones or spaces that are identified for specific purposes such as a wet area for painting or 'messy' activities. This approach can be successful but it is important that the dividers are moveable so that there is flexibility in making the separate areas bigger or smaller to meet the children's needs.

The outdoor space is as important as the indoor space. Bilton (1999) highlights the need for practitioners to view the outdoors as a teaching and learning environment with the same attention to organisation, resourcing and planning as for the indoor environment. There is also the need for flexibility and therefore smaller, moveable equipment often provides more opportunities for different types of play than larger fixed equipment (Johnston and Nahmad-Williams 2009). The space enables children to expand their play by making it bigger. Water trays can be joined with guttering flowing water from one to another; paintings can be done with decorators' brushes; imaginary worlds can be created that reach from one side of the outdoor space to the other. It is also useful to utilise the natural environment rather than relying on purchasing resources. Mounds can be created for running up and down, bushes and trees can provide shade and den areas, longer grass is good for exploring and short grass for running or wheeling bikes, scooters or prams, logs are good for balancing and jumping off as well as being excellent for minibeast hunting. These natural spaces also provide the type of open-ended, flexible opportunities for play that Broadhead (2010) and Nutbrown (1999) highlight and which could be seen as central in our approach to play.

Further Reading

Bilton, H. (1999) *Outdoor Play in the Early Years.* London: David Fulton.
This book provides a range of ideas for outdoor play but also includes relevant research to justify the approaches suggested.
Bruce, T. (2004) *Developing Learning in Early Childhood.* London: Paul Chapman.
Tina Bruce has written many books about play and learning and her 10 principles (now revised) are often cited by other authors. This book provides a very good overview of theories and theorists with useful summaries and comments on some of the key ideas.
Lindon, J. (2005) *Understanding Child Development.* London: Hodder Arnold.
This book considers a range of issues relating to child development with references to more recent research as well as more established theories.

Useful Websites

www.kids.org.uk/files
This is a Playwork Inclusion Project (PIP) based on inclusive play in the early years.

References

Blaiklock, K. (2008) 'Are Learning Stories Working?' Conference presentation at the Early Childhood Council Annual Conference, Wellington, May 2–4. Available at: http://www.ecc.

org.nz/conference/download/0830-1000_Ken_Blaiklock_ECC_Conference_May_2008_Are_Learning_Stories_Working.ppt

Bilton, H. (1999) *Outdoor Play in the Early Years*. London: David Fulton.

Bishop, J. (2001) 'Creating Spaces for Living and Learning', in L. Abbot and C. Nutbrown (eds) *Experiencing Reggio Emilia*. Buckingham: Open University Press.

Boud, D. (2001) 'Using Journal Writing to Enhance Reflective Practice', in L.M. English and M.A. Gillen (eds) *Promoting Journal Writing in Adult Education*. New Directions in Adult and Continuing Education No. 90. San Francisco: Jossey-Bass. pp. 9–18.

Broadhead, P. (2010) 'Making Relationships', in P. Broadhead, J. Johnston, C. Tobbell and R. Woolley (2010) *Personal, Social and Emotional Development*. London: Continuum.

Bromley, H. (2009) Storyboxes. Available at: http://www.yellow-door.net/products/products_talk_for_writing_storyboxes.html

Bruce, T. (2004) *Developing Learning in Early Childhood*. London: Paul Chapman.

Clarke, L. (2008) 'Observation, Assessment and Planning', in J. Basford and E. Hodson *Teaching Early Years Foundation Stage*. Exeter: Learning Matters.

David, T., Goouch, K., Powell, S. and Abbott, L. (2003) *Birth to Three Matters: A Review of the Literature*. Nottingham: DfES.

DCSF (2008) *The Early Years Foundation Stage: Setting the Standard for Learning, Development and Care for Children from Birth to Five: Practice Guidance*. London: DCSF.

Devereux, J. (2003) 'Observing Children', in J. Devereux and L. Miller (2003) *Working with Children in the Early Years*. London: David Fulton in association with the Open University.

Froebel, F. (1826) *On the Education of Man*. Keilhau, Leipzig: Wienbrach.

Hutt, C., Tyler, S., Hutt, J. and Christopherson, H. (eds) (1988) *Play, Exploration and Learning*. London: Routledge.

Johnston, J. and Nahmad-Williams, L. (2009) *Early Childhood Studies*. Harlow: Pearson Education.

Lindon, J. (2005) *Understanding Child Development*. London: Hodder Arnold.

Macintyre, C. (2001) *Enhancing Learning through Play*. London: David Fulton.

Marsh, J. and Hallet, E. (eds) (1999) *Desirable Literacies*. London: Paul Chapman.

McMillan, M. (1911) *The Child and the State*. Manchester: National Labour Press.

Moyles, J. (1989) *Just Playing? The Role and Status of Play in Early Childhood Education*. Milton Keynes: Open University Press.

Nahmad-Williams, L. (2010) 'Language for Communication', in N. Callander and L. Nahmad-Williams *Communication, Language and Literacy*. London: Continuum.

Nutbrown, C. (1994) *Threads of Thinking*. London: Paul Chapman.

Nutbrown, C. (1999) *Threads of Thinking: Young Children Learning and the Role of Early Education* (2nd edn.) London: Paul Chapman.

Palmer, S. (2007). *Toxic Childhood: How the Modern World is Damaging our Children and What We can Do About It*. London: Orion.

Piaget, J. (1976) 'Mastery Play' and 'Symbolic Play', in J. Bruner, A. Jolly and K. Sylva (eds) *Play – Its Role in Development and Evolution*. Middlesex: Penguin.

Podmore, V. and Carr, M. (1999) 'Learning and Teaching Stories: New Approaches to Assessment and Evaluation'. Paper presented at the AARE – NZARE Conference on

Research in Education, Melbourne, 1 December, 1999. Available at: http://www.aare.edu. au/99pap/pod99298.htm

Rousseau, J.J. (1911) *Emile*. London: J.M. Dent and Sons.

Siraj-Blatchford, I., Sylva, K., Muttock, S., Gilden, R. and Bell, D. (2002) *Researching Effective Pedagogy in the Early Years*. Nottingham: DfES.

Vygotsky, L. (1962) *Thought and Language*. Cambridge, MA: MIT Press.

Vygotsky, L. (1978) *Mind in Society: The Development of Higher Psychological Processes*. Cambridge, MA: Harvard University Press.

ENABLING ENVIRONMENTS

Jane Johnston

Learning objectives

- To understand what an enabling environment is
- To be able to plan for enabling environments to support learning indoors and outdoors, promoting effective, safe and stimulating provision for young children
- To understand how enabling environments support cooperation and collaboration, enhancing the progress and development of children

ENABLING ENVIRONMENTS IN THE EYFS

Enabling Environments is one of four complementary themes of the Early Years Foundation Stage (DCSF 2008a). In the EYFS the environment is recognised as of key importance in children as it supports learning in all key areas of development. The environment that supports learning can be both the physical (indoors and outdoors) and the ethos/ambience of the setting. It is reliant on the social interactions between the child and adults and peers and wider interactions between the child's microsystem (immediate family, carers and community) and their mesosystem (wider childcare, setting, extended family, etc.), as in Bronfenbrenner's ecological systems theory (Bronfenbrenner 1995; Bronfenbrenner and Evans 2000). The interactions between these two systems influence the children's behaviour development and learning, extending cognitive development, encouraging creativity and physical development, and supporting language through social discourse (Alexander 2008) and other areas of development (Johnston and Nahmad-Williams 2009). For example, an enabling environment is one where children interact with others (adults and peers) in a rich learning environment that encourages them to explore the world around them, learn to relate to others and become well-rounded individuals, who are socially and emotionally able to interact in the wider world.

The enabling environment is therefore one that encourages individuality (DfES 2003), supports children through transitions, providing continuity in their lives, and where adults (parents, carers and professionals from a range of backgrounds) work together in an effective way that sees the child at the centre of the environment (Alexander 2009). The development of integrated services aims to provide 'a hub within the community for parents and providers of childcare services for children of all ages' (Sure Start 2004: 9) and encourage effective relationships between professionals to promote enabling environments.

Also of importance is the approach to learning and development within the early years setting, as this plays an important part in establishing the overall environment. Didactic, controlling approaches are not enabling and have an adverse affect on behaviour, motivation and development. More effective are play, discovery and exploratory, child-centred approaches (Johnston 2004; Moyles 2005; Bruce 2009) that encourage the child to gain independence and be motivated to want to learn, are flexible to accommodate individuals (DfES 2003) and are well supported by adults (Vygotsky 1962). Play is recognised by theorists (Froebel 1826; Rousseau 1911; Vygotsky 1962; Piaget 1976; Steiner 1996) and modern professionals and academics (BERA 2003; Moyles 2005; Bruce 2009; Johnston and Nahmad-Williams 2009), all of whom recognised play as supporting emotional, social and cognitive development. Play-based approaches within an enabling environment need to be motivating, creative and interactive and also supported by adults who understand how to develop children in this way. Motivating practical approaches support emotional and physical development, and adult interaction supports social development. In this way play-based approaches can be fully enabling.

INDOOR ENVIRONMENTS

The indoor environment is very important for children in the EYFS. It should be familiar and comforting, easing transitions from home care to early years settings. This may involve equipping the physical environment with soft furnishings, small rooms and quiet spaces. The best settings ease transition by catering for all children. They may provide routine for those who are used to it and easing those who are not into a routine. They may provide food for those who arrive without breakfast and healthy snacks and drinks on demand. They may have bathing facilities, so children can enjoy bath-time and learn about floating and sinking, volume of water, how materials change and develop skills of pouring, etc. while they bathe. They will have plenty of opportunities for activities that support all areas of development, such as creative pursuits, fine and gross motor activities, language development, vocabulary and knowledge about the world they live in. There will be plenty of opportunities to interact with others, developing language and socialising (EPPE 2003), but also quiet places where children can go and engage in solitary play, sit, read or sleep when they want to. They will have a key carer who is a constant in their lives and good home–setting liaison, with parents playing a full part in the early years setting, so that the emotional traumas of transitions (Bowlby 2007) can be taken into account and ameliorated. Children can be encouraged to become independent by making them feel secure and supporting their move to independence. The full use of integrated services (Sure Start 2004) with professionals and parents working together will help to ensure that the atmosphere in the setting is conducive to good learning and development (Sylva et al. 2004). In this way the early years setting can become an extension of home and positively affect the home-life of some children. Once the early years setting is a really enabling environment, the challenge is to make the transition from the EYFS to Key Stage 1 as effective.

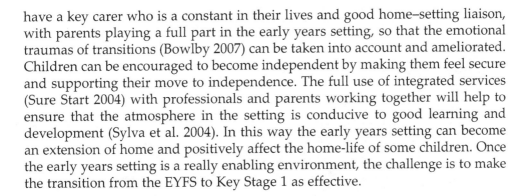

Questions for Discussion

How do you currently facilitate transition into and out of your setting?
How could you improve facilities to support individual children?

 Case Study

Darryl is two years of age and has just started attending a nursery. He finds it difficult to settle when he arrives but his mother sits and reads with him when he arrives in the morning. His key worker, Michele, will sit in a quiet corner with her story apron on and use this to tell a story. When telling the story of the three little pigs, the pockets of the apron have the three pig glove puppets, some straw, wooden bricks, twigs and a wolf mask. As Michele starts to tell the story and remove things from her pockets, Darryl begins to take notice and, after a few minutes, he starts to move nearer to Michele and take part in the story telling. His mother is able to leave him and waves goodbye.

After the story Michele leaves the puppets and resources for children to re-enact the story, but Darryl chooses to play with the bricks and build a 'strong' house for 'pig number 3'.

Indoors, the setting should be an environment that encourages children to be independent and curious, following their own avenues for exploration. Some professionals believe that an enabling environment is one that has a vibrant, bright physical setting with primary colours and plenty of colourful interactive displays and motivating objects to touch and explore. Others feel that muted colours and a quieter feel is more enabling. Probably a mixture of the two is sensible, accounting for differences in children's preferences and the need for some to be active and others to be quiet.

Figure 10.1 A quiet place to share a story

An environment that is rich in language, with signs, symbols, notices, rhymes and word displays and quiet areas for browsing books (DCSF 2008b) will encourage development in communication, language and literacy. Feely boxes, unusual objects, bright colours, sounds, etc. will help to provide an environment that promotes curiosity and questioning, that is, an environment where children feel confident enough to ask questions to find out about the world around them. However, too much choice and too many activities can be overwhelming and lead to sensory overload or even de-motivation. It is best to provide a mixture of quieter and noisier, familiar and novel activities, with a well thought out rationale for what is offered and some resources being put aside for a while and then re-offered.

Opportunities for learning through role play can enable children to use and develop their imagination (Johnston and Nahmad-Williams, 2010). Children can help to develop the role play area, suggesting what theme it should have and what resources they need, and helping to resource and develop it.

Figure 10.2   Role play in the pirate ship

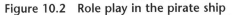

📁   **Case Study**

The children in a reception class decided to create a pirate ship in their classroom. Their teacher provided a wooden rowing boat and the children sorted through the dressing-up box for suitable clothes for pirates and made masks, hats, treasure maps and telescopes, as well as bringing resources from home.

The role play encouraged Joe, who usually engaged in solitary play, to work with other children. He and Wayne donned masks and hats and 'rowed' the boat to an island where they buried some treasure and had a picnic. Both boys then created a treasure map so that they could find their buried treasure in the future – this was the first time that both boys had independently engaged in mark-making, helping them to see writing as a purposeful activity.

OUTDOOR ENVIRONMENTS

An enabling outdoor environment is also one that encourages curiosity, enquiry and exploration, having a number of sensual experiences for children to encourage them to use all their senses, where safe (Johnston 2005). In the early stages of the EYFS children will be naturally curious and want to touch, taste, smell and listen to things they encounter in the world around them. The outdoor environment can enable the development of gross motor skills through the provision of quality outdoor play resources, such as tricycles, balls, beanbags, as well as

Figure 10.3 Exploring the outside environment

outdoor play equipment (see Cooper and Doherty 2010). The resources should allow for individual use as well as sharing, as too few wheeled vehicles (tricycles, cars, chariots, etc) can cause arguments as children learn to take turns and share, although Broadhead (2004) believes that children need to engage in social negotiation to support their social development. The resources need to provide the correct level of physical challenge for the children (DCSF 2008b) and also be capable of being used in a variety of creative ways, so a tricycle can be a horse or a car or an aeroplane in different play contexts. In an integrated setting, there may be professionals who support individuals with physical and other disabilities (physiotherapists, speech and language therapists) who may work with the children in context.

As with the indoor environment there needs to be sufficient space outdoors for 'energetic play' (DCSF 2008b: 91) and also quiet places so that children can play

Figure 10.4   Opportunities to develop the outside environment

quietly, enjoy the outdoor experience and engage in contemplation and reflection. Sensory gardens can provide:

- Colour in leaves, flowers, stones
- Smells through herbs and flowers
- Tastes through vegetables and fruit grown
- Things to touch and experience different textures, for example bricks, bark, leaves, etc.

Children with sensory disabilities can be encouraged to use other senses and every child can focus on specific senses by closing their eyes to highlight smells, tastes, sounds and touch. Even a concrete and brick outside play area can provide an enabling environment, as flowers, vegetables and herbs can be grown in pots, planters or grow-bags and plants and animals living in between cracks and brickwork can enable children to explore the living world.

Question for Discussion

How could you develop your outside environment to make it more enabling?

Wet sand, mud, drying puddles, outdoor sounds, lights and shadows can all be enabling experiences. Role play can be set up outside, as can painting, water play, etc. The Forest Schools initiative (http://www.forestschools.com) aims to provide positive outdoor experiences and believes that the whole curriculum can be delivered through outdoor experiences. It motivates children and provides positive learning experiences which often we deny children because we worry about the weather, their clothes or their safety. In a society where children's outdoor experiences are considered less enabling (Palmer 2006) we need to consider ways we can enhance the learning environment to provide children with opportunities to explore the world around them, play safely outside, develop levels of independence and to develop socially and emotionally.

Exploration of the wider, local environment, experienced through a sensory/ historical/geographical walk, can support children in developing knowledge and understanding of their world (see Cooper et al. 2010), as well as providing opportunities for counting, finding shapes, measuring distances, and developing vocabulary and speaking and listening skills. This development will only happen when the children are supported by knowledgeable adults (Vygotsky 1962).

Case Study: Planning Enabling Environments

The case study uses the story book *The Owl Who Was Afraid of the Dark* (Tomlinson and Howard 2004) with three-year-old children. In the story Plop, a young barn owl, has a problem with the dark, but has positive experiences about the dark, realising that it is kind, fun, necessary, fascinating, wonderful and beautiful.

Key Learning Outcomes

Personal, Social and Emotional Development

- Understand fear as an emotion in yourself and others.

Communication, Language and Literacy

- Be able to retell a story
- Be able to articulate fears and listen to others.

Knowledge and Understanding of the World

- Understand the difference between dark/light and day/night.

Creative Development

- Be able to express emotions through creative media (paint, music, role play).

Introductory Experience/Activity

The story of *The Owl Who Was Afraid of the Dark* (Tomlinson and Howard 2004) can be told to children and the emotions within the story can be examined. Children can be encouraged to tell each other and the key adult their fears. A toy owl or a puppet owl can be used to encourage quiet children to articulate their fears, as they are more likely to speak to or through a toy than to an adult or group of children.

Follow-on Experiences/Activities

- The puppet/toy can be left with the book for children to play with, retell the story, talk about his fears of the dark.
- Emotions can be expressed through colour wash paintings.
- Day and night or shadow pictures can be created; that is, the same scene in the day and at night.
- Music can be composed to accompany the story and express the emotions. Children can decide which instruments best express the feelings at different times in the story.
- Light and dark can be explored with torches, a projector and shadow puppet owls made with different materials (black card, white card, clear acetate, greaseproof paper, coloured acetate, etc.).
- Children can explore what makes a shadow and how to make a dark shadow. An outdoor tent or shed can provide a dark place to explore light and dark. Shadow pictures can be drawn on the ground with chalk and the difference between these shadows at different times of the day can be explored.

Differentiation

The professionals will provide appropriate support for individuals encouraging them to articulate their emotions to peers, adults or to the toy. The professionals will also differentiate their questioning of the children asking challenging questions of the more able about the shadow they are making, such as 'Why is the shadow dark?' or 'How can you make the shadow less dark?' Less able children may be supported through questioning, with professionals asking more direct questions, such as 'What happens to the shadow when you use this puppet?' or 'Which puppet makes the darkest shadow?'

Assessment

Some children will be able to articulate things that scare them and describe the similarities and differences between light and dark using their own words. They will be able

(Continued)

(Continued)

to produce both day and night pictures and express emotion in creative media and explain what they have done and why. Most children will be able to identify why Plop is scared and when they have felt like this in their own lives. They will be able to identify what makes a puppet make a good shadow and provide some explanation for this (it does not have to be correct). They will be able to produce either a day or night picture and use colour or music to express an emotion such as fear.

A few children will need support to show why Plop is scared and the professionals may need to provide them with some words to help them. They will be able to say if a shadow is dark or light but not give reasons. They will be able to paint a light or dark picture or use colour or a sound to express this.

In this case, after telling the story, the professional asked the children why they thought Plop was frightened of the dark. Dean said 'It's scary in the dark. My mum leaves a light on in my room.' Zoe said that she did not need a light as her mum 'left the curtains open and the light from a street lamp comes in'. A few children identified things that frightened them, such as when they lost their parents or when they had fallen over and hurt themselves. The professionals asked them what made them feel better. The responses ranged from their parents or siblings comforting them to a favourite toy as a comforter. Sophie and Francesca listened to the story intently and later played with the puppet, making owl hooting noises. The professional suggested that they tried to make the same noise with a musical instrument and so they tried out a variety of different instruments before Sophie decided that a recorder was best. Francesca 'flew' the owl and Sophie made the noises. Dean chose to explore the shadow puppets and when asked, before he started, which puppet would make the darkest shadow, he replied 'the black one' pointing at the owl made of black card. He and two other children used a torch to try out their ideas and found that all the puppets made shadows but some were darker than others. He decided that his original idea, that the black card owl was best, was correct. He then painted a dark owl picture saying 'This owl is in the tree at night.'

The next day one child brought in an owl pellet that his father had found and he explained to all the children what an owl pellet was. This led to questions about owls and a few children went to look for some books about owls, whilst Dean went to the computer to look up owls there. The professional began a display with paintings produced by the children and an interactive table underneath with the puppets, torches, the story book and factual books about owls.

 Questions for Discussion

How did the children achieve against the learning outcomes?
How can you extend the activities to incorporate other key areas of development?

When planning for an enabling environment, we need to plan in a cross-curricular way, encompassing as many key areas as possible, and utilising the indoor and outdoor environment in a relevant and holistic way (see de Bóo 2004). We need to not just plan learning outcomes and activities but also to plan the children's role in the activities to ensure that the learning outcomes can be achieved. We should consider what questions will challenge the more able and what actions will support the less able. In order to do this effectively, we need to be clear what the outcomes will look like in different learners, so that when we see differentiated outcomes we can be clear that children have met, or exceeded or not achieved our expectations. We need to be flexible enough to modify our plans if learners are too challenged or not challenged enough and also to enable children to make their own learning decisions and decide what they want to do and how they intend to do it.

In this way enabling environments can be a reality and support every child to achieve their full potential.

Further Reading

Alexander, R. (ed.) (2009) *Children, their World, their Education: Final Report and Recommendations of the Cambridge Review*. London: Routledge.
This is a comprehensive report of the Cambridge Review and emphasises the importance of enabling environments on holistic development. It recognises the part played by children's social and emotional development on their cognitive development and the recommendations are supported by research.

DCSF (2008) *The Early Years Foundation Stage: Setting the Standard for Learning, Development and Care for Children from Birth to Five*: CD ROM. London: DCSF.
The CD ROM that accompanies the Practice Guidance and Statutory Guidance contains a wealth of research and professional articles which are designed to support all aspects of the EYFS provision. Reading such articles encourages reflection and can help professionals to develop their practice and improve provision for early years children.

de Bóo, M. (ed.) (2004) *The Curriculum Partnership: Early Years Handbook*. Sheffield: Geography Association.
This book was developed by a group of diverse professionals to provide cross-curricular support for learning and development within the Early Years Foundation Stage. Each activity considers how to provide an enabling environment in which children learn in an holistic relevant way.

Johnston, J. and Nahmad-Williams, L. (2009) *Early Childhood Studies*. Harlow: Pearson Education.
This is a comprehensive book that focuses on all aspects of early years development using the international definition of early years (from birth to eight years of age). It is firmly rooted in good practice, building on early years theories to give practical support for professionals of today.

Useful Website ⌇🖱

www.thegrid.org.uk
This website provides information from the University of Hertfordshire Grid for Learning.

References

Alexander, R. (2008) *Towards Dialogic Teaching: Rethinking Classroom Talk* (4th edn). York: Dialogos.

Alexander, R. (ed.) (2009) *Children, their World, their Education: Final Report and Recommendations of the Cambridge Review*. London: Routledge.

BERA (British Educational Research Association) Early Years Special Interest Group (2003) *Early Years Research: Pedagogy, Curriculum and Adult Roles, Training and Professionalism*. Southwell, Notts: BERA.

Bowlby, R. (2007) 'Babies and Toddlers in Non-parental Daycare Can Avoid Stress and Anxiety If They Develop a Lasting Secondary Attachment Bond with One Carer who is Consistently Accessible to Them', *Attachment & Human Development*, 9(4): 307–19.

Broadhead, P. (2004) *Early Years Play and Learning: Developing Social Skills and Cooperation*. Abingdon: RoutledgeFalmer.

Bronfenbrenner, U. (1995) 'The Bioecological Model from a Life Course Perspective: Reflections of a Participant Observer', in P. Moen, G. H. Elder Jnr and K. Lüscher (eds) *Examining Lives in Context*. Washington, DC: American Psychological Association. pp. 599–618.

Bronfenbrenner, U. and Evans, G.W. (2000) 'Developmental Science in the 21st Century: Emerging Theoretical Models, Research Designs and Empirical Findings', *Social Development*, 9: 115–125.

Bruce, T. (2009) *Early Childhood* (2nd edn). London: Sage.

Cooper, L. and Doherty, J. (2010) *Physical Development*. London: Continuum.

Cooper, L., Johnston, J., Rotchell, E. and Woolley, R. (2010) *Knowledge and Understanding of the World*. London: Continuum.

DCSF (2008a) *The Early Years Foundation Stage: Setting the Standard for Learning, Development and Care for Children from Birth to Five: Statutory Guidance*. London: DCSF.

DCSF (2008b) *The Early Years Foundation Stage: Setting the Standard for Learning, Development and Care for Children from Birth to Five: Practice Guidance*. London: DCSF.

de Bóo, M. (ed.) (2004) *The Curriculum Partnership: Early Years Handbook*. Sheffield: Geography Association.

DfES (2003) *Every Child Matters*. London: DfES.

EPPE (2003) 'Measuring the Impact of Pre-School on Children's Social/Behavioural Development over the Pre-School Period', *The EPPE (Effective Provision of Pre-school Education) Project Technical Paper 8b*. London: Institute of Education.

Froebel, F. (1826) *On the Education of Man*. Keilhau, Leipzig: Wienbrach.

Johnston, J. (2004) 'The Value of Exploration and Discovery', *Primary Science Review*, 85: 21–3.

Johnston, J. (2005) *Early Explorations in Science* (2nd edn). Maidenhead: Open University Press.

Johnston, J. and Nahmad-Williams, L. (2009) *Early Childhood Studies*. Harlow: Pearson Education.

Johnston, J. and Nahmad-Williams, L. (2010) 'Developing Imagination and Imaginative Play', in A. Compton, J. Johnston, L. Nahmad-Williams and K. Taylor (2010) *Creative Development*. London: Continuum.

Moyles, J.R. (ed.) (2005) *The Excellence of Play* (2nd edn). Maidenhead: Open University Press.

Palmer, S. (2006) *Toxic Childhood: How the Modern World is Damaging our Children and What We Can Do About It*. London: Orion.

Piaget, J. (1976) 'Mastery Play' and 'Symbolic Play', in J. Bruner, A. Jolly and K. Sylva (eds) *Play – Its Role in Development and Evolution*. Middlesex: Penguin.

Rousseau, J. J. (1911) *Emile*. London: J.M. Dent and Sons.

Steiner, R. (1996) *The Education of the Child and Early Lectures on Education*. New York: Anthroposophic Press.

Sure Start (2004) *Working Together: A Sure Start Guide to the Childcare and Early Education Field*. Annesley, Notts: DfES.

Sylva, K., Melhuish, E., Sammons, P., Siraj-Blatchford, I. and Taggart, B. (2004) *The Effective Provision of Pre-School Education (EPPE) Project: Final Report: A Longitudinal Study Funded by The DfES, 1997–2004*. London: DfES.

Tomlinson, J. and Howard, P. (2004) *The Owl Who Was Afraid of the Dark*. London: Egmont.

Vygotsky, L. (1962) *Thought and Language*. Cambridge, MA: MIT Press.

11 LEARNING AND TEACHING STYLES

Alison Jakins

Learning objectives

- To be aware of the breadth of teaching and learning styles and how different styles develop different skills
- To be aware of teaching and learning strategies that will help to strengthen the provision for all learners and promote independent thinking
- To consider how learning can be supported through effective use of the learning environment and adult involvement

Engaging children fully in learning and ensuring they develop the necessary skills, knowledge and understanding can be very challenging yet the rewards for both the children and the teacher are high. How the brain works is a significant factor in what types of teaching and learning strategies are successful with children. As we learn more and more about brain function we find that achievement in the classroom is not simply down to intelligence and effort but a child's ability to be an effective learner. Many researchers and practitioners consider lessons which rely heavily on directed teaching and where children remain in a passive role to inhibit their ability to remain attentive. Children's attention will wane if they cannot see the relevance of an activity or they view it as impersonal and removed from their own context (Caine and Caine 1995; Jensen 1998; Smith 2004).

As parents will testify, all children are individuals and what sparks curiosity and interest in one child will not always grip a second child in the same way. However, as practitioners, it is paramount that we do not cater solely for a child's preferred learning style but that we expose him or her to other strategies and experiences to help develop key skills and knowledge, enabling the child to become an independent, life-long learner.

THEORIES LINKED TO TEACHING AND LEARNING STYLES

Accelerated learning is a model widely used in early years and primary education. There are key principles which underpin the learning opportunities offered to children through the model. A definition of accelerated learning presented by Hughes (2001: 11) illustrates the links to brain function – he calls it an umbrella term that 'encompasses approaches to learning that are compatible with the way in which the brain operates and learns most effectively'.

Some schools have fully adopted the ALPS approach (Accelerated Learning in Primary Schools) – a collaborative work of Smith and Call (1999). Other schools and educational settings have adopted aspects of the approach which fit firmly with the ethos of their school and the needs of the children they have on roll. Multi-sensory stimulation is at the heart of the model, where children are challenged cognitively and given choices and effective feedback upon their learning. This view of learning can be enhanced through an appropriate learning environment to cater for all learning styles. The previous chapter gave examples of ways in which this can be achieved.

The model draws heavily from Howard Gardner's *Theory of Multiple Intelligences.* Gardner suggests that intelligence is not fixed and can change throughout our lifetimes. The multiple intelligences model recognises different types of intelligence which we all possess but in different proportions (Gardner 2004). Table 11.1 illustrates the key skills shown by young learners possessing each intelligence type and considers a brief introduction to the learning experiences which will help to interest and motivate the children.

Although you may recognise a child as having a highly developed spatial intelligence it is important to remember that the child will have other developed intelligences. Early years practitioners need to also offer opportunities for the child to practise skills from the other areas for the future. If the challenge is at a suitable pitch, practitioners can initiate opportunities for a child to refine motor skills, communication skills, and more, in order for them to access learning across the curriculum. Curriculum areas and subjects internationally do not rely on one intelligence but need children to use the skills and attributes linked to a number of Gardner's intelligences in order to access the learning effectively and add to their knowledge and understanding. The practitioner that builds in a variety of activities whilst offering sufficient challenge through the school day, week, month and year will enthuse and motivate the learner. Practitioners will also recognise their own preferred methods of learning from Gardner's categories. Recognising preferences and attributes is essential to ensuring that we can reflect with forethought and be vigilant to times when our own preferences begin to dominate our teaching and learning styles at the expense of varied methods to capture all types of learner.

Table 11.1 The multiple intelligences: characteristics and associated abilities

Intelligence	Characteristics	Abilities
Linguistic	Enjoys learning through discussion, reading and writing	Good listener Effective communicator
Logical-mathematical	Enjoys learning involving sequencing, number work and analogies	Problem-solving Mathematical reasoning
Musical	Enjoys learning through songs, raps, poems and word play	Sense of rhythm Enjoyment of music and improvising with sounds
Spatial	Enjoys learning through observation and where visual aids are used	Can imagine pictures easily and often in 3-D Construction skills
Bodily-kinesthetic	Enjoys learning through movement, touch, role-play and outdoor experiences	Good co-ordination Dexterity
Interpersonal	Enjoys collaborative learning and opportunities for taking on different roles and responsibilities	Effective communicators Empathy with others
Intrapersonal	Enjoys learning independently and the use of diaries and draft books to note down thinking and ideas	Good self-awareness Strong, self-motivation
Naturalist	Enjoys working with nature and learning about it	Good knowledge of the natural world and has an understanding of the natural environment
Existential	Enjoys learning about religious ideas and thinking about spiritual possibilities	Awareness of spiritual and religious ideas

Sources: Gardner (2004) and Smith (1996).

The principles of accelerated learning have been used in a two-year project called Dancing with Words which has been developed by the Astra Zeneca Science Technology Trust. Using methods linked closely to the bodily-kinesthetic, spatial, music and linguistic intelligences, the Science-Physical Approach helped primary-aged pupils to remember and understand scientific concepts (Mason 2008). Children used dance and movement to represent aspects of a concept through words and phrases spoken at the same time. The accelerated learning cycle was adopted to give structure to the various stages of the lesson, ensure a multi-sensory approach and encourage pupils to recognise the lesson aims and outcomes. Similar methods are used widely in early language learning and can now be observed in the teaching of foreign languages in early years and primary education settings. Learning a song to consolidate the parts of the body could be used alongside actions to help children link meanings to words more readily. Using physical activity in this way can be particularly helpful to those children who learn less well in the confines of the classroom.

Accelerated learning provides useful insights into different learning styles and supports planning for children as individuals. Brain research has also given us some understanding of the different ways children learn. It is thought that the two parts of the brain, the right and left hemispheres, are responsible for different aspects – for example the left concerns language and numbers while the right includes music and pictures amongst other areas of learning. Discussions in Chapter 5 on self-esteem and motivation support our learning. However, the reptilian brain brought to the fore when we are stressed or anxious, can dispel our self-esteem, resulting in an inability to learn new ideas or be confident in our thinking. In an appropriately devised learning environment where all are valued this should not be a problem for adults or children. Awareness of this aspect for those working in a stressful environment or with individuals experiencing difficulties within it, should help to urge the importance of providing a suitably inclusive situation where all are appreciated and supported. The neo-cortex helps us to make connections with information and concepts. In a stimulating, motivating learning environment this becomes possible through interaction with the physical space by learning through the surroundings and with peers and adults through communication and sharing ideas. The emotional brain involves emotional intelligence and the ability to express emotions and interact with others. It is close to the area of the brain responsible for memory.

Recent research has considered whether the fast pace of human evolvement has resulted in the growth of the part of our brain which concerns technology and formal learning, while the other side of our brains is decreasing in influence. This could mean that we lose touch with our awareness of feelings and our ability to understand nature and the spiritual aspects of existence.

Bloom's *Taxonomy of Educational Objectives,* first developed in the 1950s, considers the existence of distinct levels of cognitive ability in relation to thinking. Bloom identified levels of cognitive ability where one level must be reached before the next level could be met. Anderson and Krathwohl (2001) have adjusted Bloom's original model to bring it up to date with current educational thinking. Table 11.2 summarises the adapted model, starting with the initial level of cognitive ability. Consideration is given to some questions that could be put to young children to try and evaluate a child's cognitive development – the questions all focus on the topic of minibeasts.

For early years educators, the planning and preparation needed to teach the upper levels (analysing, evaluating and creating) can be more challenging, but the strategies teachers use to develop these levels open up a wider set of learning experiences to children and therefore a greater likelihood that the children will be motivated and challenged.

Some authors and practitioners have made distinct links to how *thinking skills* can be utilised in the classroom by making links to Gardner's multiple intelligences

Table 11.2 Levels of learning

Levels of Learning	Related questioning
Remembering	What minibeasts did we find living under the log?
Understanding	Why do woodlice like living under stones and logs?
Applying	What parts of the woodlouse's body help it to live under stones and logs?
Analysing	How can we sort the minibeasts to show where they like to live?
Evaluating	If we put the woodlice into a tray of soil (with different conditions) which part of the tray do you think they will move to?
Creating	What else do we want to find out about woodlice homes? What experiment could we do to find this out?

(Lazear 2004) and accelerated learning principles (Staricoff and Rees 2005). The importance and relevance of promoting thinking skills in the learning environment is discussed in Chapter 8. Strategies can be devised which actively incorporate this aspect of learning into planning. During the early years key consideration needs to be given to how best to incorporate thinking skills into the school day:

- Will it be through a distinct subject area (as outlined in Table 11.2)?
- Is it to develop children's use of creativity and imagination?
- Is it to practise key transferable skills at the beginning or end of the school day?

Allowing children to practise thinking skills in a non-threatening environment will help children to use various thought processes and levels within Bloom's hierarchy in subject-specific ways. Incorporating general thinking skills activities into the timetable opens up the chance for children to practise these skills in open-ended ways where there is no right or wrong answer. From my own experience, children looked forward to the general thinking challenges which I would normally set after lunchtime. Many aspects of learning identified in the *Excellence and Enjoyment* document (DfES 2003) include thinking skills, and depending on the strategies initiated by the teacher or children when undertaking an activity, the children can often practise other key skills such as collaborative working, improving on past performances and problem-solving. Thinking-skills activities which involve the use of visualisation, imagination and improvisation can be particularly useful with younger children. For instance, it never ceased to amaze me how differently children would interpret and use a large square which had been drawn onto a piece of paper (an activity adapted from Staricoff and Rees 2005). When asked to use the square as a starting point, the shape became a spaceship, television, treasure chest, robot, picture frame and emergent word search all within the same 10 minute timeframe.

GENDER

Much has been made of the differences in attainment between boys and girls, with a great deal of time and effort put into bridging the gap between boys and girls when it comes to reading and writing. Research highlights the way in which boys and girls view their successes and failures and the impact this has upon their learning. How each of the sexes views their achievements is very different. Boys who evaluate that they have performed badly will try to blame outside factors and may only consider themselves a failure in the specific aspect or subject in which they did not perform well. However, girls are more likely to blame their failures or errors solely on themselves which will also affect their perception of their general abilities (Pomerantz et al. 2002; Eccles et al. 1993).

Children's own self-worth coupled with adults' interpretation of the successes and failures can influence and reinforce the perceptions held by boys and girls of their own abilities. Recognising differences between the genders enables practitioners to think carefully about the children's own self-awareness and self-esteem, therefore ensuring consideration is given to both the interpersonal and intrapersonal intelligences within Gardner's model. However, care is needed not to stereotype boys and girls due to a statistical likelihood but to always keep in mind the individual and the plethora of factors that will influence a child's capacity to learn.

IMPACT OF THE LEARNING ENVIRONMENT

Children learn from the moment they are born, and perhaps even before that. The environment they enter therefore influences their learning and development, as testified by cases occasionally brought to the public domain where children are isolated from others and fail to learn basic human accomplishments, such as speaking or moving using what appear to be healthy limbs. Understanding of children's development and theories of learning can be helpful when gaining perceptions and knowledge of the child as an individual, thus giving appropriate support for their needs. As younger children they might find out about the world through their senses, exploring tastes, textures, sounds and feelings as they extend their knowledge of their world. Practitioners can enhance children's learning through an understanding of what the child is trying to achieve and the ways in which it is attempted. Sometimes it is better to observe and let a child experience and try out challenges, to take risks and find out what works and what does not. Children learn from the context in which they are placed – the social mores, the rules of the setting – how to interact successfully. Care needs to be taken that the learning environment is inclusive and supports individuals who might need extra provision in certain areas. Teaching and learning styles can be devised which promote a personalised approach within the inclusive ethos.

The learning environment created in Early Years' settings goes beyond the use of display and general classroom layout; it should encompass the ethos of the establishment and the practitioner's values and beliefs. For some children, pre-school, nursery or school is the one stabilising factor in their lives. Children may have come from home environments which offer little or no consistency in day-to-day routines, relationships or affection. Creating a learning environment which is safe and where children feel valued is essential for young learners to develop.

The BASICS model breaks down one of the key principles of accelerated learning – that positive self-esteem and a low stress environment are factors in the brain's ability to gather information, remember and reason. BASICS is a mnemonic which identifies the factors which need to be considered to ensure the best mind state for effective learning to take place:

Belonging – feeling valued in all activities including contributions and responses offered

Aspiration – encouraging learners to set and work on achievable goals

Safety – rules and expectations are used consistently

Individuality – individuals and individuality are celebrated

Challenge – extend children suitably and recognise their success

Success – where success is reinforced and children understand the value of making errors and learning from their mistakes

(Smith and Call, 1999).

Consider how the BASICS model could be met through:

- behaviour management strategies
- verbal and written feedback
- relationships with the children and other adults in the classroom
- display of the children's work
- classroom organisation.

Case Study

A combined reception and Year 1 class in a school with a mixed catchment area incorporated a number of routines into the school week to celebrate the individual. For a weekly show and tell session called 'Class 2 has Talent' the children were encouraged to share their successes. The children presented a variety of successes, including a drawing of their favourite character from their favourite story, their latest swimming badge, and a composition on the bongos learnt at an out-of-school club. After several weeks it became apparent that children within the class from more deprived backgrounds were less involved in the session and were rarely forthcoming in sharing any success. The teacher introduced different activities and strategies across the timetable to help develop the children's self-esteem. Roles and responsibilities were given to individuals on a fortnightly rota, including watering the classroom plants and changing the visual timetable at the beginning of the school day. Learning achievements were celebrated with parents informally at the end of the school day and a success tree was created whereby children earned leaves for various positive values and actions displayed in and out of the classroom. The show and tell session was transformed in a short space of time as the successes were more easily spotted by individuals and their peers; a greater number of children were willing to present their achievements and those with less confidence but eager to play a part were allowed to stand up with a buddy.

ADULT INVOLVEMENT

By implementing many of the learning and teaching styles considered so far in this chapter, early years practitioners move to a position of facilitator. However it would be very easy to slip in and out of this role and lead children frequently through the learning without giving consideration to how much of the session developed the children's ability to take ownership of the learning.

Bernadette Russell found herself in a similar position when reflecting on her practice which promoted enquiry-based learning (Colcott et al. 2009). She found that although the children were involved directly it was recognised that the children still needed to actively make the link between practising a skill and thinking about the skills they needed to use. As a result, Bernadette found she was the one who was always correcting the children, the children were not able to do this independently or recognise when they had made an error. This led to the creation of a pedagogy called 'Visible Thinking'. Each child had a toolkit which they constructed and from which they could pull out a number of skills needed to complete a task, thereby getting the children to identify which skills would help them creatively or in solving a problem. For young children the tools would be in the form of simple pictures or symbols which were both visual and tactile. For example, if we were asking a group of early years children to describe simple properties of an object in a feely bag, we would get the children to identify which skills from their toolkit they would need to use in order to complete the activity effectively – taking turns, listening, describing, using the sense of touch and asking questions.

This process of learning how to learn has become common practice in various forms in both early years and primary education, particularly since the introduction of *Excellence and Enjoyment* published by the DfES in 2003. This document encouraged greater creativity by ensuring educators gave pupils opportunities to develop skills and understanding which included problem-solving tasks and enquiry-based learning. The sharing of child-friendly learning objectives can be extended further by the use of 'success criteria' or 'learning tools'. The more children are involved in the creation of these criteria the more chance they have of understanding the skills they use are multifunctional and can be called upon in various lessons and circumstances. Such a strategy ensures children are not passive in the learning process and aids the practitioner to move from teacher-led activities to teacher-initiated activities.

A number of early years approaches, including the HighScope curriculum and the Early Years Foundation Stage framework, place emphasis upon child-initiated learning. The term child-initiated simply means that opportunities are given to allow children to engage in activities which are driven by the children themselves. Children can take ownership of their learning through a carefully planned environment which enables them to explore and investigate. Celebrating children's achievements through books and displays and encouraging daily routines which promote this approach, such as self-registration and taking responsibility for collecting their snack, can enhance this. By establishing a learning environment which encourages children's curiosity and choice making we can fuel young children's desire to explore, experiment and think independently with greater confidence. A practitioner introducing child-initiated activities would need to evaluate the way in which adults are involved in the learning and teaching as well as reflect upon the organisation of the children and how resources and areas of the classroom are utilised.

To the observer, child-initiated activities can seem no more than exploratory play, yet exploration and play are essential tools for children to carve out new experiences which stimulate their interest. Practitioners can gain valuable information about a child's cognitive and social development through observing them during child-initiated situations. Building Learning Power (BLP) (Claxton 2002) is a learning how to learn approach which has been tried and evaluated in all phases of education and where the research is firmly grounded in science and how our brains are wired to learn. The BLP approach identifies four key aspects a child needs to become an effective learner. The first of these (resilience) identifies the need to find out about things, finding pleasure in learning whilst not being distracted so that notice is taken and perseverance is demonstrated to complete the exploration in full. The child-initiated approach allows children to learn through exploration and play in a way that suits their own learning style(s) thereby helping children to work upon the key characteristics outlined for initial learning power.

Child-initiated activities allow children to learn at their own level of understanding and, as discussed earlier, remain attentive for longer as they are fully involved and in charge of where their activity leads them. A child discovering that the tube needs to be tilted at an angle for the water to run into the barrel will be more likely to remember than if they had been told. Being actively engaged and playing the central role in the learning experience makes important connections in the brain which are strengthened. For such valuable learning experience to take place, the adult plays a vital, supporting role.

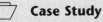 **Case Study**

Two, four-year-old children are observed playing in an area where there is a tub containing various sized balls and marbles. The children begin rolling the balls to each other simultaneously; one child changes tack and tries to hit the other child's ball as it rolls forwards. The following day the adult adds some cardboard tubes, plastic ramps and sticky discs to the tub of balls. The same children are observed; one child arranges the discs, ramps and tubes to form an obstacle course while the second child uses the tubes and sticky discs as targets for the ball to reach. The second child has to persevere in reaching the targets he has placed furthest away, shouting in excitement as he succeeds. The adult goes over to the second child and joins in. The child enters into an explanation of the game he has created and about what he has found he needs to do to get the ball to reach the furthest target.

Questions for Discussion

How important do you feel it is to accommodate children's preferred learning styles? Why? When devising activities for children, do they incorporate a variety of learning styles or do activities tend to become focused on a few styles?
If the latter, what factors hinder the use of a range of styles? Can they be overcome?

Visual, auditory and kinesthetic teaching and learning styles can often dominate in early years and primary education. And whilst the three styles ensure a basic multi-sensory approach, the balance between the three methods can be distorted and very easily learning can take place using one dominant method for a large chunk of time. Practitioners must always keep in mind that teaching and learning styles go beyond visual, auditory and kinaesthetic and that reflecting upon any imbalance is essential so that variety across the day can be maintained. Even having an imbalance across a session can lead to some learners' attention wandering and so they have lost their readiness to learn.

According to Burnett (2002: xiv) sessions should consider all areas that might influence children's learning. These include the right environment, connecting the learning, using the context for learning, incorporating visual, auditory and kinaesthetic stimulus, making meaning through multiple intelligences and discussing with children what they have learned to help them make meaning of their experiences.

Learning objectives, increasingly developed nationally from birth to five or six, can be used to formulate what is to be learned and provide guidance on how children can be supported in their learning when progressing through their next steps. This can be developed from the child's interests to motivate them in their learning. Children can voice their opinions when discussing new themes and devise ideas for future experiences to be planned into their learning. In this way they can take ownership of their achievements and become totally immersed in the activities they have devised. Records of achievement can be maintained to give children the opportunity to discuss their experiences with others and celebrate what they have learned.

Teaching in the early years can incorporate adult-led, adult-initiated or child-initiated activities. Adult-led tasks often include specific requirements from national frameworks for practitioners to cover as a progression towards formal schooling. There is much debate as to the validity of such practice, but it can be positive in the way in which it is delivered, for example in an interactive, enjoyable manner. Discussions of activities can lead to adult-initiated work where children seize an initial idea and use it in their tasks or play. Children devise their own activities through child-initiated play, both indoors and outdoors. Sensitive adult involvement can enhance children's learning with support through open questioning to aid children's thinking, and resources to support the development of the learning.

Teaching and learning styles are intrinsically linked and therefore practitioners need to give great consideration to all the areas discussed in this chapter. Having a multi-sensory approach will not be conducive to learning if the children are anxious or exposed to a learning environment which is constrained by conflicting factors, whether it be a limited amount of resources to be shared between a number of children or the lack of routines established between the adults and the children.

Helping children to become effective learners goes beyond developing children's cognitive abilities; allowing children to work collaboratively, with realistic challenge, will enable them to develop socially too. Setting open-ended tasks and giving suitable enquiry-based learning will assist young children to explore through trial and error. The practitioner can help children come out of their comfort zone and feel safe to do so when the adults ensure they get involved in the children's discoveries and offer effective, appropriate and timely feedback. So, observe the children in the class carefully to consider the individuals within the group and discover what will engage and interest them. The information you collect will be a powerful tool and help you on your way to creating motivating learning experiences for all the children in your care.

Further Reading

Bayley, R. (2002) 'Thinking Skills in the Early Years', *Gifted Education International*, 16: 248–60.

Call, N. and Featherstone, S. (2003) *The Thinking Child: Brain-Based Learning for the Foundation Stage*. Stafford: Network Educational Press Ltd.

Featherstone, S. (2008) *Like Bees, Not Butterflies: Child-initiated Learning in the Early Years*. Lutterworth: Featherstone Education Ltd.

Nutbrown, C. (2011) *Threads of Thinking: Young Children Learning and the Role of Early Education* (4th edn). London: Sage.

Nutbrown, C. and Page, J. (2008) *Working with Babies and Children from Birth to Three*. London: Sage.

Useful Websites

www.acceleratedlearning.com
Accelerated Learning

www.azteachscience.co.uk
Astra Zeneca Science Technology Trust

www.brainboxx.com
Theory and practice related to the brain and learning

www.lotc.org.uk
Learning Outside The Classroom

References

Anderson, L.W. and Krathwohl, D.R. (eds) (2001) *A Taxonomy for Learning, Teaching and Assessing: A Revision of Bloom's Taxonomy of Educational Objectives*. New York: Longman.

Burnett, G. (2002) *Learning to Learn*. Carmarthen: Crown House Publishing Ltd.

Caine, R.N. and Caine, G. (1995) *Making Connections: Teaching and the Human Brain*. Massachusetts: Addison Wesley Longman Publishing Company.

Claxton, G. (2002) *Building Learning Power*. Bristol: TLO Limited.

Colcott, D., Russell, B. and Skouteris, H. (2009) 'Thinking About Thinking: Innovative Pedagogy Designed to Foster Thinking Skills in Junior Primary Classroom', *Teacher Development*, 13(1): 17–27.

DfES (2003) *Excellence and Enjoyment: A Strategy for Primary Schools*. Nottingham: DfES Publications.

Eccles, J., Wigfield, A., Harold, R.D. and Blumenfeld, P. (1993) 'Age and Gender Differences in Children's Self and Task Perceptions during Elementary School', *Child Development*, 64(3): 830–47.

Gardner, H. (2004) *Frames of Mind: The Theory of Multiple Intelligences* (20th anniversary edition). New York: Basic Books.

Hughes, M. (2001) *Strategies for Closing the Learning Gap* (3rd edn). Stafford: Network Educational Press Ltd.

Jensen, E. (1998) *Teaching with the Brain in Mind*. Virginia: ASCD.

Lazear, D. (2004) *High-Order Thinking: The Multiple Intelligences Way*. Carmarthen: Crown House Publishing Ltd.

Mason, S. (2008) Science-Physical Approach. Available at: http://www.azteachscience.co.uk/resources/cpd/the-science-physical-approach.aspx (accessed 25 September 2010).

Pomerantz, E., Alterman, E. and Saxon, J. (2002) 'Making the Grade but Feeling Distressed: Gender Differences in Academic Performance and Internal Distress', *Journal of Educational Psychology*, 94(2): 396–404.

Smith, A. (1996) *Accelerated Learning in the Classroom*. Stafford: Network Educational Press Ltd.

Smith, A. (2004) *The Brain's Behind It: New Knowledge about the Brain and Learning*. Stafford: Network Educational Press Ltd.

Smith, A. and Call, N. (1999) *The ALPS Approach: Accelerated Learning in Primary Schools*. Stafford: Network Educational Press Ltd.

Staricoff, M. and Rees, A. (2005) *Start Thinking: Daily Starters to Inspire Thinking in Primary Classrooms*. Birmingham: Imaginative Minds Press.

12 LEADERSHIP AND MANAGEMENT IN EARLY YEARS SETTINGS

Pat Beckley

Learning objectives

- To be aware of the differences between leadership and management
- To give suggestions of factors to consider when working in an early years setting
- Practical examples provided

This chapter explores the many aspects of leadership and management to be considered within the early years setting. This includes questions of what makes an effective leader and what issues should be covered to ensure good management. These elements will be discussed with the incorporation of practical examples.

LEADERSHIP AND MANAGEMENT IN AN EARLY YEARS SETTING

An early years setting poses unique challenges for leadership and management. In the postmodern world leaders and the teams they work with respond flexibly to the changing demands and challenges of early years provision. Early years practitioners work as teams to support children and devise strategies to care for individuals within this group of children. The smooth running of the setting often belies the hard work and organisational skills required to facilitate it. Many, for example Goleman (2002), suggest emotional intelligence is the capacity for recognising our own feelings and those of others, for motivating ourselves and others, and for managing emotions well, both in ourselves and in our relationships with others. It has been noted in previous chapters on the importance of self-esteem, different learning styles and the learning environment, that factors planned for and provided in an early years setting can have a crucial impact on an individual and how they progress and develop. An effective leader and manager can play a vital part in these aspects of the well-being of the children in their care.

AN EFFECTIVE LEADER

An effective leader demonstrates qualities that respond to the individuals within the setting. Effective communication skills are vital to ensure misunderstandings do not take place and information is shared with a common understanding between team members. Practitioners should enjoy their work and develop professionally. In this way teams are able to draw on one another's strengths to form awareness of each other's abilities and promote bonds that can withstand the challenges faced by early years provision on a daily basis and through long-term concerns. This promotion of individual strengths within the team encourages motivation and personal attachment which fosters a desire to present the highest quality of work in the individual concerned.

A positive role model can have an impact on our behaviour at the time and into the future. Sometimes words spoken, or even the tone of voice, can be remembered and used as a way of speaking and responding to others. The leader can create a feeling of being special as an individual while being a valued part of the team.

> ### 📁 Case Study
>
> In a busy setting a visit was planned to the city centre with a class of older children. It had been agreed that the children would return later than usual from the outing and meet parents at the local train station. On returning to the class the leader was waiting for the practitioner, despite having to pick up his own children, to let her know that she had won an award.

PERSONAL QUALITIES

Consideration should be given to developing personal qualities, gaining further self-awareness and understanding of one's own strengths and weaknesses and how these are transmitted when working with others.

Self-awareness can cover issues such as an understanding of personal responses to emotional factors, knowledge of strengths and weaknesses in academic ability or other learning styles, and qualities such as commitment, motivation or determination. Consideration could also be given to how change is addressed, whether positively or feared, and whether situations are used to advantage to seize opportunities. Self-awareness includes an understanding of personal reactions when events are not working as hoped or there was disappointment in your work, or behaviour by yourself or others. Reflections could consider personal reactions to situations in the past, from previous experiences, how they were dealt with and the consequences of those actions. Social aspects vary, encompassing the ability to network and share experiences with others, to judge social situations and respond appropriately and to interact with others in groups or on an individual basis. The ability to listen is relevant to gaining an understanding of the other person's viewpoint and perception of situations. However, it is useful to know how to influence others by stating your viewpoint too and expressing your ideas and plans. It might be necessary to compromise and agree on a mutually acceptable solution.

KEY LEADERSHIP ROLES

According to Goleman (2002), emotional intelligence is the capacity for recognising our own feelings and those of others, for motivating ourselves and others, and for managing emotions well, both in ourselves and our relationships with others. Bush and Middlewood (2005: 19) suggest a people-orientated approach where 'people are valued in their own right and not simply because they can "deliver" an appropriate level of performance'. They go on to state that this stance 'assumes a more dynamic relationship in which people can be developed and motivated to produce higher levels of performance'. In this way people working in the setting can work together to promote a vision for the setting and have an instrumental part in achieving the vision for its development. According to Busher (2006: 65) a leader's values include 'taking account of the expressed needs of other people with whom he works ... by listening to their voices and creating a culture of interdependency'. Good role models have a positive impact on us and can influence our practice both at the time and into the future.

Case Study

Relationships can cause situations to deteriorate if leadership falters, despite the best intentions. In a setting three colleagues had caused such a situation, where relationships had become so bitter that the lack of collaboration between staff was resulting in an unpleasant atmosphere which children and their parents/carers did not want to be part of. The leadership role was the early years teacher's dream and she was determined to work as hard as she could to promote the children's learning and progress. The team of three consisted of an older practitioner, a younger practitioner and the leader. The new leader planned the organisation of the setting before term started and devised work for the staff. She gave the older practitioner the greater amount of work believing her to be the most experienced. However, when unpicking the situation it became clear that the lack of liaison had led to misunderstandings of experience and roles. The older practitioner was

(Continued)

(Continued)

struggling to cope with the amount of work given and had increasing demands on her personal time too. The younger practitioner was a highly capable woman, whose strengths were not being utilised. A great deal of bridge-building was needed by the leader to listen to and understand the people she worked with. As the leader it was essential to lead the team, rather than working in isolation. On reflection, she was able to learn lessons from the mistakes she had made at the start of her practice, and children stopped leaving the setting.

LEADERSHIP STYLES

According to the Hay Group there are six leadership styles. These are coercive; authoritative; affiliative; democratic; pace-setting; and coaching. These terms cover a range of strategies and mean that in a given situation, for example, a coercive person would wish to take control and be forcefully demanding to get what was wanted, achieved. An authoritative person would firmly suggest a viewpoint and due to the strength of the leadership, achieve what was desired. An affiliative person would wish to please the members of the team and take a friendly standpoint, listening to others and sharing plans, giving way to others at times and wanting to give others the lead too. A democratic system ensures that all participants share decisions and plans, working cooperatively through items that might need addressing. The pace-setting ethos requires the leader to set goals and targets to focus the team on reference points to be achieved in the future. A coaching style suggests the leader gains ideas for action from the rest of the team, hoping that they might think of similar solutions to challenges that the leader has. No one single style of leadership is desirable. A mix of, or perhaps all, the leadership styles would be useful in different situations. An effective leader should be able to judge when a certain style is most useful in supporting the team and the work to be achieved in the setting.

ACCOUNTABILITY

The principles for accountability in public life, as described by the Nolan Committee in 1994, consist of qualities such as selflessness, integrity, objectivity, accountability, openness, honesty and leadership. By reflecting this leadership role model practitioners can be motivated to work well with the team. The leader is accountable to his/her own understanding of what constitutes a leader's role, the children and staff in the setting, parents/carers and the wider community. Leading an early years setting is a crucial aspect of community life and can have long-term effects on the well-being of those who attend. The pressures are immense yet hugely rewarding and worthwhile. Networks with other leaders can be forged to share ideas and plans, view the organisation and layout of the environment and discuss new resources or introduce fresh initiatives. It is vital in the early years team to work as a team, sharing ideas and valuing and respecting others' views and thoughts. In this way accountability can become something to be proud of, a way to celebrate achievements and plans for the future. In a stifling atmosphere work can become something to be 'got through' with the minimum of satisfaction in the work achieved. However, with a supportive, dynamic ethos individuals can discuss, revise and implement ideas in an honest manner, admitting mistakes and sharing success.

LEADERSHIP IN AN EARLY YEARS SETTING

Early years practitioners work as teams with the leader providing the planned direction for the setting. This vision works as a way forward and long-term planning can be organised to work towards the proposed outcomes. This requires everyone's cooperation and commitment to the vision, and involves deciding on roles for the implementation of the plans. The leader therefore needs to have an understanding of the capabilities of the team, an awareness of the roles to be undertaken and the ability to motivate colleagues to work towards the vision. This cannot be achieved without the agreement of all concerned.

Once the shared vision has been agreed by the team, planning for each person's work to accommodate it, the time scale and the intended outcomes can be decided. These should be achievable goals within specified time limits, with individuals involved in the cooperative plan. All stakeholders can take part in this where appropriate, for example parental involvement can be included, with specific roles given if desired. This could include such practices as supporting volunteers to participate, drawing on the individual's strengths and abilities, and accommodating their commitment and time constraints. When individual members of the team have been given specific responsibilities according to their roles, strengths and abilities then the dynamic, learning environment can be considered to facilitate the smooth running of the setting and everyone's involvement in it.

In a setting where relationships are well established, strong performance management can be a welcoming sharing of achievements and concerns. Planned targets for the forthcoming year can motivate individuals striving to develop professionally. Learning can be strong and the leader can encourage high standards. Bush (2008: 6) notes: 'The significance for self-management for leadership development is that the scope for leadership and management is much greater'. Leaders of the provision, while exercising emotional intelligence and interpersonal and intrapersonal skills, also require self-management skills to organise their time and work. It is beneficial for the children's learning, the smooth running of the setting and the professional development of the adults working there, that responsibilities are devolved to others, drawing on their strengths and abilities. This responsibility and leadership for certain areas enhances the teamwork, shared vision in the setting, attention to specific aspects by a number of people, and pride in personal work achieved as part of the early years team. Bush and Middlewood (2005: 78) assert 'job satisfaction and motivation are inextricably linked because staff need to feel they are doing a good job and, when that is established, the leader can build on that to try to motivate them to move forward'. After all, adults working in the setting spend a great deal of their time in that setting, along with the children. It is up to the leader to ensure others working there are enjoying their challenges and gaining fulfilment in their work. If those working in the setting have no say in what happens there and are not valued, they do not have a reason to become totally engaged with the work, appearing in the role of a passive helper. If they have shared ownership of aspects of learning it promotes feelings of fulfilment and pride in a job well done. An astute leader can ascertain what supportive frameworks are needed for those working in the team, while the team appreciate the leader's empathy in their situation. This in turn can promote children's engrossment in their work, using the adults working with them as role models, so they make good progress in their learning. Achievement is very high. Teaching and learning are stimulating, enthusiastic and consistently challenging, stemming from expert knowledge of the Early Years Foundation Stage framework. Practioners know how the framework can be incorporated into sessions and how children learn. A range of approaches to learning are used, including child-initiated, adult-led and adult-initiated. Social interactions and collaborative work are valued. Activities are sensitively matched to children's individual needs. Children's learning and development are carefully tracked. Adults in the provision work successfully as members of a team.

DESIRABLE KNOWLEDGE AND UNDERSTANDING FOR EARLY YEARS PRACTICE

A thorough and perceptive knowledge and understanding of the Early Years Foundation Stage framework is important. There should be expertise in basic skills, for example talk. Practitioners challenge and inspire children, with high expectations of their performance. An understanding of a range of learning strategies can be developed. It is important to build trusting relationships and use praise, support and collaboration. A balance can be maintained between adult-led and child-initiated activities. Adults can encourage children to attempt new experiences, with activities devised to suit children's needs and abilities. The leader can ensure behaviour is maintained with respect for others fostered. Timings, management of staff, resources and the accommodation need to be considered. Assessments of children's achievements can be incorporated into daily routines and this formative tracking leads into knowledge of children's progress towards the Early Learning Goals while providing evidence to inform the Early Years Foundation Stage Profiles.

 Questions for Discussion

How would you promote effective leadership in a setting?
What strategies would you use to ensure all those in the setting were reaching their potential and supporting children's learning and development by doing so?
What do you feel are your strengths as a leader?

Reflections of practice can include consideration of children's learning, for example whether they are able to make choices and explore, work with and learn from each other. They should be able to acquire new skills from the environment provided, including the six areas of learning and development identified in the Early Years Foundation Stage framework, namely, personal, social and emotional development; communication, language and literacy; problem solving, reasoning and numeracy; creative development; physical development; and knowledge and understanding of the world.

The leader can encourage the enhancement of planning and practice through an enthusiastic commitment to meaningful experiences planned for the children in the setting. This philosophy will cascade into communications and interactions between children and staff and encourage their enthusiasm. When all involved in the learning and development of those in the setting feel they have a voice that is heard in decision-making, engagement with the setting increases. This applies to all stakeholders of the setting, including governors, parents/carers, staff and children. The inclusive manner of the leader, whose interactions with others demonstrates respect when they are treated as valued individuals, proves a positive role model for the children and secures a loyal, hardworking team. Through the interactions with the learning environment, social interactions and adult interventions, children can acquire and increase their knowledge and understanding, make links with their learning and consolidate new skills and understandings. Questions posed, particularly the use of open-ended questioning, can encourage children to problem solve and think, enhancing self-assessment and awareness.

A POSITIVE ENVIRONMENT

Where practitioners work effectively and well together, with the leader ensuring this is maintained, they can model this behaviour to the children, who feel safe to develop to their utmost. Doyle and Smith (1999: 48) discuss this as a notion of a sense of well-being for those involved. They state, 'leadership should work so that people can flourish'. A leader has to create a social context where each individual flourishes and feels appropriately challenged and fulfilled with respect to their personal development. This can be identified in a number of ways, for example through the interest shown in their surroundings and in the available activities, demonstrating curiosity and enthusiasm. They behave appropriately and show consideration for others. This growing confidence supports children's abilities to become independent and offer their own views and opinions. It is reflected in the atmosphere of the setting where children work well together.

QUALITY OF LEARNING AND TEACHING

In a well run setting, practitioners should have a clear understanding of how young children learn. They plan, cooperate and work well together. Activities and resources are carefully devised for a range of strategies. There is a balance of adult-led and child-initiated activities. Practitioners work directly with the children. Children's play and interests are supported and extended sensitively, enabling them to grow in confidence and learn from their mistakes. Good use is made of space, materials and equipment to give children a broad, stimulating and interesting range of activities. Practitioners are flexible and exploit opportunities that occur spontaneously. They have high expectations for each child in the setting. Children are helped through talk and relevant questioning to evaluate what they have done.

GOOD MANAGEMENT

Management concerns how the provision is organised and managed.

A DYNAMIC, MOTIVATIONAL ENVIRONMENT

A dynamic, motivational environment can only occur if all the participants are happy to be there and feel a valued part of the organisation of the setting. This naturally needs careful planning and, while appearing effortless in well-organised provision, it nevertheless needs thought and consideration to achieve. An understanding of those in the team is a start with an appreciation of the strengths, gifts and talents they can bring to the provision, drawing on experiences to promote a broad base of knowledge and awareness to build on. This can be facilitated in a number of ways, through working together as a team, allocating various responsibilities or carefully identifying aspects of the provision for individual accountability within the team. Stakeholders could be given a role in the smooth running of the provision, according to their level of responsibility and concern, in order to develop a team with many diverse strengths, whose members complement each other. In this way ideas are constantly being developed for improvement, growing through shared dialogue and interactions.

This can be achieved through informal, ongoing discussions in planning meetings and teams or as formal reflective practice resulting in the compilation of written action plans to share with the wider community. The format for use could take the form of a perceived need for improvement of a particular aspect, such as provision for child-initiated activities. Observations of practice could lead to identifying ways of promoting this approach to learning, for example through changing the height of resources to enable ease of access for children. Further observations could assess the success of the changes and identify further ones if needed.

The leader would also need a vision of what could be possible in the setting to use the facility to its best advantage. Building on established relationships, the leader would need to ensure all participants are agreeable, or at least willing to support the implementation, to ensure the new initiatives are successfully implemented. Therefore, the dynamic, motivational environment is inclusive with well-organised structures in place so that everyone is fully aware of their responsibilities and roles within the team. It is based on an appropriate culture of mutual trust and respect. Effective leadership within this ethos is encouraging, enthusiastic for the learning and development that is taking place, keeps up-to-date with relevant initiatives and is prepared to devise an action plan to implement them. Interest is shown in others, giving praise when appropriate and effective leaders inspire those who work with them. The effective leader has high aspirations for those who work with them, encouraging their professional development as well as the development of children they are responsible for. Effective leaders and teams can respond successfully to the needs and requirements of the community they serve, while focusing on the individual needs of the children in the setting. The holistic approach promoted in this book emphasises the importance of community involvement with the setting to enable it to be seen as an important part of the area, participating as a part of the values and culture of its surroundings.

To achieve the well-organised provision, each area of the setting should be scrutinised to assess whether it is being used to its full advantage. This has financial implications and the leader must appreciate the necessity of maintaining secure financial means, carefully scrutinised through audits on a regular basis. The money that must be used for resources must be budgeted over a number of years to develop good quality furniture and resources for the children to use imaginatively. Items can be bought according to an action plan devised to assess which resources are most needed and how they can be purchased through careful planning over two or three years. If a plan for the resources is organised, implemented and shared between governors and colleagues and at an appropriate level, with the children, care can be taken of the new purchases and delight generated at the growth of the bank of equipment available. The area can be viewed as sections of the environment, indoors and outdoors, or learning areas. Responsibility for the daily upkeep of these areas can be shared between practitioners. This can also help to promote professional development as practitioners aim to improve the areas they are responsible for. The areas can be considered in turn to ensure resources are adequate and at an appropriate level for child-initiated learning or easily accessible if adult resources are part of the perceived needs for learning in that section. Further points for consideration can include interactive, informative, table-top or on-going displays, and the provision of opportunities for development of the areas of learning from the Early Years Foundation Stage framework, such as mark-making equipment, artefacts for investigation and the provision of an environment where children can explore and share experiences with their peers.

In this positive atmosphere those working in the teams can be inspired to have high aspirations for learning and teaching. This awareness of the context can help to forge networks and partnerships to promote children's learning and enable them to be excited and motivated when making progress in their learning.

MANAGING THE LEARNING ENVIRONMENT

Leaders and their teams should routinely consider the upkeep of the learning environment to ensure it remains an attractive and welcoming place to be. This includes a stimulating, engaging range of two and three dimensional displays. The print-rich environment should have a variety of accessible and appropriate resources. Care should be taken to check that resources are appropriate and of sufficiently good quality and in a satisfactory condition for children to use. The team can discuss the best use of the environment for relevant learning areas and their position in the space available. These can include a mark-making/graphics/writing area, a reading corner/book corner or library space, an imaginative role-play area, a wet and dry water/sand area, a mathematics area, an investigative science/living things/growing things area, small and large construction area, a creative media area including paint/clay/wood and junk materials, a musical instruments and listening centre, collections of objects to feel, sort, draw, write about, investigate or count, artefacts and pictures reflecting the wider community and inclusion, small world play computers, language masters, programmable toys, and specific outdoor equipment including wheeled toys or climbing frames.

REFLECTIONS OF PRACTICE

Management involves continually reflecting on existing practice and changing areas when appropriate. This could involve such aspects as daily incidents that occur, changes to the learning environment of the setting, consideration of ways to promote links with parents/carers and the community, or collaboration with multidisciplinary teams. There are many theories of reflective practice. There can be shared reflections and evaluations of practice to devise agreed considerations of happenings, points of change when necessary and ways to manage the changes, with the agreement of all concerned. Reflection can greatly enhance teaching and learning by identifying areas of strength and considering possible means to improve certain aspects where appropriate. This can be beneficial to everyone in the team and those involved with the setting.

According to Schön (1983: 63) the study of reflection-in-action is critically important. The dilemma of rigour or relevance may be dissolved if we can develop an epistemology of practice which places technical problem-solving within a broader context of reflective enquiry. This shows how reflection-in-action may be rigorous in its own right, and links the art of practice in uncertainty and uniqueness to the scientist's art of research. Reflection-in-action suggests doing the right things by value judgements and balancing perspectives. There is also a desire to ask 'what if' and 'what if not', to challenge assumptions, forge theory and make further explorations of practice. Reflection in action consists of doing things right with guidance and review and includes asking questions such as what, why, and how to use theory and gain more control. Reflection on action consists of a 'plan, do, review' cycle which draws reflections from existing practice. The practitioner plans as usual and uses both personal reflections and those from people who are involved in the setting, to identify areas for improvement. Findings from this review of practice can then be transformed into an action plan or recommendations implemented on a daily basis. Reflection-in-action can occur when an area for development has already been identified.

Reflections could incorporate:

Your perspective	Internal reflection
	Pupils' responses and work
	Post-it notes – journal
	Video – audio – photo
Colleagues	Lesson observation
	Review of your data
Pupils	Interview – group discussion
	Photo selection and presentation
Adults other than teachers	All of the above …

Reflections on the range of events happening in the setting could include reflections on practice, to identify changes needed if appropriate, reflections on policies to update or revise, reflections on processes concerning how the provision is delivered to the children and those concerned with their welfare, and reflections on theory to change practice in the light of new initiatives and findings, for example recent research regarding brain development.

When reflections have identified actions to be taken, resulting in a modification of practice, these can again be reflected upon and adjustments made. Findings of the changes can be disseminated and shared to promote good practice and collaborative work.

Bleach (1999: 79–80) identifies stages to consider when new members of staff learn about the setting through an induction period. These include the identification of an area of professional interest/concern by articulating an issue. A focus can be made on one aspect through auditing evidence. Consideration of what can be done about it can take the form of design intervention. A plan can be implemented and monitored for improvement where practice is modified. Further evaluation of varied sources of evidence could result in establishing a claim for improved practice and disseminating findings to others. Researchers who highlight the importance of an educative adult's interaction with his/her children include amongst others, Bruner (1966), Vygotsky (1972 in Pound 2005), Donaldson (1978), Rogers (1983) and Athey (1990). Therefore, the importance of an adult's responses and the reflections that have taken place are crucial for a child's development.

Questions for Discussion

What do you feel is important when managing an early years setting? Why?
How can the factors you have noted be implemented in practice?

Reflections could cover consideration of your work as part of the team and how each member relates to the others. Responsibilities undertaken within the roles would be discussed as well as how teamwork has promoted the learning environment with each person responsible for aspects of it. Policies would need to be considered to keep up to date and to incorporate new initiatives or ideas. Diversity issues would also be included in this remit.

Within the setting, decisions need to be made constantly. To be an effective leader and manager reflections form an essential part of the sustainability of the successful environment. Personal reflections of practice include consideration of what happened in incidents, particularly if they are of a critical nature and determine and impact on the atmosphere in the environment. Thoughts could include reflections on what had happened and why it might have occurred, whether others were involved and how the situation and events felt and appeared on reflection. It is difficult sometimes to honestly come to terms with what was said or occurred in certain situations. Further reflection at a later date can add to perceptions of the incident with less of the 'raw' feeling that can hamper true and honest reflections of the incident; it is necessary to come to terms with the situation first. The outcomes form a powerful indicator of the crucial nature of the incident and, if negative, calm reflection of possible ways personal practice could be done differently if faced with a similar situation.

Further Reading

Bruner. J.S. (2006) *In Search of Pedagogy: The Selected Works of Jerome S. Bruner.* London: Routledge.

Donaldson, M.C. (1978) *Children's Minds.* London: Fontana.

Goleman, D. (1999) *Working with Emotional Intelligence.* London: Bloomsbury.

Harris, A. Day, C. Hopkins, D. Hadfield, M. Hargreaves, A. and Chapman, C. (2005) *Effective Leadership for School Improvement.* London: RoutledgeFalmer.

Miller, L. and Cable, C. (2011) *Professionalisation, Leadership and Management in the Early Years.* London: Sage.

Pound, L. (2005) *How Children Learn: From Montessori to Vygotsky.* London: Step Forward Publishing.

Rogers, C.R. (1983) *Freedom to Learn from the 80's.* Columbus, OH: Charles E. Merrill.

Southworth, G. (2004) *Primary School Leadership in Context: Leading Small, Medium and Large Sized Schools.* London: RoutledgeFalmer.

Useful Website

www.eyfswarwickshire.co.uk

This website contains information from the Early Years Department in Warwickshire County Council.

References

Bleach, K. (1999) *The Induction and Mentoring of NQTs*. London: Fulton.

Bush, T. and Middlewood, D. (2005) *Leading and Managing People in Education*. London: Sage.

Bush, T. (2008) *Leadership and Management Development in Education*. London: Sage.

Busher, H. (2006) *Understanding Educational Leadership: People, Power and Culture*. Maidenhead: Open University Press.

Doyle, M.E. and Smith, M.K. (1999) *Born and Bred? Leadership, Heart and Informal Education*. London: YMCA George Williams College for the Rank Foundation.

Goleman, D. (2002) *Emotional Intelligence*. New York: Bantam Books.

Schön, D. (1983) *The Reflective Practitioner*. New York: Basic Books.

PART 4

ISSUES IN PRACTICE

The pedagogy and philosophy discussed in earlier parts of the book and considered as implications for implementation into practice in the previous section are developed and expanded in Part 4. This section explores aspects of practice concerning contemporary issues, the importance of the social context, multi-agency working and implications of practice as an awareness of children's future well-being and ability to cope with future challenges.

Chapter 13 is written by Becky Glenton who identifies the many challenges she faces in promoting an holistic approach in the early years setting where she works. She describes practical activities and provides suggestions of ways she has found to successfully implement an holistic approach. She examines appropriate planning procedures to enable children's interests and ideas to be used as a stimulus for relevant themes and as a tool to support their development through exploration and investigation of their ideas.

Chapter 14 identifies important aspects of the social context of learning and development. The use of the whole environment, both indoors and outdoors, has significance as a place where interactions between adults and children take place. To promote an holistic approach there needs to be an awareness of children's needs, both their immediate ones and those reflecting academic progress. To do this a suitable, happy and secure environment has to be created. The outdoor environment can have a profound impact on children's development and welfare. Individuals respond to the natural environment in many ways, but it does seem to influence children's emotional well-being. Children explore and investigate, making their own meaning and understanding of the world around them, scrutinising natural features and learning about life. They become calm in their constructions and social constructions of their world. Issues regarding transition are considered in this chapter. Suggestions are made to ensure children's first experiences of education and care in settings other than home are happy ones. This helps children to make a smooth transition to school and fosters ease in dealing with new experiences. In an increasingly global world these abilities could become of vital importance if children are to meet future demands and changes.

Chapter 15 is written by the educational psychologist Anita Soni. Anita has extensive experience working in multi-agency teams. In this chapter she provides a rationale for multi-agency working and its historical development. She relates multi-agency working to early years provision and looks at how it can support an holistic approach for the children concerned. Skills and knowledge needed for practice are identified and the challenges and dilemmas posed in practice are examined. The drive to multi-agency working was led by the Every Child Matters (2003) agenda. This agenda strove to ensure that agencies within Children's Services worked collaboratively around a preventative agenda. It also sought to provide 'an effective way of supporting children and families with additional needs and helping to secure real improvements in their life outcomes' (Every Child Matters 2006: 1). This support can range from a group of practitioners deciding informally to work together to help a child or family through to a large-scale venture of different services coming together, as in a Sure Start local programme or a Children's Centre. Three distinct models of multi-agency working – multi-agency panel, multi-agency team and an integrated service – are described. The Inter-Departmental Childcare Review *Delivering for Children and Families* (DfES 2002) found that: 'an integrated approach, that ensures the joining up of services and disciplines, is a key factor in determining good outcomes for children' (2002: 32–3). Multi-agency working is one of the six key areas of skills and knowledge in the *Common Core of Skills and Knowledge for the Children's Workforce* (CWDC 2005). Anita notes that the skills and knowledge listed in this chapter form a useful foundation for practitioners in the early years to reflect upon when considering their strengths and areas for development within the area of effective multi-agency working.

The final chapter, written by Liz Creed, promotes an awareness of issues concerning aspects of practice which support children's social, emotional and behavioural needs from an holistic stance, including children's mental health. It considers factors such as emotional resilience as a way of coping with future changes and challenges. Human development is itself a complex issue with numerous factors existing to influence this. Bronfenbrenner (1979) stated that a number of systems exert influences on a child as they develop, through environments in which a child is both directly involved and indirectly influenced. A child is not only influenced by their immediate environments, such as the home or school environment and individuals within these settings, but also by settings within which they are not directly involved themselves. This includes such situations as a parent's work environment, for example. The child is not directly involved with and therefore not directly influenced by this situation. However, the child may be indirectly influenced by this situation through the effects of this situation on their parent.

Optimal social, emotional and intellectual development can be encouraged through positive experiences in early life, a supportive and encouraging upbringing, positive role models, and low levels of stress and distress during childhood. All of these factors can act as facilitators of good mental well-being and function as protective factors against developing mental health problems in adolescence and adulthood. The chapter also covers negative experiences which might impact on a child's development. Children who are better able to cope with difficult and stressful situations in life are much more likely to go on to reach their full social, emotional and intellectual potential. It is necessary to consider all aspects of a child's life in order to better understand the unique child and cater for their needs effectively. Most important for future practice is the consideration of an holistic approach to caring for and supporting children, facilitating social, emotional and intellectual development by exploring the impact of differing and varied factors upon children. This, while not being able to define what might happen in the future, this should help practitioners to understand the reasons why the challenges are occurring and support their strategies to cope with them for the benefit of the young children concerned.

References

Bronfenbrenner, U. (1979) *The Ecology of Human Development.* Cambridge, MA: Harvard University Press.

Children's Workforce Development Council (CWDC) (2005) *Common Core of Skills and Knowledge for the Children's Workforce.* Leeds: CWDC. Available at www.cwdcouncil.org.uk/common-core (accessed 10 February 2010).

Department for Education and Skills (DfES) (2002) *Delivering for Children and Families.* The Inter-Departmental Childcare, Strategy Unit, London (accessed from: www.surestart.gov.uk/publications).

Every Child Matters (2006) *Multi-agency Working Factsheet* (accessed from EYFS CD ROM). Nottingham: DfES.

13 ENGAGING EARLY LEARNERS

Becky Glenton

Learning objectives

- To become aware of early years practice through the eyes of an early years teacher
- To consider points for successful practice when working in a Foundation Stage Unit
- To examine ways to devise assessment and planning for young children

This chapter discusses issues in an Early Years Foundation Stage Unit from the perspective of an early years teacher. It includes reflections of the importance of the learning environment, areas of learning, including outdoors, relationships, assessment and planning for the young children and the wider community. According to Scott, 'It is characteristic of human beings to explore their environment and to reflect on what they discover' (cited in Fisher 2002: 75).

As a Foundation Stage teacher, I feel that play is vital for a child's development, both emotionally and academically. The Foundation stage curriculum allows children to learn in an inspiring way and should lead the way for primary schools, particularly in Key Stage One. Being a Foundation Stage teacher is exhausting but incredibly rewarding. Having 60 five-year-olds in your care for six hours a day provides happiness and laughter. These children are in their prime and need care, comfort and safety. If these things are provided, the opportunities are endless and learning is unlimited.

AN EARLY YEARS TEACHER IN ACTION

As a Foundation Stage teacher, the roles include being an educator and also, seemingly, a mother, nurse, actress, police officer, social worker, singer and secretary. 'Effective early years educators know that it is through play that children come to terms with new knowledge and can explore and confront their feelings' (Fisher 2002: 77). Young children are supported by the practitioners working in the setting and it is important they do everything they can to make children feel happy and secure there. Happiness is the key; children learn more, are more enthusiastic and contribute more if they are happy. When the children skip out of school with a smile on their faces, it is most rewarding for those working with them.

THE LEARNING ENVIRONMENT

The classroom environment should be warm, welcoming and exciting. This may sound simple but getting the balance right can be difficult. According to Bruce (2006: 112), 'children use their senses to learn about materials, and they learn from feedback from their movements in relation to them (kinaesthetic learning)'. The best way to ensure the children enjoy being in their setting is to involve them in creating it. It is, after all, their classroom, not the practitioner's. It is important that the learning environment develops and extends independence. Children should be given the opportunity to select resources independently. Practitioners should try not to lay resources out for the children whenever they can. Children should be encouraged to find and select the resources as and when they need them. Children may start school being unable to be independent as they have had everything done for them. Children can be supported to learn to look after themselves, dress themselves, feed themselves and play with what they choose. Setting the right learning environment can help to develop this independence. The children can be involved in creating the learning environment. Regular sessions with the children enable them to interact and develop their communication skills. It might not be possible to change the colour of the walls or buy new furniture on a regular basis, but the children can be included in discussions about their learning environment and any changes that could be made. Building relationships with the children is vital in order to learn about their interests. Children love talking about themselves, the world around them and the things they enjoy. Their ideas can be amazing when asked questions such as, 'How would you like to change the classroom?'

Involving the children in setting up areas of provision linked to particular themes is vital to engage and interest their minds. For example, they could be questioned about an area of the provision such as, 'How could we develop the water area to link it to our under the sea theme?' This supports their suggestions and enables them to be involved in any dynamic changes that could be made.

This focus of attention to an area can create a 'Hot Spot'. As the area is new, and they have developed it, they are motivated to use the activities in the area. The challenge is to create new 'Hot Spots' on a regular basis and maintain them. Children become engrossed in investigating, floating and sinking, asking questions about sea creatures and wanting to role play a pirate adventure. They have created the situation for their own learning and because of this, skills are developed and children are engaged. The children could perhaps be given too much choice if all areas are changed at one time and they could become unable to focus on one activity in the indoor or outdoor area, rather than spending extended periods of time at a task and challenging themselves by extending their learning. Too much choice can perhaps confuse children, who need time to explore and investigate before being drawn to another area.

📁 **Case Study**

Children were set a problem to solve. They were asked to build a boat out of junk modelling materials which would carry a toy across the water tray without sinking. This created huge excitement which spread to others. Eventually everyone decided to create a boat.

Examples such as making boats provide opportunities which develop and extend learning. Children will then be much more open to recording their findings and methods, thus establishing a situation where children are creating writing possibilities.

💬 **Questions for Discussion**

Are strategies for children's engagement in their learning the focus of the early years provision?
How can this promote children's learning?

AREAS OF LEARNING

The variety of the areas of learning also provides a key factor in developing an exciting early years environment. Children need opportunities to explore, investigate, research, let off steam, relax, talk and build relationships. Children experience a range of emotions throughout the day and practitioners can provide areas for children to be comfortable at different stages of their development.

Exploring and investigating involves allowing children to problem solve, complete practical activities, challenge themselves and discuss solutions with each other. Investigation areas can prove to be very popular in the classroom and children enjoy using magnifying glasses to explore all kinds of objects and creatures. Through such activities children can be given the opportunity to record their findings. Observing children in these situations can prove to be most beneficial and children can be encouraged to ask questions, researching, exploring and finding out about their surroundings. 'Educators who watch and interact with children who incorporate all that they know in purposeful play can learn much about those children' (Nutbrown 2011: 118). This prepares the children for the start of their Key Stage One education. Transition into Year 1 can be carefully planned to meet the needs of the children – particularly the summer term entrants who may continue the Foundation Stage framework in the first term of Year 1. Watkins (2006: 44) suggests 'classrooms rarely operate as separate islands, and one of the major influences on them is the culture of the school'. In the school where I work early years provision is valued and contributions respected. The sense of community within the school supports activities undertaken in the Foundation Stage Unit. Liaison with local playgroups and nurseries and colleagues working with older children in the school builds a strong sense of collaboration and a culture of sharing ideas.

OUTDOOR LEARNING

The school day for older children, often begins with intense literacy sessions such as phonics and children are expected to participate and concentrate for sustained periods of time. Children then need the opportunity to stretch and use some energy, and this is often best achieved in an outdoor area. Children need equipment which allows them to be physical such as bikes, balls and climbing equipment. Many children prefer to learn (and learn better) outdoors. Activities can be adapted to outdoor provision. Children can paint, write, draw, construct, explore, read and develop number skills in an outdoor environment and providing the children with these experiences encourages them to develop their knowledge of the outdoor world. The outdoor area can be accessible at all times and weathers. If it is raining, children should be provided with the correct clothing to be outside in these conditions.

Good partnerships with parents and carers can be established through liaison with children prior to the child's entrance to the setting. This could be through parents bringing their children to the nursery or playgroup or via a home visit. Parents and carers can also be invited into the setting, to observe their child and the activities they pursue. This provides an opportunity for the practitioner to discuss any concerns or queries the adult responsible for the child, might have. If the setting where the open morning or day is taking place is linked to a school, time can be productively spent showing the children around the premises, if appropriate, and sharing a coffee break while considering aspects of school life. This enables parents and carers to see, at first hand, the range of experiences accessed by the children in the school and the seamless transition between classes.

A QUIET AREA

Children appreciate some quiet time and need some time out from the hustle and bustle of the day. Some early years settings, including Foundation Stage classrooms, have a quiet area which allows children to relax comfortably. Sofas are extremely popular, and allow children to take some time out. This is often a good opportunity to talk to them, and provides a place where they can express any concerns or worries. These situations sometimes lend themselves to enabling assessment, whether or not young children have a problem, or just require some time out.

RELATIONSHIPS

Providing young children with the opportunity to build relationships with others is vital. Language is an important part of development, and communication skills can be developed through play. Children extend their vocabulary through talking to others and listening to others.

They develop the skill of sharing and negotiating, and even the quietest children gain a lot from spending time with others, adults as well as children. It is important that the adult models appropriate language and new vocabulary, and this often means the practitioner plays alongside the children. Demonstrating new experiences is often a good way for children to learn new skills. Children enjoy an adult participating in their play, for example in role play.

The role of the adult is key in children's learning. The practitioner can support the scaffolding of children's understandings and concepts, as the provider and challenger. She/he extends the children's learning through questioning and discussion. Open-ended questions, allowing the children to think and explore new words, support this learning. This then, after time, gives children the skills of asking questions themselves. Children can be supported in the skills of thinking and questioning. Initially children may make a statement. However, through questioning, the children develop this skill and become inquisitive. This skill can be maintained throughout the primary school as children increasingly take control of their learning. If they are investigating something they want to find out about, they are much more likely to be interested and look deeper into the question.

CHILDREN'S DEVELOPMENT

During these first few years of education, huge strides are made in children's learning. They, more often than not, learn to read and write, key skills needed for surviving in a literate society. Children interact with intensive programmes of phonics and shared reading.

ACTIVE LEARNING THROUGH PLAY

Practical involvement is a key element. Children enjoy being motivated, enthusiastic and interested in their learning. Short bursts of activity can maintain this momentum. Anything more than 20 minutes of intense formal work and the children usually wish to participate in active learning. Children seem to enjoy hearing which sound matches which letter or how to write a high frequency word, as long as it is achieved in an enjoyable and interactive way. Children do not seem to tire of repeating sounds and often find it very rewarding when they understand. A good home–school partnership is an important element in developing reading and writing skills. Children can be supported at home learning the basic skills of reading and writing. It requires parents to be dedicated and reinforce any work that has been completed at school. Children respond much better to work with an individual adult. Small steps taken by parents to reinforce reading and writing skills in their daily lives can provide children with further understanding of the importance and meaning of literacy in everyday life.

From pupil questionnaires, it is clearly apparent that children enjoy, and learn the most, when they are 'doing'. Children enjoy practical activities as they allow them to see situations for themselves. Activities can be adult-led, adult-initiated or child-initiated. This gives a variety of experiences for children in their learning.

Case Study

Yasmin was finding it very difficult to understand the concept of volcanoes when reading about them in a book or finding out information from the internet. Yasmin's class decided to make a volcano, and then watched it explode together. This created many learning opportunities and Yasmin was eager to explore what had happened. Children were fascinated by the simple scientific procedures, and the activity allowed them to investigate and explore these. The children then wanted to learn more about volcanoes and they became interested in written information and short clips from the internet. Beginning a lesson with a practical activity inspired the children and promoted their motivation.

FORMAL ACTIVITIES

There are times when more formal education is needed and the expectations for children by the end of Key Stage One are extremely high. Therefore, when children are ready, a more formal approach is appropriate. There are always going to be those children who choose to sit at a table and make marks and write. Through their play, children can develop their imaginations and this is something to treasure. If children develop a good imagination, they will be able to create inspiring pieces of writing at a later stage, and with the development of technology, children have the opportunity to note down their ideas in different ways.

Home life has a huge impact on developing imagination. Society has, in recent years, changed dramatically. It was not that long ago when children spent their entire summer holidays out in the fields and parks and would only return when they were hungry. There were no mobile phones and parents would only worry if they did not see their child by nightfall. Today, children are watched much more closely, and sometimes they lose the opportunity to explore or use their imaginations.

DEVELOPMENT OF TEACHING STYLES

Another factor for practitioners to consider in their planning for the provision is the development of new technologies. Children often have access to technological tools such as a Nintendo DS or a Wii. Children from the age of four are given these electronic games and become adept at using them. Many children in the Foundation Year spend a lot of time watching and playing these games, or listening to their iPods and some have their own television. Early years practitioners have the challenge of using technology in appropriate ways to extend children's learning. Technology is part of the modern-day world, and we can help children by providing a range of activities, including those involving technological equipment.

Practitioners can interest and inspire children through practical and physical activities. Children are, generally, safe in a school and developing imagination and role play can form a daily part of their school day. Aspects of learning, such as those to develop imagination, can be incorporated into activities and tasks devised for the children and those where the child takes the lead and devises imaginative play themselves. The ethos of the Foundation Stage is therefore crucial for children's development, providing play-based activities where children can thrive and make progress in their learning.

ASSESSMENTS

Observational assessment is a valuable tool to gain an informed picture of a child's development. For example, a child can participate in role play of the story of Little Red Riding Hood. A cottage in the woods can be created, and children's responses, language and imagination can be observed and assessed. Much can be gained from these experiences, as children show their abilities, skills and ideas in a relaxed atmosphere, playing with friends.

PLANNING

It is from these observations that the planning can begin. Planning can be centred around the children's interests. Some examples are listed below:

- Observing children making space rockets in the construction area could lead to a space theme.
- Children talking about visits to the seaside they had made in the summer holidays may lead to an under the sea theme.
- Children asking questions about distance to other countries may lead to a theme about airports and transport.
- Whilst reading a story about dinosaurs, children ask what a volcano is. This then leads to a geography based theme centered on volcanoes.
- Observing children role playing a traditional story such as Jack and the Beanstalk, could lead to a fairy tale theme.
- Asking children to bring in their favourite story could lead to a Book Week.
- Learning that a child in your class has a new baby sister could lead to a theme about babies and changes as we grow older.

This list could be endless. Observations open the door to many opportunities and children then feel involved and responsible for their own learning. They are much more enthusiastic and interested and learn much more than if a theme was prescribed for them.

When a theme is decided, practitioners are able to create a plan which will inspire the children. Reflections of children's learning can include 'What do they already know?' and 'What do they want to learn?'.

This forms the basis of the plan and learning objectives and activities can fit around the theme. Links can be made to a learning objective from national guidelines and frameworks and are important and require careful planning. Each activity can be valuable and give children different experiences. At the end of a theme, it can be evaluated appropriately. The children can be asked 'What have you learned?' and the practitioner can gain understanding and useful information about their progress from the children themselves. This can often lead to another theme the children are interested in or it could inspire children to ask a question as the theme has motivated them to be interested in something else.

LEARNING ABOUT THE WIDER COMMUNITY

If something occurs, in the news, nationally or globally, children are often exposed to this and want to learn more about it. Duffy (2008: 148) observes: 'The local environment is part of the children's everyday experience'. She continues, 'Exploring the local environment and sharing the creative and imaginative representations of adults in the community inducts children into their own culture and exposure to the representations of other communities introduces them to cultures other than their own' (2008: 147). Children overhear things and can be inquisitive about natural disasters they have seen on the news such as earthquakes or volcanoes. They also mention things which may not be desirable to talk about such as kidnapping and abduction. Flexibility is sometimes required as planning may need to be put aside to discuss or research such events. Children are generally interested and keen to learn and it can be extremely important to reassure them if they are unsettled by events. Researching volcanoes or earthquakes may take a few days and completely take over a weekly timetable but it is important children learn about global events and understand things which can change the world we live in. Children might ask about other events in the news such as a pending election or a celebration. By talking about these things, insights are developed into the world around them and their place within it. This method of planning can seem daunting at first.

Asking children to contribute to the corporate life of the provision, such as a school, can be rewarding. It is interesting for them to participate and have a say in events in the setting. Children respond very well to initiatives such as a School Council. They have an open-mindedness which allows them to think outside the box and their suggestions are often the most creative. Children can be involved in charity events, competitions and other school activities as it gives them a sense of importance and maturity which prepares them for the rest of their education.

Networks of early years professionals can form bonds for support and sharing of new ideas and initiatives. These can be arranged at a mutually convenient time, perhaps once a term, and can enhance discussions of practice. An agenda can be arranged to cover issues which are relevant to the participants, speakers invited or links made to wider networks such as TACTYC: The Association for the Professional Development of Early Years Educators.

PROGRESS

Progress is a very important part of development. Without progress, nothing changes or develops and everything stays the same. Children progress at a very fast rate at a young age and the changes seen over a year can often be quite astounding. In the first year of school, many children learn how to read and write. This is not the case for all, as development differs for different children at different rates and stages. There are, however, children who develop very quickly and it can amaze those involved in the child's development, just how much progress children can make in a year.

PRAISE

Praise is an important part of developing a positive outlook and self-esteem. Children need to feel proud of themselves, and they respond so well to praise.

A lot of praise can sometimes appear to be over the top, but it can never be over-used. A reward system, of any shape or form, is essential for maintaining a calm and happy classroom. Children need to know the boundaries for the setting. Creating a celebration of success is important for all children, no matter how small the progress. It is this that encourages children to try harder and value their efforts and achievements.

Children can be excited and interested, promoting a positive outlook about themselves. Praising children on a regular basis from the start promotes good behaviour and gives them positive attention. Getting to know the children and their interests shows them that we want to find out about them as individuals and care about them.

It is interesting to see the reaction of older children entering a Foundation Stage classroom. Children in all years in the primary school often find themselves entering a Foundation Stage classroom for many reasons and they always react in the same way. They are inspired, interested and captivated by the different activities and areas of learning. The question 'Can I play?' might be heard. When hearing they may spend some time in the classroom, the joy on their faces is quite intriguing. They resort to being young children again and would spend a significant amount of time in the sand, play dough, role play area and construction and art areas. They particularly enjoy the freedom and opportunity to explore. This joy and enthusiasm surely only tells us one thing? Children enjoy being children and like to be hands on. Surely there is a place for this in all years of primary education?

 Questions for Discussion

What is it about the learning environment in an early years setting that older children find interesting?
Could this approach be developed throughout the primary age phase?

CONCLUSION

In my opinion, there are key pieces that are needed to complete the jigsaw of a successful Foundation Stage Unit. These are: imagination, safety, comfort, happiness, friendships and inspirational learning. If these things are solid in a unit, then a learning environment can be created which will inspire and motivate young children. It can be exhausting, difficult, stressful but extremely rewarding. Play is vital for a child's development and we can provide them with experiences to stretch and develop creativity.

Further Reading

Morrison, G.S. (2009) *Early Childhood Education Today*. New Jersey: Pearson Education.

Useful Website

www.education.gov.uk/publications

References

Bruce, T. (2006) *Developing Learning in Early Childhood: 0–8 Years*. London: Sage.

Duffy, B. (2008) *Supporting Creativity and Imagination in Early Years*. Maidenhead: Open University Press.

Fisher, J. (2002) *The Foundations of Learning*. Buckingham: Open University Press.

Nutbrown, C. (2006) *Threads of Thinking: Young Children Learning and the Role of Early Education* (3rd edn.) London: Paul Chapman.

Nutbrown, C. (2011) *Threads of Thinking: Schemas and Young Children's Thinking* (4th edn.) London: Sage.

Watkins, C. (2006) *Classrooms as Learning Communities: What's in it for Schools?* London: Routledge.

THE SOCIAL CONTEXT

Pat Beckley

Learning objectives

- To identify important aspects of the social context
- To consider issues to promote an inclusive early years environment
- To discuss ways to develop provision as a part of the community
- To consider the child as a member of the wider community

This chapter considers how to help children build relationships and manage emotions, supporting those who are learning English as an additional language, newly arrived families and those from the Traveller community. It provides suggestions to support visits and visitors to enhance an holistic approach. Consideration is given to the child as a member of the wider community and shared dialogue fostering a child's social construction of the world.

THE SOCIAL CULTURAL CONTEXT

There are many definitions about what culture is. According to Sutherland et al. (2005: 6) culture represents 'core understandings of a group of people who are in communication with each other, and who share, knowingly or not, some common sense of values and purposes'. Fukuyama (1996: 41) believes culture concerns the 'highly developed ethical rules by which people live, nurtured through repetition, tradition and example'. However, Wagner (cited in Bray et al. 2007) argues that 'culture is not a fixed entity that shapes the lives of the individual', while Mason (cited in Bray et al. 2007) claims that 'Culture functions more as a productive force constituted by a relatively amorphous aggregation of loosely bounded factors that both influence the lives of the individuals who share in it and are influenced by those individuals'. Therefore, culture is not static, but evolves and changes. Williams (cited in Bray et al. 2007) states that culture is 'a particular way of life, whether of a people, a period, a group, or humanity in general'. Keesing (cited in Bray et al. 2007) develops the symbolic nature of culture as 'concerned with actions, ideas and artefacts which individuals in the tradition learn, share and value'.

SOCIAL INTERACTIONS

Trevarthen's (1977) focus on the communication of babies during their first six months of life concluded that a pattern of development in social behaviour was forming in all five infants in the study (cited in Nutbrown, 2006: 7). The importance of the family as a child's influential social context is discussed in Chapter 3 on partnerships with parents. Theories of learning include consideration of children's cognitive development through social interactions. This includes children's constructions of concepts and meaning through their experiences in the early years setting. It is aided by children's social interactions with others, including their peers and concerned adults. Johnston and Nahmad-Williams (2009: 208) state: 'The emergence of language plays a large part in early social development by copying others and recognising sounds, and developing independence through making our needs and intentions known to others'. These interactions promote children's thinking and reasoning. The Early Years Foundation Stage framework encourages practitioners to devise a learning environment which supports children's interactions through child-initiated activities. Children's interests can be used to provide the basis of their learning through the planned observations of play. Play can be a wonderful way of promoting children's social development. They are able to consolidate their understandings of happenings in the 'real' world through role play of events, act out scenarios of imaginary plots adapted from life events, interact with constructions of play and learn to negotiate the give and take of working with others. They learn how to react appropriately in different situations and the consequences of their actions and reactions for others.

📁 **Case Study**

Two young girls enjoyed playing with dolls in the role play area and choosing tasks such as jigsaws, building blocks, playing on the outdoor climbing equipment or emergent writing. They enjoyed each other's company. Both girls were only children. When they disagreed and wanted to have their own way they were heard to argue 'I will never play or speak to you again'. This assertion lasted a few minutes before they realised they would not get their own way and needed to negotiate to take their play further and come to some agreement. They quickly stopped complaining about each other to maintain their friendship and had learned of their own volition that compromise works.

The culture of the setting has an impact on the attitudes, values and ways of behaving of those participating in it. This is particularly important in early years as it can have a lasting impact on attitudes and values gained and developed throughout the child's later life. This perception is used as part of the reflections in Chapter 16.

THE SETTING AS A VENUE FOR HOLISTIC PROVISION

To promote an holistic approach there needs to be an awareness of children's needs, both their immediate ones and those reflecting academic progress. To do this a suitable, happy and secure environment has to be created. Learning, underpinned by the principles of a unique child, enabling environments and positive relationships, uses the six areas of learning and development to support children's progress, that is: personal, social and emotional development; communication, language and literacy; problem solving, reasoning and numeracy; knowledge and understanding of the world; physical development; and creative development. Transition should be carefully considered to ensure children's first experiences of education and care in settings other than home are happy ones. This helps children find transition to school smooth and fosters ease in dealing with new experiences. Inclusive practice should support equality of opportunities for all, including provision for those with special educational needs, those for whom English is an additional language or those who are gifted and talented. Tracking children's learning progress, through observations and assessments can initiate suitable resources when needed. The provision can be part of on-going reflections and evaluations of practice. Effective collaboration with other agencies and disciplines and those involved with children's learning in the community is important. Close collaboration with parents supports this work. This should be achieved on a daily basis if possible, through routines and procedures. In this way appreciation of the child as a unique person can be established and independence encouraged. This can enable the child to grow in confidence and competence as ideas and skills are practised and developed. Children can grow in a safe and secure environment, in what for most will be their first experience of a prolonged separation from home.

INCLUSIVE PRACTICE

The provision should be carefully considered to ensure inclusive practice is taking place. It is easy to become familiar with existing practice and miss ways of inclusion or be unaware that certain practices might not be inclusive, for example the omission of bilingual information, or pictorial information for those with English as an additional language.

DIVERSITY

Children learn the values and cultural mores of those around them through interacting, talking, gaining feedback about events and experiences and observing people and the community in which they live.

However, expecting children to be supported in an early years environment simply through immersion in their surroundings is not enough. Settings need to adapt their provision to involve and make welcome all who are there. Further discussions concerning diversity issues can be found in Chapter 7.

AN HOLISTIC APPROACH IN THE SOCIAL CONTEXT

International drivers highlight a broad, or holistic, approach towards learning.

> [The] 'holistic ideology values the whole child and endeavours to understand each young child as an individual within the context of his or her family, community and culture. With this approach, professionals endeavour to be sensitive and responsive to all of a child's needs and aspects of development – that is physical, intellectual, social, emotional, cultural, moral and spiritual'. (Woods, 2005: x)

Petrie (2005: 294) suggests 'there is a growing awareness of the "whole" child or young person, rather than the child as the output of the formal curriculum.' To enable individuals to cope with future challenges, skills such as self-reliance and creative thinking will be necessary. This inner resourcefulness will enable individuals to access new technologies and innovations, whilst having the social skills to disseminate them and work with others. Life-long learning would be part of this process.

These are laudable aims. However, there are different interpretations as to how an holistic approach can be achieved. Vadeboncoeur states that 'throughout the twentieth century, two competing views of child development' have been prevalent (quoted in Richardson 1997: 15). One considers it important to 'educate the individual child in a manner which supports the child's interests and needs', while a second concerns a 'social transformation and the reconstruction of society aligned with democratic ideals'. These differences influence how an holistic approach could be implemented.

Waller (2005: 59) contends: 'There are multiple and diverse childhoods and in order to study childhood one has to consider a range of perspectives.' Nativism stems from the belief that a child has innate capabilities while children learn from an appropriate environment. Empiricism incorporates the notion of a child being rather passive in their learning with a professional delivering the appropriately devised learning environment. This includes an instructivist approach with an emphasis 'on preparing for school and focusing on literacy … aiming for equality of educational opportunity and the means to improve later education'. (McQuail et al. 2003: 14) This approach is taken 'where early childhood services for children 3–6 are seen as the initial stage of schooling' (McQuail et al 2003: 14). Instructivism argues that children should be instructed in predetermined facts to enable them to progress in their learning. In a constructivist approach early childhood is seen as a stage in its own right, with children viewed as competent learners and co-constructors of their learning.

> [Constructivism] acknowledges that children are born with cognitive capabilities and potential, and sees each child constructing knowledge and developing through cognitive activity in interaction with his/her environment. Children create their own meaning and understanding, combining what they already know and believe to be true with new experiences. (Woods 2005: 5)

Social constructivist views emphasise the need for children to use social interactions with their peers and adults to formulate constructions of their world and develop their concepts. The inclusion and pursuit of one of these learning theories in early years settings has major implications for the learning and development of the child. Through a devised strategy a child gains an understanding of the world in which he/she is located. Brannen and Moss (2003: 37) state 'Young children are viewed as active subjects with rights and voice, members of a social group and located both in the family and the wider society'. Therefore the strategy used in the setting is crucial for the way in which children respond to the world around them.

ALBERT BANDURA (1925–)

Bandura was born in Canada. He became a psychologist and is known as the originator of social learning theory and the theory of self-efficacy. He is also responsible for the influential 1961 Bobo Doll experiment. This concerned a study he conducted with three groups of nursery children. They observed a film which showed a plastic doll called Bobo being hit with a mallet. Each group of nursery children viewed a different ending. One saw where the behaviour was rewarded, another where it was punished and another where nothing was done at all. The children were then allowed to play with the doll and their behaviour observed. Their behaviour demonstrated a higher likelihood of aggressive behaviour towards the doll if they themselves had observed a reward given for aggressive behaviour or nothing was done about it. The children were responding to their perceived views of what was thought to be appropriate, valued behaviour.

CONSTRUCTIVIST AND SOCIAL CONSTRUCTIVIST THEORIES

Piaget (1896–1980) believed children construct their meanings and make sense of the world through their constructions from their experiences. This is discussed further in Chapter 2 on theories of learning.

Vygotsky (1896–1934) was born in Russia (Belarus). He graduated from Moscow State University in 1917. At the Institute of Psychology and other educational, research and clinical institutions in Russia he worked extensively on ideas about cognitive development. He died in 1934 in Moscow of tuberculosis.

Vygotsky believed that social interaction leads children to values and beliefs that reflect those interactions and those of the society or culture they represent. An aspect of play that Vygotsky referred to was the development of social rules that can be seen, for example, when children play house and adopt the roles of different family members. Vygotsky cites an example of two sisters playing at being sisters. The rules of behaviour between them that go unnoticed in daily life are consciously acquired through play.

As well as social rules, the child acquires what we now refer to as self-regulation. For example, when a child stands at the starting line of a running race, she may well desire to run immediately so as to reach the finish line first, but her knowledge of the social rules surrounding the game and her desire to enjoy the game enable her to regulate her initial impulse and wait for the start signal.

Vygotsky developed a socio-cultural theory which was based on the notion that children internalise the ideas and beliefs of the adults and peers they interact with, using language to develop thinking and cognitive skills to make sense of the world. For example, a baby learns the meaning of signs through interaction with its main care-givers, such as crying or gurgling to get what is wanted. How verbal sounds can be used to conduct social interaction is learned through this activity, and the child begins to utilise, build, and develop this ability to communicate. Vygotsky considered language in thoughts differed from spoken language. Speaking developed along two lines, the line of social communication and the line of inner speech, by which the child mediates and regulates their activity through their thoughts, which in turn are mediated by the semiotics (the meaningful signs) of inner speech.

BEHAVIOURISM

There are a number of behaviour theories, some of which are described in this section.

Konrad Lorenz (1903–1989)

Some animals are attached or imprinted to the first thing they see after birth and will follow it. Lorenz demonstrated that ducklings could be imprinted to the first thing they saw, which was himself. This process was irreversible.

Ivan Pavlov (1849–1936)

Pavlov was a famous Russian physiologist and is notable for his theory of classical conditioning which is a form of associative learning. The typical procedure for inducing classical conditioning involves presentations of a neutral stimulus along with a stimulus of some significance. The most famous example of classical conditioning involved the salivary conditioning of Pavlov's dogs.

B.F. Skinner (1904–1990)

Skinner was an American psychologist. He received a PhD from Harvard in 1931 and remained there as a researcher until 1936. While at Harvard, B.F. Skinner invented the operant conditioning chamber to measure responses of organisms, which were most often rats and pigeons, and their orderly interactions with the environment. He used positive and negative feedback to gauge responses. He invented the operant conditioning chamber, innovated his own philosophy of science and founded his own school of experimental research psychology.

Skinner suggested that any age-appropriate skill can be taught using five principles to promote learning:

1. Give the learner immediate feedback.
2. Break down the task into small steps.
3. Repeat the directions as many times as possible.
4. Work from the most simple to the most complex tasks.
5. Give positive reinforcement.

Thorleif Schjelderup-Ebbe (1894–1982)

Schjelderup-Ebbe was a Norwegian zoologist who described the pecking order of hens in his PhD dissertation of 1921. The work in his dissertation was partly based on his observations of his own chickens that he had recorded since the age of 10. The dominance hierarchy of chickens and other birds that he studied led him to the observation that these birds had established the order in which individuals would be allowed to get to food while others would have to wait for their turn.

Clark L. Hull (1884–1952)

Hull was an American psychologist who sought to explain learning and motivation by scientific laws of behaviour. He is also known for his work in drive theory. Hull's model concerns the needs of organisms to achieve goals for survival value. Deprivation of the goals creates deprivation which in turn creates a need. Behaviour is driven to satisfy the need and achieve the goal.

Urie Bronfenbrenner (1971–2005) and Ecological Systems Theory

Bronfenbrenner was a Russian-American psychologist, known for developing an ecological systems theory. He was the co-founder of the Head Start programme in America for disadvantaged pre-school children.

His ecological systems theory contains four types of nested systems. He called these the *microsystem* (such as the family); the *mesosystem* (which is two microsystems in interaction); the *exosystem* (external environments which indirectly influence development, for example, parental workplace); and the *macrosystem* (the larger socio-cultural context). He later added a fifth system, called the *chronosystem* (the evolution of the external systems over time).

AN EFFECTIVE SOCIAL CONTEXT

Social development occurs when children learn to live with others in a social environment. Therefore, consideration needs to be given to ways of promoting an effective social context in the early years to help children thrive and support each other's well-being. This requires those involved in the organisation of the provision to plan for aspects which concern this outlook. The provision should consider children's prior experiences. Have links been made with other providers in the neighbourhood to share good practice and liaise about children? This is particularly relevant if children experience a number of different providers, such as private childcare arrangements, private daycare or nurseries, nursery school, Children's Centre, nursery, reception, early years admissions or Key Stage One class in a school. Activities to promote liaison early in a child's development can be organised, through, for example, home visits, family learning sessions or parent /carer toddler groups.

When in the setting those involved in its running can devise ways to ensure the social context is continually being reviewed to assess whether changes need to be made to accommodate changing requirements. This can be achieved in a variety of ways, for example team work and sharing ideas, respectful responses to views and values held, mistakes viewed as learning opportunities (with no fear of ridicule) professional development to assimilate findings into practice and a commitment to reflection and reviewing performance to bring about change and progression in practice. Doyle and Smith (1999: 65) suggest that while the aims of the provision may change 'the fundamental purpose remains the same. Educators should be working so that all may share a common life'. They feel that this should contain:

- Mutual respect and a concern for others' needs
- Readiness to take and share responsibility
- Commitment to conversation and community
- Knowledge of the issues and situations facing them
- Particular skills.

Practitioners should be prepared to share their strengths as part of the strength of the setting. This is developed to benefit the children and form personal celebrations of achievement. Decisions should be made through agreed guidelines and procedures, notifying appropriate staff in a meaningful way which enhances the smooth running of the facility.

Children's voice plays a part in this. Reflections on practice, besides concerns for individual children's progress, can incorporate the well-being of groups of children and how they can interact effectively together. Children can develop their social awareness through interactions and inclusion within the social environment and learning to live amicably within it. It is often said that a provision can exude an atmosphere or ethos which is apparent in the first few minutes of entering the setting. This has a profound effect on those working there and the children who attend, as well as influencing new arrivals in the community or visitors to the facility. It is a crucial aspect to consider and should be collectively thought about to ascertain an honest and realistic picture of the atmosphere in your setting. It is easy to only see the positive aspects, or points which might be sympathetic personally, but to really make appropriate improvements a reliable audit needs to be taken and issues addressed to provide a worthwhile action plan. A supportive atmosphere can be one where stakeholders are appropriately challenged, develop their learning and experience, feel valued, look outwards for new initiatives and experiences, value others and have the children's interests and wellbeing at the heart of all they do. This atmosphere would quickly become apparent to any visitor coming into the setting and helps those involved to enjoy and be enthusiastic about their time spent there. Specific strategies can be used to promote this ethos, for example bi-lingual posters to welcome children and their parents/carers as they enter the building. It is also apparent in slightly hidden ways, such as care taken with resources around the setting which have been maintained well or children's on-going models or creations stored or displayed to indicate their importance and valued as part of their learning process. The organisation of furniture is also a factor. If cupboards are communally used and resources accessed collaboratively, it reflects the ethos of the setting where practitioners share and cooperate.

Case Study

In one setting each adult was responsible for an area of the provision, according to their interests. Team work ensured that all areas were covered. Resources for the individual areas were determined by the person responsible, who devised a plan for the purchase of new items, costing them and assessing when they could be purchased. These plans were shared at team meetings with open discussions about costs, which areas had priority for funding due to needs, changes to plan, and overall directions for the setting to take. The individual responsible for an aspect of the provision also maintained that area and was accountable for it.

Visitors coming to help in the setting were given an option to support an aspect of the provision, depending on their skills or interests, for example a particular parent helper was gifted in retelling stories. She agreed to do a number of recordings of stories much loved by the children in the setting to enable children to access and listen to them in the reading area or include them as part of a shared home/setting partnership scheme where storysacks, incorporating the recordings of the stories inside, could be borrowed. This was a positive experience for all concerned: the storyteller, who enjoyed having her skills utilised, the staff, and the children who valued the recordings which enabled them to listen to their favourite story when they wished. It also encouraged children to make their own recordings of stories they enjoyed.

Question for Discussion

What strategies can be implemented in a setting to promote children's thinking and ideas and enable them to be heard as valued members of the community?

THE WIDER SOCIAL CONTEXT

As has been discussed earlier, culture is not a static state but one which is constantly changing and adapting to new and evolving happenings. 'Cultures in societies, communities and organisations are constructed by their members and manifested in the symbolic, practical, linguistic and interpersonal interactions of their members and in the social structures that are constructed, upheld and modified by them' (Busher, 2006: 6). Interactions within an early years setting occur within a collection of groups, such as children and different groups of children, children and adults, adults to adults, staff and parents /carers, staff and governors all creating their own networks. Around these the culture for the provision pervades to support those living within it and the learning and development that takes place there.

This culture, including ways of working, interactions, routines, procedures can provide a powerful sense of belonging to those involved and part of the supportive provision. Members of the provision can also reflect different wider social contexts as individual members belong to different groups in the wider community. Cultures 'are fluid, forever changing as people move in and out of organisations and the formal and informal groups within them, and as change occurs in response to internal and external pressures' (Busher, 2006: 88).

The wider social context can be considered to promote an outward looking organisation that responds well to the changing needs of the children and the locality in which it is based. This requires an ability to be aware of the locality and have some understanding of how it works. The provision can then respond appropriately to needs, for example of timings of the sessions or can utilise skills and opportunities which might arise to benefit the children. This could take the form of links with a local bakery, restaurant or garden centre.

VISITS AND VISITORS

It is essential for the safeguarding of children to ensure visitors to the provision have CRB checks. The adults in the setting are responsible for the safety of the children. When visitors come to the setting they could be perceived by the children as being trusted and approachable, both while in the provision and outside. It is therefore essential to be satisfied, through appropriate checks, of a person's reliability and trustworthiness in the presence of children.

Visits can form part of the ongoing routines for the setting. Risk assessments need to be carefully written. Outings can include explorations in the neighbourhood, such as visits to the park or local shops, observations of simple plans of the area, a religious centre, museum, natural area, farm or countryside area. Some settings plan outings to 'natural' areas once a week, possibly drawing inspiration from the Scandinavian model where the use of the outdoor, natural environment is well known. This use of the outdoor environment has a profound impact on children's development and welfare. Individuals respond to the natural environment in many ways, but it does seem to influence children's emotional well-being. Children explore and investigate, making their own meaning and understanding of the world around them, scrutinising natural features and learning about life. They become assured in their constructions and social constructions of their world. In an increasingly global world these abilities could become of vital importance if children are to meet future demands and changes, where communities are interconnected and share resources.

THE CHILD AS A MEMBER OF THE WIDER COMMUNITY

The provision can be promoted as an integral part of the community. This supports the notion of helping children to feel like valued members of the setting. Nutbrown (2006: 6) suggests that 'worries about children's safety and urban living now inhibit the freedom of children to explore their world'. She continues 'adults who wish to support children's learning now often bring the stuff of the world into safe, defined but falsely created boundaries'. Fears of health and safety issues often make practitioners err on the side of caution and keep children within perceived 'safe' environments. In an age of litigations and individual blame, practitioners might choose to have the children not taking risks in their learning or participate in a learning event outdoors, for example visit a farm. This is a contentious issue. Of course, it is up to the adults concerned to undertake risk assessments and not expose children to unnecessary dangers. However, sometimes withdrawing opportunities for children to take risks themselves, for example exploring a woodland area, can spoil the possibility for young children to find out for themselves what they are capable of, including assessing the associated risks. Taking measured risks helps them to become aware of their strengths and limitations, so that they do not undertake too difficult a task based on their own perceptions of the situation, rather than relying on someone else to say whether a task is possible or not. This supports their learning through their childhood, helping them to understand the nature of risks involved and to become 'streetwise'.

A hands-on approach to experiences in the wider community also helps children to appreciate the wonders of our world! A sand tray might be great fun but it does not compare with the sights, sounds and smells of a beach. A few carefully chosen natural artefacts might interest the children but not in the same way the exuberance of a run through the trees on a summer's day might.

A NATIONAL CONTEXT

National policies form the framework and guidelines for activities deployed in the early years settings. These can underpin the activities planned and the principles guiding this planning. They provide the framework, often statutory, for the work occurring in the settings. This influences the culture of the setting, for example the Early Years Foundation Stage Profile results can alter activities through a desire by practitioners to fulfil the perceived need to provide evidence for profile points achieved by the children. The work achieved in the setting, however, depends on the context of the provision. As has been considered earlier in this chapter, practitioners should have their children at the heart of the planning and respond to their needs, accessing resources around them. It is up to the practitioners to use their professional expertise, experience and judgement to interpret the national guidelines in appropriate ways for their setting. This is no inconsiderable undertaking! There is a wealth of excellent practice and practitioners are fortunate that if they are unsure of an aspect they can contact colleagues in the locality who will support their endeavours. Important resources and sources of information can be found in: differing networks, interactions and communications with families, other, early years settings, the local community, professional associations, and national agendas and initiatives, as well as global influences. The changing challenges for early years learning and development are reflected in the dynamic social context it is part of.

Further Reading

Askew, S. and Carnell, E. (1998) *Transforming Learning: Individual and Global Change*. London: Cassell Publishers.

Forman, E. A., Minick, N. and Addison Stone, C. (1993) *Contexts for Learning: Sociocultural Dynamics in Children's Development*. Oxford: Oxford University Press.

Light, P. and Littleton, K. (1999) *Social Processes in Children's Learning*. Cambridge: Cambridge University Press.

Moyles, J. (2010) *Thinking about Play: Developing a Reflective Approach*. Maidenhead: Open University Press.

Useful Website

www.tactyc.org.uk
This is the website of the Association for the Professional Development of Early Years Educators and covers a range of issues pertinent to early years provision.

References

Brannen, J. and Moss, P. (2003) *Rethinking Children's Care*. Buckingham: Open University Press.

Bray, M., Adamson, B. and Mason, M. (eds) (2007) *Comparative Education Research: Approaches and Methods*. Hong Kong: Comparative Education Research Centre.

Busher, H. (2006) *Understanding Educational Leadership: People, Power and Culture*. Maidenhead: Open University Press.

Doyle, M. E. and Smith, M. K. (1999) *Born and Bred? Leadership, Heart and Informal Education*. London: YMCA George Williams College for the Rank Foundation.

Fukuyama, F. (1996) *Trust*. London: Penguin Books.

Johnston, J. and Nahmad-Williams, L. (2009) *Early Childhood Studies*. Harlow: Pearson Education Limited.

McQuail, S., Mooney, A., Cameron, C., Candappa, M., Moss, P. and Petrie, P. (2003) *Early Years and Childcare International Evidence Project*. London: Thomas Coram Research Unit, Institute of Education.

Nutbrown, C. (2006) *Threads of Thinking: Young Children Learning and the Role of Early Education*. (3rd edn). London: Sage.

Nutbrown, C. (2011) *Threads of Thinking Schemas and Young Children's Learning* (4th edn). London: Sage.

Petrie, P. (2005) 'Extending Pedagogy', *Journal of Education for Teaching*, 31(4): 293–6.

Richardson, V. (ed.) (1997) *Constructivist Teacher Education*. London: Falmer Press.

Sutherland, R., Claxton, G. and Pollard, A. (2003) *Learning and Teaching: Where World Views Meet*. Stoke-on-Trent: Trentham Books Ltd.

Waller, T. (ed.) (2005) *An Introduction to Early Childhood: A Multidisciplinary Approach*. London: Sage.

Woods, T. (1999) *Beginning Postmodernity*. Manchester: Manchester University Press.

MULTI-AGENCY WORKING

Anita Soni

Learning objectives

- To understand what multi-agency working is and how it relates to integrated working
- To consider the reasons for undertaking multi-agency working
- To have an understanding of the historical background to multi-agency working
- To consider how multi-agency working relates to the Early Years Foundation Stage (EYFS)
- To identify the skills and knowledge needed for multi-agency working
- To examine the challenges and dilemmas within multi-agency working
- To reflect on how transition can be supported by multi-agency working

WHAT IS MULTI-AGENCY WORKING?

It is important to begin by having a clear understanding of what multi-agency working is. Most recently, the drive to multi-agency working was led by the Every Child Matters, 2003, agenda. This agenda sought to ensure that agencies within Children's Services work collaboratively around a preventative agenda. Therefore multi-agency working is stated to be: '... an effective way of supporting children and families with additional needs and helping to secure real improvements in their life outcomes' (Every Child Matters, 2006a: 1).

Multi-agency working falls within the umbrella term of 'integrated working' which is defined by the Children's Workforce Development Council (CWDC) (2008: 2) as: '... when everyone supporting children and young people work(s) together effectively to put the child at the centre, meet their needs and improve their lives'. As a result, multi-agency working sits alongside other integrated working tools, guidance documents and approaches such as the Common Assessment Framework (CAF), information sharing and the lead professional role.

The Every Child Matters fact sheet on multi-agency working (2006a) states there are many different ways of approaching multi-agency working. These can range from a group of practitioners deciding informally to work together to support a child or family through to a large scale venture of different services coming together as in a Sure Start local programme or a Children's Centre. The fact sheet suggests these different ways of multi-agency working can be grouped into three distinct models:

1. Multi-agency panel

   - Practitioners remain employed by their home agency
   - Practitioners meet as a panel or network on a regular basis to discuss children who may benefit from multi-agency input
   - In some panels casework is carried out by panel members and in other instances the panel takes a strategic role employing key workers to lead on casework.

   Examples of the multi-agency panel include Youth Inclusion and Support Panels (YISP) and Pre-school Special Educational Need (SEN) Panels.

2. Multi-agency team

   - The practitioners are seconded or recruited into the team
   - The team has a leader and the team work to common goals and purposes
   - Practitioners may remain linked to their home agency through supervision and training.

   Examples of multi-agency teams include Behaviour and Education Support Teams (BESTs) and Youth Offending Teams (YOTs).

3. Integrated service

   - A range of separate services share a common location and work together in a collaborative way
   - Visible service hub for service users
   - Has a management structure that facilitates integrated working
   - Commitment by partner providers to fund/facilitate integrated service delivery.

   Examples of integrated services include Sure Start Children's Centres and extended schools that offer access to a range of integrated, multi-agency services.

Multi-agency working is one of the six key areas of skills and knowledge in the Common Core of Skills and Knowledge for the Children's Workforce (CWDC 2005). The Common Core sets out the basic essential skills and knowledge needed by all people, including volunteers, whose work brings them into regular contact with children and young people. This highlights the importance and value placed upon multi-agency working for all practitioners within the Children's Workforce.

Multi-agency working operates at a range of levels, from the policy level that has restructured Children's Services in local authorities, to the agency and individual professional level. It represents a profound shift in the approach to work within the Children's Workforce and has led to many changes at professional, child and family level. This means that all those practitioners who work with children and families have to be prepared to pool resources and knowledge with others, whilst maintaining confidence in their own professional role and being open to other perspectives from other professionals. This is particularly relevant for practitioners who work with children who have additional needs or who are deemed to be at risk from significant harm. This is because these are the children and families most likely to have a range of professionals working with them. Effective multi-agency working means professionals need to:

- Work together
- Have a clear understanding of each others' roles and expertise
- Place the families, the child and the parent/carers, in a central role as equal and active partners in the process of working together.

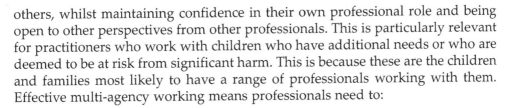

Question for Discussion

Can you think of instances where you have worked within or had contact with one of the three models of multi-agency working?

WHY SHOULD THERE BE MULTI-AGENCY WORKING?

Whilst there are legal imperatives to working within an integrated framework, there is evidence to support the shift to multi-agency working. The Inter-Departmental Childcare Review Delivering for Children and Families (DfES 2002: 32–3) found that: 'an integrated approach, that ensures the joining up of services and disciplines, is a key factor in determining good outcomes for children'.

The Early Support programme is reported to be needed (Early Support website) because research over time in the UK delivered consistent messages about the experience of service provision for families with young disabled children. These families often reported that they find it difficult to:

- Find out about the services that are available to help them
- Make sense of the role of the different agencies and the many different people they meet
- Manage multiple contacts with service providers
- Get professionals to understand their child's needs in the context of the whole family
- Have their own knowledge of their child recognised
- Negotiate a better service where delay and bureaucracy seem to be affecting their child.

These findings have led to the development of Early Support, an approach (including materials and training) that takes a family- and child-centred approach to working with families of children with complex health needs and/ or a disability.

Within universal services, Sylva et al. (2003) report from the Effective Provision of Pre-school Education Project (EPPE) that the integration of services contributes to high quality education and care for children aged three to five years. The EPPE research reported that certain types of pre-school, namely LEA nursery schools, nursery classes and 'combined centres', delivered the best outcomes and higher attainment in primary schools. This combined approach, where education and care are combined, was one of the primary drivers towards the establishment of the Early Years Foundation Stage where education and care are combined within one document.

In the Early Excellence Centre evaluation, Bertram et al. (2002) identified the following benefits of providing integrated services:

- Services being more easily available to parents if they are on one site – especially in poor and disadvantaged areas
- Breaking the cycle of poverty
- Providing diversity and more choices of services in a non-judgemental way
- Benefits for children in terms of enhanced social and emotional competence, and cognitive development.

This research provides an evidence base to advocate integrated and multi-agency working.

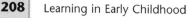 **Question for Discussion**

Reflect upon times where you feel use of a multi-agency model may have benefited the child or family involved.

HISTORY OF MULTI-AGENCY WORKING

The idea of effective multi-agency working is not new. Multi-agency working and the integration of services for children and families have been central across all disciplines including Health, Social Care and Education for over a decade. Within Health, the Health Act (1999) set out requirements for the National Health Service to strengthen partnerships with the Local Authority. Similarly the report *Making a Difference: Strengthening the Nursing, Midwifery and Health Visitor Contribution to Health and Welfare* (DoH 1999) advocated for midwives to expand their role. A similar approach was advocated within Social Services with the White Paper *Modernising Social Services* (DoH 1998) which pushed for a more effective co-ordination of services for children. Within early years, Early Years Development Partnerships (DfEE 1998) were set up to expand education and care at local authority level and local Sure Start programmes were established to narrow the gap for disadvantaged families and children through joined up services.

The Green Paper *Every Child Matters* (2003) was a significant driver for integrating services for children and families that built upon the previous legislation. The Green Paper was the response to Lord Laming's report of the inquiry into the death of Victoria Climbié. Every Child Matters has four key themes:

1. To increase the focus on supporting families and parents/carers
2. To ensure the appropriate intervention was given to children before crisis point and to prevent children falling between different services
3. To address the issues identified by Lord Laming about weak accountability of services and poor integration between agencies
4. To ensure that those who work with children are valued, rewarded and trained.

As a result Every Child Matters legislation was introduced to restructure children's services and give local authorities the primary responsibility to deliver integrated services to children and families. Multi-agency working is stated to be: '... an effective way of supporting children and families with additional needs and helping to secure real improvements in their life outcomes' (Every Child Matters 2006a: 1).

Government departments also began working together to produce guidance. An example of this is 'Together from the Start – Practical Guidance for Professionals Working with Disabled Children (Birth to Third Birthday) and their Families' (DfES and DoH 2003). This guidance, issued jointly by the Department of Health and the Department for Education and Skills, contains key themes including:

- Co-ordination of multi-agency support for families
- Better information for families and services
- Improved professional knowledge and skills
- Partnership across agencies and geographical boundaries.

It was this guidance that informed the Early Support programme. 'Together from the Start' (DfES and DoH 2003) identified that whilst there were examples of effective service delivery and partnership working, many parents of young disabled children identified inconsistent patterns of service provision and a lack of co-ordination between multiple service providers.

The Early Support materials, training and approach are intended to help families by:

- Taking a family-centred approach
- Giving materials that can aid with the co-ordination of services
- Supplying a range of background information booklets on a range of difficulties and disabilities

- Providing standard information about what to expect from services
- Encouraging partnership working.

 Questions for Discussion

What do you think are the difficulties and strengths of multi-agency working?
Can you think of other tools that support multi-agency working, for example, Individual Education Plans (IEPs), care plans?

MULTI-AGENCY WORKING IN THE EARLY YEARS FOUNDATION STAGE

The Early Years Foundation Stage (DfES, 2007b) states on 'The Wider Context' card that practitioners need to work together across services to help children achieve the Every Child Matters outcomes. This places a responsibility on all practitioners in early years settings to be able to engage in effective multi-agency working with other settings and professionals, and with individuals and groups in the community to support children's progress and development. The Early Years Foundation Stage makes it clear that multi-agency working is a key aspect in delivering improved outcomes for all children in their learning and development. This is emphasised within the commitment on card 3.4 of 'The Wider Context': 'Working in partnership with other settings, other professionals and with individuals and groups in the community supports children's development and progress towards the outcomes of Every Child Matters: being healthy; staying safe; enjoying and achieving; making a positive contribution and economic well-being'.

This card highlights the importance of multi-agency working alongside transitions, continuity and the community. It emphasises that practitioners need to work together across services and gives examples of services that practitioners could engage with, going beyond health, social care and education staff, to include local libraries and artists. The card emphasises the importance of these groups communicating well, listening to all concerned and placing the needs of the children as the primary focus. However, there is also recognition that workers from different professional backgrounds may use different jargon and take differing approaches. It also recognises the challenges that exist in finding sufficient time to fully involve parents in decisions regarding their children.

The EYFS is viewed as being instrumental in creating a greater degree of coherence between the wide range of providers of services to children aged birth to five. The EYFS ties in with the Early Support programme via the information on the CD ROM through links to the materials and the Early Support buttons on the grids for areas for learning and development. These development and learning grids build upon what is printed within the Practice Guidance to offer additional development matters statements, further guidance for 'look, listen and note', effective practice and planning and resourcing. The links between the EYFS and Early Support are vital to create a common language that can be shared by the range of professionals who work with children with additional needs. In addition this is useful to help demonstrate where children are achieving in terms of universal guidance, as assessments on children with additional needs are sometimes conducted using tools not frequently used on typically developing children. It is this form of curriculum-based assessment that is useful to examine children's progress at an individual or group level over time but also in comparison to other individuals and groups.

The in depth article on multi-agency working on the EYFS CD Rom (DfES, 2007) reminds practitioners working in early years of the importance of multi-agency working alongside the difficulties that exist: 'Multi-agency working is … an essential and integral part of early years work. However, multi-agency working can be a challenge to individuals' professionalism …' (DfES 2007b: 2).

Questions for Discussion

Why do you feel multi-agency working is essential but challenging?
When has or could multi-agency working be a challenge to your professionalism?

WHAT ARE THE SKILLS NEEDED FOR MULTI-AGENCY WORKING?

The Children's Workforce Develpment Council identify the following as key areas to consider for effective multi-agency working at an individual level:

> To work successfully on a multi-agency basis you need to be clear about your own role and be aware of the roles of other professionals; you need to be confident about your own standards and targets and respectful of those that apply to other services, actively seeking and respecting the knowledge and input others can make to delivering best outcomes for children and young people. (CWDC 2005: 18)

The skills of multi-agency working are identified as:

1. Communication and teamwork
   - Communicate effectively with other practitioners and professionals by listening and ensuring that you being listened to
   - Appreciate that others may not have the same understanding of professional terms and may interpret abbreviations such as acronyms differently

- Provide timely, appropriate, succinct information to enable other practitioners to deliver their support to the child or young person, parent or carer
- Record, summarise, share and feed back information, using IT skills where necessary to do so
- Work in a team context, forging and sustaining relationships across agencies and respecting the contribution of others working with children, young people and families
- Share experience through formal and informal exchange and work with adults who are parents/carers.

2. Assertiveness

- Be proactive, initiate necessary action and be able and prepared to put forward your own judgements
- Have the confidence to challenge situations by looking beyond your immediate role and asking considered questions
- Present facts and judgements objectively
- Identify possible sources of support within your own working environment
- Judge when you should provide the support yourself and when you should refer to another practitioner or professional.

(CWDC 2005: 18–19)

Questions for Discussion

Which of the skills of multi-agency working do you currently have?
Which of these skills is well developed and which require further development?
How could you further develop these skills?

WHAT KNOWLEDGE IS NEEDED FOR MULTI-AGENCY WORKING?

The knowledge base needed for effective multi-agency working is identified as:

1. Your role and remit

- Know your main job and responsibilities within your working environment
- Know the value and expertise you bring to a team and that are brought by your colleagues.

2. Know how to make queries

- Know your role within different group situations and how you contribute to the overall group process, understanding the value of sharing how you approach your role with other professionals

- Develop your skills and knowledge with training from experts, to minimise the need for referral to specialist services, enabling continuity for the family, child or young person while enhancing your own skills and knowledge
- Have a general knowledge and understanding of the range of organisations and individuals working with children, young people and those caring for them, and be aware of the roles and responsibilities of other professionals.

3. Procedures and working methods

- Know what to do in given cases, for example for referrals or raising concerns
- Know what triggers are for reporting incidents or unexpected behaviour
- Know how to work within your own and other organisational values, beliefs and cultures
- Know what to do when there is an insufficient response from other organisations or agencies, while maintaining a focus on what is in the child or young person's best interests
- Understand the way that partner services operate – their procedures, objectives, role and relationships – in order to be able to work effectively alongside them
- Know the Common Assessment Framework (CAF) and, where appropriate, how to use it.

4. The law, policies and procedures

- Know about the existence of key laws relating to children and young people and where to obtain further information
- Know about employers' safeguarding and health and safety policies and procedures, and how they apply in the wider working environment.

(CWDC 2005: 19–20)

The skills and knowledge listed in this section and the preceding section form a useful foundation for practitioners in the early years to reflect upon when considering their strengths and areas for development within the area of effective multi-agency working.

Question for Discussion

Do you have sufficient and relevant knowledge to support your role in multi-agency working? Find out about the agencies in your locality and the responsibilities and roles of these services.

HOW TO WORK WITHIN A MULTI-AGENCY SERVICE

When working within a multi-agency service, it is suggested that practitioners need to recognise the differences in expectations, language and ethos that may exist in other members of the multi-agency service. There needs to be a willingness to engage in open discussions of these differences in order to assimilate the differing perspectives within the service. It is also important for all members of the multi-agency service to have a common vision for their work with children and young people, and be clear about each individual's role and contribution. Guidance from the Every Child Matters website (www.ecm.gov.uk) suggests working within a multi-agency service is easier when practitioners:

- value the views of others and take them seriously
- treat all members of service with respect
- celebrate the diversity of practice, experience and personality within the service
- are open about their own perspective and practice
- have the resilience to challenge other perspectives and practices in a constructive way
- question, reflect and suggest possible alternatives.

Whilst these guidance points are considered relevant for those working in a multi-agency service, they are also useful for all practitioners to reflect upon when engaging in any type of multi-agency work at an informal or formal level.

BENEFITS OF MULTI-AGENCY WORKING

The benefits of multi-agency working can be difficult to isolate, however research has identified three main advantages of multi-agency working.

1. Multi-agency working improves outcomes for children and families

   Atkinson et al. (2002) reported a range of outcomes for children and families including:

   - Access to a wider range of services or services previously unavailable
   - Easier or quicker access to services or expertise
   - Improved educational attainment or better engagement in education
   - Earlier identification and intervention
   - Better support for parents
   - Children's needs addressed more appropriately
   - Reduced need for more specialist services.

   In addition, within healthcare, Sloper (2004) associated multi-agency working with better patient outcomes. Within multi-agency projects targeting children's mental health, Kurtz and James (2002) reported a reduction in the proportion of those with clinically significant problems and better engagement in schools.

2. Multi-agency working leads to benefits for staff and services

   Fitzgerald (2004) reports that practitioners with backgrounds in traditional, single agencies report high levels of satisfaction with multi-agency working. They report that practitioners find the cross-fertilisation between different agencies stimulating and it also allows a more holistic approach to the needs of the child.

The 'On Track' evaluation identified positive impacts for staff (NFER 2004) that were primarily associated with working within multi-agency teams including:

- Less replication between different service providers
- Better links between service providers and understanding of what the services provide
- Opportunities for professional development and career progression
- More involvement in community involvement
- Increased awareness of different services.

3. Multi-agency working provides what children, young people and families say they want

Families with children with additional needs are likely to be in contact with a range of agencies and professionals. However families do not always understand the roles and responsibilities of the different agencies and professionals, and do not know who to go to for what service, get conflicting advice or may get passed between agencies. Mukherjee et al. (1999) state that families wanted a single point of contact with services and a trusted named person to co-ordinate assessments, information sharing and care pathways to help ensure quicker access to the right kind of support. It is this approach that is supported by effective multi-agency working using integrated working tools such as the CAF, Early Support and lead professional roles.

Question for Discussion

Can you identify any other benefits to multi-agency working?

THE CHALLENGES OF MULTI-AGENCY WORKING

Whilst the value and benefits of multi-agency working have been discussed, it is important to acknowledge the barriers and difficulties faced. Anning (2001) identifies two significant challenges:

1. For practitioners to create new professional identities (who I am) in the new multi-agency services
2. For practitioners to articulate and share their personal and professional knowledge in order to create a new version of knowledge (what I know) for the new ways of working.

In order to meet these challenges within the Early Excellence Centres where practitioners from care and education backgrounds were working together, Anning (2001) emphasises the value of:

- regular meetings for staff to share ideas on how best to work together
- observation and evaluation of each other's practice
- shared decision making about key issues such as purchase of resources and arrangement of furniture.

These key features required time and prioritisation, however importantly they allowed the practitioners to understand each other's perspectives and modify practices in order to create new professional identities and a new version of knowledge.

Chandler (2006) also identifies the following challenges to integrated services at Pen Green that are relevant to multi-agency working:

- Conditions and pay for different agencies varying significantly
- Providing a range of services that parents can access and not be confused by.

Chandler (2006) advocates a well established and commonly held philosophy and ethos, a set of beliefs and values, for effective working within multidisciplinary teams. In addition he highlights the importance of the structures surrounding these teams having policies and procedures that support integrated working. For those within the teams he highlights the need for workers to be empowered and enabled through additional training. In order to improve access for parents he suggests that a clearly identified theoretical framework is shared with parents so that a common language is used by all to further dialogue and understanding. Throughout, the importance of a responsive and reflective approach is encouraged in order to evaluate the effectiveness of work undertaken.

Chandler (2006: 148) states that:

> The agenda for change is complex on many levels, but is also very simple. As long as we remind ourselves of the vision and values upon which our work is based then we can cut through much of the complexity of interdisciplinary and multi-agency work.

The information to support multi-agency and integrated working also focuses on the central importance of having a shared vision and values. The Every Child Matters outcomes offer this shared vision, but it is important that all practitioners in early years understand and own these outcomes in order to work towards them.

 **Question for Discussion**

How easy or challenging do you find or expect to find multi-agency working?

TRANSITIONS AND CONTINUITY

The *Ten Year Strategy for Childcare* (HM Treasury 2004) aimed to give parents greater choice through more flexible working conditions, a wider range of childcare that suited local community needs in terms of affordability and flexibility, and the assurance that all childcare is of a high quality in order to ensure every child achieves the best start in life. Whilst this diverse system of childcare has benefits in that it enables families to pick and mix according to their needs, it also means there are challenges whereby children face both vertical and horizontal transitions. Vertical transitions are transitions that a child may make over time, possibly from a playgroup to a nursery class or from a Children's Centre to a primary school. Horizontal transitions are those that a child may experience within a day or week, for example a child may spend two days with a grandparent and three days with a childminder who may take him to a stay and play group.

The effective practice article on card 3.4 'The Wider Context' (DfES, 2007b) identifies that where experiences are different but complementary there can be a positive contribution to a child's development and learning. However in transitions where children feel unsettled or confused, there is a negative affect on the child's ability to thrive and develop.

Whilst children and babies get stimulated and excited by new events and experiences, these need to be set within a context or setting where they feel secure and able to learn. This sense of security is dependent upon having a close and loving relationship with one carer or a small number of carers at the setting, that is having a key person to depend upon. This sense of security is threatened by change, and times of transition, of either people or setting. However, it is not that settings should be identical, as each offers a unique and valued contribution, but that there should be a shared understanding of what is high quality in early years provision for children. The EYFS provides consistency in what is identified as high quality within each setting. The Every Child Matters framework provides the five outcomes that all professionals working with children are aiming to achieve with all children.

Therefore to maintain a sense of security, there need to be good links between all the settings the child attends, the child and the family. These can be created in the following ways:

- The child's key person at the each setting needs to cooperate with the child's key person at other settings. They need to share information about the child's learning and development, needs and interests. This can be done through meeting in person or by using a communication book. It is important to remember to involve the parent and child in this information sharing process.
- When the child is experiencing different settings on the same day it is important to share information to ensure a balance of activity and rest, sufficient opportunities to eat and drink and to link learning opportunities. An example of this may be a childminder seeking opportunities to liaise with a nursery class through access to the weekly newsletter and daily time to liaise with the child's key person to ensure this balance occurs.

> ### Case Study
>
> A child experiencing speech and language challenges was supported in the setting by a Speech Therapist who visited the provision once a week and gave practitioners valuable systems to support the child. The case was reviewed each term by those concerned with his welfare, for example the person with responsibility for Special Needs in the setting, the child's key person and parents. This ensured the child was supported in his interactions with adults and other children in the provision.

O'Connor (2007) makes some valuable suggestions to help practitioners make transitions stress-free for children and families (and therefore the staff). These include:

- Having transition as a priority for all staff, with a particular focus on managers and leaders
- Creating familiarity for the child through helping the child become familiar with the people, places and routines. This can occur through home visits and encouraging the child to make frequent visits to the new setting to build a sense of security
- Giving each child a key person so that the child and family have an adult to help them make sense of the new setting. The key person is vital to help create a bond between the child, the family and the setting
- The child's family is involved and consulted in all aspects of the child's learning and development. This needs to be a two-way dialogue between the key person and the parent where both are seen as having valuable information to share about the child and the setting
- Supporting parents during transition is vital to helping the child feel secure. Emotions are contagious so it is important to reduce the parents' anxieties as well as the child's
- Having a relaxed start where the child and parent can separate in a space and time that is comfortable and not pressured to occur at a certain moment or place. O'Connor (2007) advocates the child and parent coming into an active provision where there is continuous provision rather than a fixed registration time
- Acknowledging a child's relationships and friendships that may already exist. O'Connor identifies research that shows that children have smoother transitions where they have friends in the same class
- Having some predictability so that children know what is expected and how the setting operates. This is not to create a rigid timetable but it is important that there are clear expectations and routines.

Induction is also an important aspect of transition to consider, as starting a new setting is stressful for children and families. It is important to give children and families sufficient time to feel secure within the setting. This starts before the child begins at the setting, by helping the child and family get to know the key person and other practitioners in the setting, and giving opportunities to build familiarity with the environment. Practitioners need to be attuned to both the children and the parents to find out what works best for them. This can happen in a number of ways, including: home visits, settling in sessions, and using booklets and photographs to help familiarise the child and the family with the setting. O'Connor (2007) suggests that transition policies need to be flexible and adaptable, rather than trying to have a single model that is considered appropriate for all children and families.

Question for Discussion

What tools and approaches have you found effective to support continuity and lessen stress for children and families in transitions between different settings?

CONCLUSION

This chapter has sought to identify what multi-agency working is and to highlight the range of models within this term. It has shown how multi-agency working relates to the broader term of integrated working and why this way of working has developed in recent years. The sections on the skills and knowledge needed for multi-agency working from the CWDC (2005) offer a useful list for practitioners to reflect upon and consider their own strengths and areas of development. The final section on transition and continuity offers some suggestions on ways to approach transitions to make them smoother and reduce the stress on all involved – the practitioner, the parent and family and, in particular, the child.

Further Reading

Aubrey, C. (2007) *Leading and Managing in the Early Years.* London: Sage.

Gaspar, M. (2010) *Multi-agency Working in the Early years: Challenges and Dilemmas.* London: Sage.

Schneider, J., Avis, M. and Leighton, P. (2007) *Supporting Children and Families: Lessons from Sure Start for Evidence-Based Practice in Health, Social Care and Education.* London: Jessica Kingsley Publishers.

Siraj-Blatchford, I., Clarke, K. and Needham, M. (eds) (2007) *The Team around the Child: Multi-agency Working in the Early Years.* Stoke-on-Trent: Trentham Books.

Useful Websites

www.cwdcouncil.org.uk
Children's Workforce Development Council

www.education.gov.uk
Early Support

www.cwdcouncil.org.uk
Sure Start

www.education.gov.uk/a0067409/every-child-matters
Every Child Matters

References

Anning, A. (2001) 'Knowing Who I am and What I Know: Developing New Versions of Professional Knowledge in Integrated Service Settings', unpublished paper presented to British Educational Research Association (BERA) Annual Conference, University of Leeds, September.

Atkinson, M., Wilkin, A., Stott, A., Doherty, P. and Kinder, K. (2002) *Multi-agency Working: A Detailed Study*. Slough: NFER.

Bertram, T., Pascal, C., Bokari, S., Casper, M. and Holterman, S. (2002) *Early Excellence Centre Pilot Programme: Second Evaluation Report 2000–2001*. DfES Research Report RR361. London: HMSO.

Chandler, T. (2006) 'Working in multidisciplinary teams' in G. Pugh and B. Duffy (eds) *Contemporary Issues in the Early Years*. London: Sage.

Children's Workforce Development Council (CWDC) (2005) *Common Core of Skills and Knowledge for the Children's Workforce*. CWDC: Leeds. Available at: www.cwdcouncil.org.uk/common-core (accessed 10 February 2010).

Children's Workforce Development Council (CWDC) (2008) Integrated Working Explained factsheet. CWDC: Leeds. Available at: www.cwdcouncil.org.uk/integrated-working (accessed 10 February 2010).

Department for Education and Employment (DfEE) (1998) *Meeting the Childcare Challenge*. London: HMSO.

Department for Education and Employment (DfEE) (1999) *Good Practice for EYDC Partnerships: Developing and Supporting High Quality Sustainable Childcare*. London: DfEE.

Department for Education and Skills (DfES) (2002) *Delivering for Children and Families*. London: The Inter-Departmental Childcare, Strategy Unit. Available at: www.surestart.gov.uk/publications.

Department for Education and Skills (DfES) (2003) *Together from the Start: Practical Guidance for Professionals Working with Disabled Children (Birth to Third Birthday) and their Families*. London: DfES.

Department for Education and Skills (DfES) (2007a) *Early Years Foundation Stage.* Nottingham: DfES Publications.

Department for Education and Skills (DfES) (2007b) 'Effective Practice: The Wider Context', on EYFS CD ROM. Nottingham: DfES Publications.

Every Child Matters (2003) Norwich: The Stationery Office. Available at: www.everychild matters.gov.uk/publications.

Every Child Matters (2006a) Multi-agency Working Factsheet, accessed from EYFS CD ROM (DfES 2007). Nottingham: DfES Publications.

Every Child Matters (2006b) *Multi-agency Services: Different Professional Cultures and Languages.* Available at: www.ecm.gov.uk/multiagency working.

Fitzgerald, M. (2004) Multi-agency Working: Literature Review (unpublished), as cited in the *Benefits of Multi-agency Working.* Available at: www.ecm.gov.uk/multiagency working.

HM Treasury (2004) *Choice for Parents: the Best Start for Children: A Ten Year Strategy for Childcare.* London: HMSO.

Kurz, Z. and James, C. (2002) *What's New: Learning from the CAMHS Innovation Projects,* London: DoH.

Mukherjee, S., Beresford, B. and Sloper, P. (1999) *Unlocking Key Working: An Analysis of Keyworker Services for Families with Disabled Children.* Bristol: The Policy Press.

NFER (2004) *Qualitative Study of Early Impact of On Track* cited the benefits of multi-agency working (accessed from www.ecm.gov.uk/multiagency working on 14.2.10).

O'Connor, A. (2007) All About....Transitions. EYFS CD ROM, Nottingham: DfES Publications.

Sloper, P. (2004) 'Facilitators and barriers for co-ordinated multi-agency services', *Child Care, Health and Development,* 30(6): 571–80.

Sylva, K., Melhuish, E., Sammons, P., Siraj-Blatchford, I., Taggart, B. and Elliot, K. (2003) *The Effective Provision of Pre-school Education (EPPE) Project: Findings from Pre-school Period.* London: Institute of Education.

16 FORWARD THINKING AND FORWARD PRACTICE

Liz Creed

Learning objectives

- To promote awareness of issues concerning aspects of practice which support children's social, emotional and behavioural needs from an holistic stance
- To consider factors such as emotional resilience as a way of coping for future changes and challenges

This chapter seeks to consider issues concerning aspects of practice which support children's social, emotional and behavioural needs from an holistic stance, including children's mental health. Case studies of strategies to promote children's health, well-being, education and care are incorporated. The importance of providing opportunities for children to be creative and flexible in their learning and development to give them confidence and strength to meet the challenges of the future is discussed.

NATURE VS NURTURE: EFFECTS ON DEVELOPMENT

Discussions around the varying degrees of influence from both genetics and the world around us on human behaviour and development have existed for many years in the form of the nature versus nurture debate. Our genes provide us with certain pre-determined personal characteristics such as eye colour and skin colour, for example, and without doubt exert a major influence upon an individual's general development throughout life. We may inherit certain qualities from our parents which facilitate our development, such as our level of intelligence and ability to learn and comprehend important information. However, these inherited qualities appear to be mediated by a number of other complex factors, such as our personality development and experiences throughout our lives. For example, should we be fortunate enough to inherit a good level of intelligence from our parents we would hope this would lead to increased success throughout life. However, this inherited capability alone may not be enough to ensure that this is so. Should our personalities develop throughout life in a way which leaves us with a lack of motivation or confidence to strive, or should early experiences lead us to believe we cannot succeed, we may be less likely to achieve our full potential than if we are motivated and given the confidence in our own abilities to do so. It is also important to consider factors outside of ourselves and their influence upon our ability to strive to reach our full potential. Should there be little opportunity to access support or develop our knowledge within society, it could be said that this may also act as a barrier to developing intellectually, furthering our knowledge, and achieving our goals. It is important that we do not ignore the influence our environment has on our social, emotional and intellectual development.

ENVIRONMENTAL INFLUENCES ON DEVELOPMENT

Human development is itself a complex issue with numerous factors having an influence on this, some of which will be discussed later in the chapter when considering ways in which children learn and develop. It is important to initially discuss the many and varied influences of our environment on development, considering the number of different situations and contexts that exist within our own lives. Bronfenbrenner (1979) developed his 'ecological model of human development' to emphasise the importance of considering human development in context. Bronfenbrenner stated that a number of systems exert influences on a child as they develop, through environments within which a child is both directly involved and influenced by indirectly. A child is not only influenced by their immediate environments such as the home or school environment and individuals within these settings, but also by settings within which they are not directly involved themselves. This includes such situations as a parent's work environment for example. The child is not directly involved with and therefore not directly influenced by this situation. However, the child may be indirectly influenced by this situation through the effects it has on their parents. Here we can consider the possible negative impact a parent's stressful work environment can have on their quality of care at home, illustrating how the child may be indirectly affected negatively by this situation.

From this we can see that it is necessary to consider not only a child's direct experience in situations, but also the wider context of a child's experiences in examining their development. The influences exerted by different individuals, such as family members and peers, upon child development will be expanded upon later in the chapter. However, to increase our understanding of the developing child it is perhaps necessary to initially discuss ways in which children have been found to learn and develop.

THEORIES OF CHILD DEVELOPMENT

Jean Piaget (1929) proposed a theory of child cognitive development. Here, Piaget stated that children develop intellectually over time progressing through a number of different stages, increasing their knowledge and understanding primarily through activity and interaction with objects around them and with ideas held about those objects. Piaget emphasised the importance of active learning for a child, suggesting that children learn much more effectively when able to interact with objects around them rather than when passively listening to information about those objects. Piaget also believed social interaction to be of great importance for cognitive development, as through this children not only learn how to use language to describe their own ideas, but also learn about other people's differing perspectives. Piaget's conclusions regarding child development came from a number of studies and observations he made during his career, in which children were able to demonstrate increased cognitive development through interacting with their environment and with other people around them, highlighting the importance of the opportunity for such activities in current teaching practice and education.

Vygotsky (1962) further emphasised the importance of social context and interaction in children's cognitive development, proposing that children learn primarily through cooperating with others in a variety of social situations. Vygotsky also highlighted the importance of a child's culture in their development, suggesting that children learn by using language to interpret the world around them, and that the language they use is determined by their wider cultural experiences. Here, it may be important to consider the implications of cultural influences on children and their development. As this is a multi-cultural society, it is necessary to consider that there are often a number of cultural influences being exerted upon children and their development, including cultural factors such as religion, familial traditions and expectations of family members, wider societal culture and demands, and possible conflicts between such areas. For an individual, cultural influences may create an environment in which striving for success and further development is valued as important, however for others such influences may act to create further demands upon that individual, placing the values of others as more important than their own individualistic achievements. It is necessary to increase our own understanding of the differential influences an individual's culture may have upon their motivation and desire for further development, and respect each individual's values regarding this, so as not to impose our values upon others.

Such theories as those outlined by Piaget and Vygotsky describe how children develop cognitively, highlighting social interaction as a key component within this development. This indicates the importance of cooperating with others and the valuable role this plays in facilitating academic learning. Therefore, being able to interact appropriately and productively with others is not only beneficial for our social and emotional development and well-being, but also appears to be able to aid our intellectual development and achievement. So how do children learn to interact effectively with others?

SOCIAL INTERACTION AND CHILD DEVELOPMENT

Social Learning Theory

As we grow and develop during childhood, we are constantly learning new information about the world around us and our own relationship to and role within that environment, which includes learning how to interact and cooperate socially with other people. A powerful way of learning new social behaviour as we grow occurs through observing and imitating the behaviour demonstrated by role models around us, such as our parents, siblings, peers and other adults.

Social Learning Theory developed by Bandura (1969), outlines that as children we often learn how to behave through observing other people's behaviour and imitating this ourselves, therefore modelling our behaviour upon those we have observed. Through this mechanism, we may learn appropriate, pro-social ways of behaving from others. By observing others cooperating with each other in order to achieve a mutually valued goal, and their achievement of that goal, we learn that this is not only a positive way of behaving but that it also leads to beneficial results for those involved. However, much of Bandura's work centred on children modeling unhelpful, aggressive behaviours after observing others displaying such behaviours. Therefore, it could also be said that learned behaviour through modelling may be inappropriate or indeed harmful, highlighting ways in which unhelpful ways of coping or responding to difficulties in life may be learned (Bandura et al. 1961). Bandura and colleagues (1961) identified that children would more frequently display anti-social, aggressive behaviours after observing adults displaying this behavior. This research highlights the importance of role models in child development, and the need for the existence of positive role models during childhood for a child to be able to learn appropriate, helpful and cooperative social behaviour in order to facilitate the forming of adaptive relationships with others, centred around mutual respect and support. However, human behavior is far too complex to be explained simply through learned behaviour alone. It is important to consider other factors which have been shown to influence our behaviour and development.

Familial Relationships

Research has indicated the important role relationships with our parents, siblings, other relatives and peers play as we develop during childhood, and has outlined ways in which negative early experiences can be detrimental to a child's social and emotional development, which in turn can lead to compromised cognitive development. The relationship between mother and child has been extensively studied during recent decades, with emphasis placed on the positive effects a good mother–child relationship can have on a child's development. John Bowlby (1969) developed an 'Attachment Theory' highlighting the importance of this early relationship, indicating that should the mother not be available to bond with the infant after birth, and within a short period of time after birth, the infant will suffer greatly in being unable to form good quality relationships with others in later life. Further research has indicated that a less than optimal attachment bond between a mother and her young infant can lead to negative effects on the child's emotional well-being and behaviour (Ainsworth et al, 1978). Ainsworth and colleagues identified a number of different 'attachment types' between mother and child, highlighting a secure attachment versus different forms of insecure attachment. A secure attachment was proposed to lead to a child becoming increasingly confident in their own capabilities whilst also recognising they have adequate support from their mother when needed; and an insecure attachment was suggested to lead to later problems with developing and maintaining supportive relationships, difficulties in developing life skills, and greater risk of becoming vulnerable to problems with emotional development and regulation. Research has also identified the long-term positive benefits of maternal affection in childhood, with high levels of affection towards babies aged eight months being associated with reduced anxiety and good mental health in adulthood (Maselko et al. 2010).

A great deal of research conducted initially focused on the relationship between mother and baby, considering the impact of this relationship on a child as far more important than any other. However, it is also important for a child to form good attachments with other family members, primarily the father and siblings, and also with other relatives and caregivers. In fact, developing multiple attachments with a number of different family members and caregivers has been found to be very beneficial for a child; increasing their social interaction with others leads to positive developmental effects (van Ijzendoorn et al. 1992). In general, positive experiences and good attachments during childhood enable a child to become more socially aware and adept, increasing the likelihood a child will be socially accepted by peers in later life. The importance of this can be seen when we understand that this can be a major factor contributing to a child's emotional well-being, in that positive social interaction with others can contribute to good mental health and increased resilience in a child's ability to cope with the challenges and difficulties faced in everyday life. It is widely understood that a good support network of friends and family, and social inclusion within a local community, can act as a powerful protector against the negative impact of difficult life events and mental health problems, whereas a common factor which increases vulnerability to, and acts to maintain, mental health problems is social isolation and loneliness. Not only is emotional well-being of value in itself, as this enables the child to become a happier and healthier adult, but it can also have a positive impact upon a child's intellectual development and academic achievement.

Effects of Deprivation

The effects of deprivation become particularly evident when we consider the effects of negative early life experiences, insecure attachments, and difficulties in peer relationships such as bullying, on a child's social, emotional and cognitive functioning. John Bowlby (1953; 1969) developed a 'Maternal Deprivation' hypothesis in which he proposed the view that a child having experienced a warm and caring bond with their mother is essential for the child's mental health. Bowlby proposed that without this, the child's social and cognitive development and capabilities would suffer. This has been illustrated in research looking into children raised in institutions and orphanages, in which such organisations were characterised by a lack of stimulation for children, with few toys and little contact and interaction with staff. Here it was found that many children in long-term care had very poor social, emotional and cognitive development (Spitz 1946; Goldfarb 1947). In addition to this, abuse and neglect experienced during childhood has been found to have a negative impact on a child's mental health (Spaccerelli 1994). However the negative effects of this can be reduced if factors such as good coping strategies and a network of support are made available.

Peer Relationships

Factors which can increase the likelihood of compromised emotional development and increased mental health problems in children are complex and numerous. As illustrated so far, the impact of parent and family relationships is particularly significant in facilitating good social and emotional development. However these relationships can act as risk factors for developing mental health problems if they are not centred on a warm and caring attachment. As suggested earlier, poor mental health can have wide ranging effects on a child's development, including upon intellectual development and achievement at school. It is also important to consider the role of peers in a child's development, as research has shown that peer relationships can play a significant part in a child's social development and in contributing to their mental wellbeing (Stocker 1994; Ladd et al. 1996).

Peer relationships can be considered beneficial for child development in a number of different ways. During early childhood, in which peer relationships involve play with other children, such relationships may facilitate increased social awareness, knowledge of appropriate social interaction and boundaries, and mastery of new skills (Bruner 1972). It is also apparent that childhood friendships and acceptance from peers can improve the likelihood of emotional well-being, whilst being rejected by peers has been associated with increased mental health problems (Cowen et al. 1973). It has been noted that being rejected by peers and bullying can be extremely detrimental to children, with victims of bullying suffering a loss of confidence, self-esteem and self-worth (Boulton and Smith 1994; Kochenderfer and Ladd 1996). Bullying has also been found to have long-term effects leading to relationship difficulties in later life, where victims of childhood bullying felt insecure as adults when considering whether other adults liked them (Gilmartin 1987). For current education and teaching practice, it is important to consider how bullying is dealt with in schools with regard to the number of negative consequences it can have upon a child, in terms of their emotional and cognitive development, and the long-lasting effects it can have.

So what are the consequences of negative social and familial contacts and interactions in later life? As we have previously seen, optimal social, emotional and intellectual development can be encouraged through positive experiences in early life, a supportive and encouraging upbringing, positive role models, and low levels of stress and distress during childhood. All of these factors can act as facilitators of good mental well-being and function as protective factors against developing mental health problems in adolescence and adulthood. In contrast, negative experiences in early life, difficult or unsupportive family relationships, poor role models, and difficulties in peer relationships can act to increase risks of developing mental health problems in later life (Malinosky-Rummel and Hansen 1993; Rubin et al. 2004). However, it is important to note that there are no simple and direct relationships between these factors and the development of mental health problems. As previously discussed, human development is far too complex to suggest that poor mental health only occurs in those who have experienced difficulties as children. Instead, it is emphasised that negative early experiences could increase the risk of poor emotional well-being. For example, if a child experiences lack of support from family and is rejected by peers this can lead to isolation and loss of confidence and self-esteem, which may in turn increase the risk of developing depression. However, we must not discount individuals' own resilience factors which may act to protect against mental health issues, which will be discussed at the end of this chapter.

EFFECTS OF EARLY EXPERIENCES IN ADOLESCENCE

It is evident that negative experiences during childhood can have detrimental effects on an individual later in life, and can impact negatively on their development

(Malinosky-Rummel and Hansen 1993; Rubin et al. 2004). For example, a child who has experienced being rejected by peers at school may be more likely to drop out of school earlier or truant from school more frequently if they fear being bullied by those peers. There appears to be a very direct link between negative social experiences and an individual's own achievements. However, this desire to be socially accepted can also appear to have a negative impact in more subtle ways.

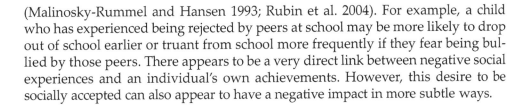

Case Study

Whilst working in Child and Adolescent Mental Health Services I observed a case where a secondary school pupil became so concerned with being accepted socially by peers that she began to focus more attention upon her appearance and dress than academic achievement. In this case, the individual began to become increasingly concerned with her weight, linking her popularity at school to how thin she could become, which escalated until she was admitted to the Child and Adolescent Mental Health ward for treatment of Anorexia Nervosa.

Here we can consider the number of negative effects of this situation on the individual's development, in terms of detriment to her physical health and to her academic achievement through reduced attendance at school due to ward admittance, as well as her mental well-being and self-esteem.

Case Study

In another case example a teenage girl who experienced childhood sexual abuse began self-harming, developed difficulties with eating, and experienced increased suicidal ideation. Her self-harming behaviour and problems with eating escalated, resulting in an admission to the Child and Adolescent Mental Health ward for treatment of depression.

From this case we can see how negative early life experiences, specifically childhood sexual abuse, can increase the risks of developing mental health problems in adolescence. This can have wide-ranging detrimental effects on the individual's later life, from relationship difficulties and risk of future mental health problems, to health issues and wider functioning difficulties in adulthood.

Adolescence can itself be a particularly difficult stage of development in an individual's life. Indeed, research seems to suggest that teenagers experiencing negative life events connected with family, school and peers often report higher rates of low mood (Larson and Ham 1993). However from the discussion so far, it appears that negative childhood experiences can exert influences upon development during adolescence, often creating further difficulties as experienced by teenagers and increasing the risks of poor emotional experiences, and adolescence can also affect our progression into adulthood. Difficulties in adolescence, whether with family members, peers, abuse and neglect, or many other factors, can lead to increased vulnerability to mental health problems as an adult (Malinosky-Rummel and Hansen 1993; Rubin et al. 2004).

EFFECTS OF CHILDHOOD AND ADOLESCENT EXPERIENCES IN ADULTHOOD

Through my own experience as a Psychological Wellbeing Practitioner I have provided therapeutic intervention to those who suffer mild to moderate mental health problems as adults, some of whom are able to link their problems back to issues in their childhood. As discussed earlier, the causes of mental health problems are far more complex than simply being triggered by an individual's early life experiences. In many situations people requiring support often find they are struggling to manage their mood or levels of anxiety as a result of current stressful life events which are not linked to their childhood experiences. However, negative childhood experiences can be considered as increasing one's vulnerability to mental health problems, often if also in conjunction with the absence of adequate protective factors, as will be further discussed later.

A great number of people who engage in therapy to address mood or anxiety problems are able to relate their current problems to early experiences, and difficulties or negative experiences as children. Whilst addressing problems with emotional well-being as an adult, through furthering their own understanding and awareness of their mood, many people find they have had certain ways of coping that they have used for a considerable proportion of their lives which they come to recognize are unhelpful, and merely contribute to their low mood and anxiety. This is often triggered as many people find they are able to cope until a stressful life event challenges their less effective, unhelpful ways of coping, at which point their emotional well-being begins to suffer. This can impact upon a wide variety of areas across a person's life, such as their home environment, employment, social and leisure activities, and relationships with others. Many of these ways of coping are often identified as being learned from role models, such as parents and other relatives, during childhood. For example, those who develop problems with anxiety and worrying often learn this as a way of coping from an early role model, which becomes problematic in later life as it can cause a great deal of emotional distress. Anger and aggressive behaviour has often been linked to such behaviour being displayed by a parent or sibling, which is observed during childhood and learned as acceptable behaviour. Some people who experience depression and low mood as adults are able to relate their problems to having poor attachments with parental figures as children, and report difficulty forming and maintaining supportive relationships with others during their adulthood, increasing their feelings of social isolation and loneliness, which in turn contributes to further low mood.

Finally, evident from my current experiences in working with people who seek therapeutic intervention for social anxiety and low self-esteem, is the negative effects of experiences such as being bullied during childhood on an individual's perception of themselves. Frequently, individuals reporting anxiety in social situations and those who hold an overall negative view of themselves as adults, state they experienced bullying as a child, leading them to view other people as threatening and themselves as unlikeable. In some cases it is evident that such mental health problems in adulthood not only have a negative impact on a person's emotional well-being, but also negative impact upon their overall sense of accomplishment and achievement in life, as they have felt less able and confident to further their development.

With this in mind, we must consider the importance of increasing the likelihood of positive early experiences through effectively aiding child development in providing caring and supportive learning environments, enabling children to increase their confidence in their own abilities and encouraging independence. We need to demonstrate appropriate and effective coping strategies, in order to provide children with resilience factors to protect against any possible risks to their social, emotional and intellectual development.

BUILDING RESILIENCE IN CHILDHOOD

To facilitate and encourage increased resilience in children is to equip them with tools and strategies to use to more effectively cope with difficult situations, situations in which those with less resilience may be more likely to develop mental health problems or suffer other negative consequences associated with a reduced ability or perceived ability to cope. Resilience appears to be fostered through a complex assortment of individual, family and community factors (Condly 2006). Research suggests protective factors, including supportive and encouraging relationships with parents and greater levels of good quality social support appear to moderate the negative effects of stressful life events and reduce the risks of inability to cope (Smith and Carlson 1997). Research has also reported on the positive effects of resilience in children within school environments. This emphasises increasing resilience through encouraging caring relationships between teacher and child; holding high expectations around children's achievements which acts to promote increased self-esteem, independence and optimism; and allowing children to be meaningfully involved in and responsible for aspects of the school environment. These factors act to create positive academic outcomes for all children, including those experiencing difficult social or familial environments (Benard 1995).

 Questions for Discussion

Think about a significant event in your early years.
What impact did this have on your outlook and positivity?
How did it affect your learning, development and self-belief?

FORWARD THINKING, FORWARD PRACTICE

So, children who are better able to cope with difficult and stressful situations in life are much more likely to go on to reach their full social, emotional and intellectual capabilities. By examining current research we can see that all environments within which a child is involved, including home and school environments, can have a significant positive impact upon a child's development. In addition, where children are experiencing difficulties in one environment, support and encouragement received in other settings can act to protect against the detrimental effects and risks associated with those difficulties. For a child who is experiencing neglect and abuse at home, for example, the school environment may act to aid that child in achieving their potential despite such adversity. Therefore, it is necessary to consider all aspects of a child's life in order to better understand that child and cater for their needs effectively.

This is demonstrated in a psychological treatment currently being used with children and adolescents experiencing mental health problems and social difficulties, known as multisystemic therapy, which has been found to be effective in improving parent–child relationships (Brunk et al. 1987). This approach highlights the need to consider the influence of a number of different systems upon an individual's behaviour and development. These systems include an individual's own characteristics, factors relating to the individual's home and family environment, peers and the school environment, and the individual's wider societal and cultural environment. As discussed at the beginning of the chapter, Bronfenbrenner's (1979) 'ecological model of human development', proposes that to understand an individual we must consider all aspects of their experiences and the differential influences of these experiences upon the person themselves. Most important for future practice is the consideration of an holistic approach to caring for and supporting children, facilitating social, emotional and intellectual development by exploring the impact of differing and varied factors upon children.

Further Reading

Woolfolk, A., Hughes, M. and Walkup, V. (2008) *Psychology in Education.* Harlow: Pearson Education.

Useful Website

www.mentalhelp.net
This considers mental health issues of young children and the impact on later life.

References

Ainsworth, M.D.S., Blehar, M.C., Waters, E. and Wall, S. (1978) *Patterns of Attachment.* Hillsdale, NJ: Erlbaum.

Bandura, A. (1969) 'Social Learning Theory of Identificatory Processes', in D.A. Goslin (ed.) *Handbook of Socialisation: Theory and Research.* Chicago: Rand McNally.

Bandura, A., Ross, D. and Ross, S.A. (1961) 'Transmission of Aggression through Imitation of Aggressive Models', *Journal of Abnormal and Social Psychology*, 63: 575–82.

Benard, B. (1995) *Fostering Resilience in Children.* Eric Clearinghouse on Elementary and Early Childhood Education. Urbana IL: ERIC Digest ED386327.

Boulton, M. J. and Smith, P. K. (1994) 'Bully/victim Problems in Middle-school Children: Stability, Self-perceived Competence, Peer Perceptions and Peer Acceptance', *British Journal of Developmental Psychology*, 12: 315–29.

Bowlby, J. (1953) *Child Care and the Growth of Love.* Harmondsworth: Penguin.

Bowlby, J. (1969) *Attachment and Loss, Vol. 1: Attachment.* London: Hogarth Press.

Bronfenbrenner, U. (1979) *The Ecology of Human Development.* Cambridge, MA: Harvard University Press.

Bruner, J.S. (1972) 'The Nature and Uses of Immaturity', *American Psychologist*, 27, 687–708.

Brunk, M., Henggeler, S.W. and Whelan, J.P. (1987) 'Comparison of Multisystemic Therapy and Parent Training in the Brief Treatment of Child Abuse and Neglect', *Journal of Consulting and Clinical Psychology*, 55(2): 171–178.

Condly, S.J. (2006) 'Resilience in Children: A Review of Literature with Implications for Education', *Urban Education*, 41(3): 211–236.

Cowen, E.L., Pederson, A., Babigian, H., Izzo, L.D. and Trost, M.A. (1973) 'Long-term Follow-up of Early Detected Vulnerable Children', *Journal of Consulting and Clinical Psychology*, 41: 438–46.

Gilmartin, B.G. (1987) 'Peer Group Antecedents of Severe Love-shyness in Males', *Journal of Personality*, 55: 467–89.

Goldfarb, W. (1947) 'Variations in Adolescent Adjustment of Institutionally Reared Children', *American Journal of Orthopsychiatry*, 17: 449–457.

Kochenderfer, B. and Ladd, G. (1996) 'Peer Victimisation: Cause or Consequence of School Maladjustment?', *Child Development*, 67: 1305–17.

Ladd, G.W., Kochenderfer, B.J. and Coleman, C.C. (1996) 'Friendship Quality as a Predictor of Young Children's Early School Adjustment', *Child Development*, 67: 1103–18.

Larson, R. and Ham, M. (1993) 'Stress and "Storm and Stress" in Early Adolescence: the Relationship of Negative Events with Dysphoric Affect', *Developmental Psychology*, 29: 130–40.

Malinosky-Rummel, R. and Hansen, D. J. (1993) 'Long-term Consequences of Childhood Physical Abuse', *Psychological Bulletin*, 114: 68–79.

Maselko, J., Kubzansky, L., Lipsitt, L. and Buka, S.L. (2010) 'Mother's affection at 8 months predicts emotional distress in adulthood'. *Journal of Epidemiology and Community Health*, 26 July doi: jech.2009.097873.

Piaget, J. (1929) *The Child's Conception of the World*. New York: Harcourt Brace Jovanovich.

Rubin, K.H., Dwyer, K.M., Kim, A.H., Burgess, K.B., Booth-LaForce, C. and Rose-Kranor, L. (2004) 'Attachment, Friendship, and Psychosocial Functioning in Early Adolescence', *Journal of Early Adolescence*, 24(4): 326–56.

Smith, C. and Carlson, B.E. (1997) 'Stress, Coping, and Resilience in Children and Youth', *The Social Service Review*, 71(2): 231–56.

Spaccerelli, S. (1994) 'Stress, Appraisal, and Coping in Child Sexual Abuse: A Theoretical and Empirical Review', *Psychological Bulletin*, 116: 340–62.

Spitz, R.A. (1946) 'Hospitalism: A Follow-up Report', *Psychoanalytic Study of the Child*, 2: 113–18.

Stocker, C.M. (1994) 'Children's Perceptions of Relationships with Siblings, Friends, and Mothers: Compensatory Processes and Links with Adjustment', *Journal of Child Psychology and Psychiatry and Allied Disciplines*, 35: 1447–59.

van Ijzendoorn, M.H., Sagi, A. and Lambermon, M.W.E. (1992) 'The Multiple Caretaker Paradox: Data from Holland and Israel', *New Directions for Child and Adolescent Development*, 57: 5–24.

Vygotsky, L. (1962) *Thought and Language*. Cambridge, MA: MIT Press.

CONCLUSION

Part 1 opened with a discussion of holistic approaches and considered how policies and practice had evolved in a country, specifically England. It continued with a consideration of relevant theories of early years education and care and the impact they had on practice. Discussions recognised the importance of parents and carers as the child's first educators. Key leaders of early years provision were noted. Pedagogical issues were considered in practice in settings in England and Norway.

Part 2 explored themes which are pertinent to the emotional well-being of children. It included discussions of children's motivation and self-esteem, inclusion and 'educating' the whole child, issues regarding diversity and the promotion of children's thinking skills. It emphasised the importance of practitioners providing an appropriate emotional atmosphere for children to thrive.

Part 3 provided practical explanations of planning, organisation and strategies to implement the pedagogy discussed in earlier chapters. It covered different approaches to play and the rationale for play as a way of learning. It continued with consideration of an appropriate enabling learning environment to promote implementing a play-based approach. Different learning styles were described with key features and learning and teaching strategies. Effective leadership of an early years setting was discussed and finally ways to successfully manage such provision were considered.

Part 4 looked to the future and began with consideration of the challenges faced by an early years teacher in a Foundation Stage Unit. This was developed through reflections of the social context, from the family, friends, the setting, the local community, wider community and international perspectives. Finally, consideration of issues that happen in children's early years were reflected on as aspects which impact on the well-being of older children and adults for the rest of their lives.

INDEX

CHILDREN'S RIGHTS IN PRACTICE

Edited by **Phil Jones** *University of Leeds* and
Gary Walker *Leeds Metropolitan University*

Considering the rights of the child is now central
to all fields involving children and to good multi-
agency working. This book offers an explanation of the theoretical issues and the key policy
developments that are crucial to all professions,
and helps the reader to understand children's
rights in relation to their role in working with children and young people. Looking at education,
health, social care and welfare, it bridges the gap
between policy and practice for children from Birth
to 19 years. Chapters cover:
- the child's right to play
- youth justice, children's rights and the voice of the child
- ethical dilemmas in different contexts
- involvement, participation and decision making
- safeguarding and child protection, social justice and exclusion.

This book helps the reader understand what constitutes good practice, whilst
considering the advantages and tensions involved in working across disciplines
to implement children's rights against a complex legislative and social policy
backdrop.

April 2011 • 256 pages
Cloth (978-1-84920-379-1) • £65.00
Paper (978-1-84920-380-7) • £22.99

ALSO FROM SAGE

PROFESSIONALIZATION, LEADERSHIP AND MANAGEMENT IN THE EARLY YEARS

Edited by **Linda Miller** and **Carrie Cable** *both at The Open University*

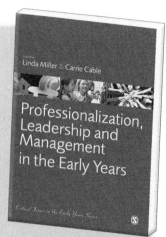

With the rapid change experienced by the early years workforce over recent times, this book considers what constitutes professionalization in the sector, and what this means in practice. Bringing a critical perspective to the developing knowledge and understanding of early years practitioners at various stages of their professional development, it draws attention to key themes and issues. Chapters are written by leading authorities, and case studies, questions and discussion points are provided to facilitate critical thinking.

Topics covered include:

- constructions of professional identities
- men in the early years
- multidisciplinary working in the early years
- professionalization in the nursery
- early childhood leadership and policy.

Written in an accessible style and relevant to all levels of early years courses, the book is highly relevant to those studying at masters level, and has staggered levels of further reading that encourage reflection and progression.

CRITICAL ISSUES IN THE EARLY YEARS
November 2010 • 184 pages
Cloth (978-1-84920-553-5) • £65.00
Paper (978-1-84920-554-2) • £22.99

ALSO FROM SAGE

THEORIES AND APPROACHES TO LEARNING IN THE EARLY YEARS

Edited by **Linda Miller** *The Open University* and **Linda Pound** *Education Consultant*

By focusing on key figures in early years education and care, this book considers the influential thinkers and groundbreaking approaches that have revolutionized practice. With contributions from leading authorities in the field, chapters provide an explanation of the approach, an analysis of the theoretical background, case studies, questions and discussion points to facilitate critical thinking.

Included are chapters on:

- Froebel
- Psychoanalytical theories
- Maria Montessori
- Steiner Waldorf education
- High/Scope
- Postmodern and post-structuralist perspectives
- Forest Schools
- Vivian Gussin Paley
- Te Whariki.

Written in an accessible style and relevant to all levels of early years courses, the book has staggered levels of Further Reading that encourage reflection and promotes progression.

CRITICAL ISSUES IN THE EARLY YEARS

December 2010 • 192 pages
Cloth (978-1-84920-577-1) • £65.00
Paper (978-1-84920-578-8) • £22.99

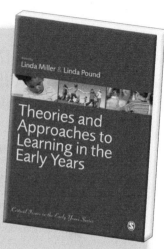

ALSO FROM SAGE